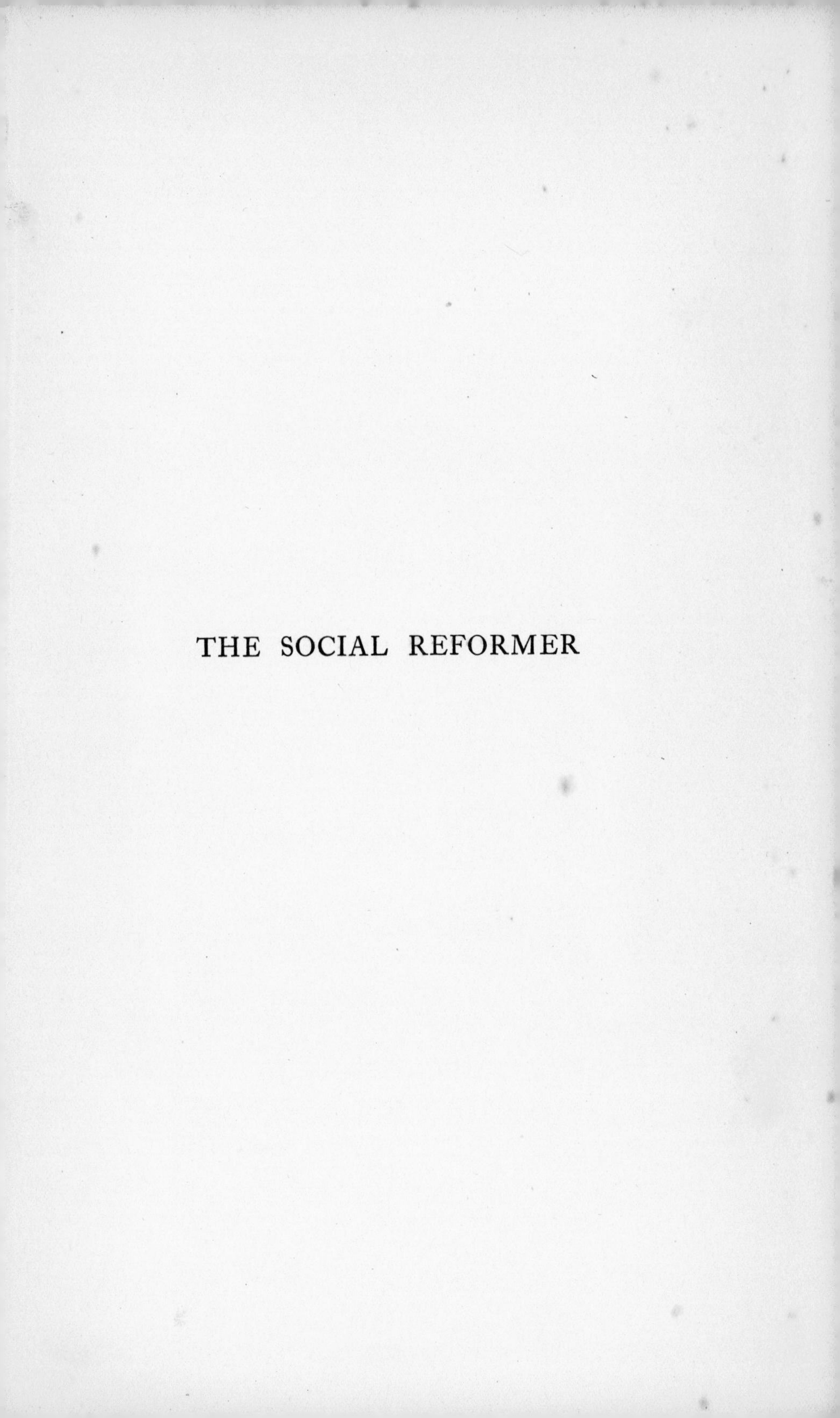

# THE SOCIAL REFORMER

MACMILLAN AND CO., LIMITED
LONDON · BOMBAY · CALCUTTA
MELBOURNE

THE MACMILLAN COMPANY
NEW YORK · BOSTON · CHICAGO
ATLANTA · SAN FRANCISCO

THE MACMILLAN CO. OF CANADA, LTD.
TORONTO

# THE WORKING FAITH

## OF THE

# SOCIAL REFORMER

## AND OTHER ESSAYS

BY

HENRY JONES

LL.D., D.Litt.

FELLOW OF THE BRITISH ACADEMY

PROFESSOR OF MORAL PHILOSOPHY IN THE UNIVERSITY OF GLASGOW

MACMILLAN AND CO., LIMITED

ST. MARTIN'S STREET, LONDON

1910

GLASGOW: PRINTED AT THE UNIVERSITY PRESS
BY ROBERT MACLEHOSE AND CO. LTD.

TO THE
MEMORY OF A GOOD CITIZEN,
ONE WHO WAS FIRST PURE, THEN PEACEABLE,
GENTLE, AND EASY TO BE INTREATED, FULL OF MERCY
AND GOOD FRUITS, WITHOUT PARTIALITY,
AND WITHOUT HYPOCRISY,

MY FATHER.

# PREFACE

THE essays and lectures in this volume have already appeared in print: "The Working Faith of the Social Reformer" and "The Moral Aspect of the Fiscal Question" in *The Hibbert Journal*; "The Child and Heredity" in a volume of The Crown Theological Library, entitled *The Child and Religion*; "Idealism and Politics" in *The Contemporary Review*; "Social and Individual Evolution" in *The New World*; and "Social Responsibilities" in a pamphlet published by James MacLehose & Sons. I wish to express my hearty gratitude to the Editors and Publishers of these periodicals for their kindness in allowing me to collect the papers together for republication.

Most of the essays were originally written in response to the incitement of some quite temporary circumstance; but they all turn around principles which, if they are valid, are of cardinal importance for our thinking and practice in social matters.

The changes I have made are both less numerous and less important than I could have wished. In particular I could have gladly eliminated some repetitions. But I was prevented, partly by the difficulty of doing so without tearing up the web of the argument, and partly by the belief that the convictions which kept recurring to my own mind might have some real value for others and even gain vitality from the changing contexts in which they stand. And, after all, while an author has no right to be monotonous, it is not necessarily a defect to be like Socrates—"always saying the same things about the same things." Neither life, nor the theoretic exposition of it, depends for its worth upon the multiplicity of its principles. We do best with very few. I am not sure that we need more than one, provided it will bear the articulation of practice.

Apart from that articulation, I am well aware, an ethical or social principle is a very shallow and poor thing. It is like the love of humanity which does not recognize a neighbour in the man who has fallen amongst thieves and has been robbed of his raiment and wounded, and which is not the force that is regenerating the world. Insistence on principle cannot be a substitute for the practical application of it, in ways that may often appear to be inconsistent, to the ever varying demands of circumstances. Nevertheless insistence on principle may, under certain conditions, be the most urgent of all a people's needs. If, on the one side, the best escape from the doubt and hesitation which reflexion brings is to follow Carlyle's maxim and "Do the duty next to hand," there are times, on the other side, where the "Duty next to hand" is just to reflect.

Observing our own circumstances at present as best I can, the conclusion is forced upon me that there is no need so imperative, none from whose fulfilment our social welfare would flow so full and free, as the convincing enunciation of a few principles which have the intrinsic right to be dominant.

The changes which have taken place in the structure of human society, the unparalleled intricacy of the relations of men to one another in the modern civilized State, the growth side by side, nay by mutual implication, of social necessities and individual freedom, have rendered many of our old formulae obsolete. The simple creed of Individualism, full of virtue as it was for many a century, will no longer work, for we know that there is more in freedom than emancipation. The creed that would not merely supplant, but sublate it, taking up its truth in correcting its errors, is hardly formulated; and, in consequence, there is much confusion. We have few, if any, hypotheses that we can employ with confidence to elucidate the social facts with which the new circumstances are flooding our lives. We appoint Commissions, some of them, like the Poor Law Commission, able in some respects to rise to the greatness of their responsibilities. Ceaseless enquiries regarding the conditions of life, in town and country, and in regard to all their greater interests, industrial and charitable, are being carried on. History, if history is an accumulation of details, description, statistics, we have in plenitude. But the principles which should not merely systematize but give the meaning of the facts, are hardly better than unexamined prejudices which split the commissions, and leave them helpless to give practical guidance. Everything is discussed except these.

And principles are very powerful, either for mischief or for good. They may appear to be remote from practice; but they are, in truth, the most practical forces of all. They warp our judgment of *all* facts, if they are false; they inform our judgment if they are true; they rule our lives consciously or unconsciously in either case. Hence, they themselves, should be constantly summoned before the bar, and required to justify themselves.

The demand that the philosopher whose main business is amongst principles should apply them to facts is altogether fair. When his turn comes, as Plato tells us, he must come out of the sunlight, and "go down to the general under-ground abode, and get the habit of seeing in the dark."

I have attempted little of that in this book. But I shall not consider that my labour has been altogether lost if anything I have said will stimulate reflexion on the part of those men whose experience of affairs is richer than my own. I know nothing, for instance, better calculated to moderate both the alarm and the hope which the mere word "Socialism" evokes than a serious attempt to examine prejudices whose very existence often escapes our notice. The social profit that would accrue from bringing the philosopher down to facts is altogether insignificant when compared to the good that would ensue from bringing the practical man to consider principles.

I have no hope except in the truth, and truth is not given to men in their sleep. It is embedded in the facts of social life as it is embedded in the material universe; but it cannot be set free by mere Empiricism in the one case any more than in the other, nor be gained without that labour of research amongst universal principles which has created the physical sciences.

HENRY JONES.

THE UNIVERSITY,
GLASGOW, *January*, 1910.

# CONTENTS

## *THE WORKING FAITH OF THE SOCIAL REFORMER*



## *IDEALISM AND POLITICS*

CONTENTS

# THE WORKING FAITH OF THE SOCIAL REFORMER

## I

## THE NEED AND CONDITIONS OF A SCIENCE OF SOCIAL LIFE

The problems of social life can be solved only by the associated will of good men, which is the true Church; and only by the "Church" if it understands as well as sympathizes.

The complexity of the social structure, and the need of enquiry. The enquiry must be conducted by many minds, for all men must share in the social virtues. Characteristics of the true reformer: insight into the needs of men, a high opinion of human nature, and trust in the good already working in the world. The British people at present lack the way rather than the will towards social reforms. A science of social life the deepest need of the times. The conditions which obstruct the attempt to establish it: distrust of theory; the notion that history is the scene of caprice and chance; the false opposition between law and freedom. How practical life refutes these objections. Society being the product of man's rational nature is capable of rational interpretation. Contrast between our attitude towards the science of social life and the sciences of physical facts. The need of the application of strict methods of enquiry greater than at any previous time. The growth of social sympathy, and how, if ill-informed, it is apt to be revolutionary. Reverence for the State best learnt from observing it as it is: example from the social life of Glasgow. The true reformer trusts the good already operating in the world, and comes not to destroy but to fulfil. The temperament of the English people, and the conditions under which they may be helped to a better life.

I

## THE NEED AND CONDITIONS OF A SCIENCE OF SOCIAL LIFE

What I have to say in this and the succeeding articles was, in substance, delivered as Lectures under the Dunkin Trust to the students of Manchester College, Oxford. The lectures were addressed primarily to young men about to devote themselves to the service of religion, and to social work as a part of that service. I have re-written them, but I have not cared to expunge all traces of their first purpose. My aim still is to speak to those who are feeling their way into social usefulness, and whose main hope of comprehending their social work lies in looking at it in the large context of religiously inspired thought.

Religion, in the degree to which it is true and worthy of man, comprises and unites the interests of his life. It is a sustained habit of contemplating human affairs in the light of ultimate issues. It therefore brings order and perspective into our conception of human life, correcting the abstraction of selfishness, the exaggeration of passion, and the urgency of desire. It throws upon the world the quiet light of a larger day, and brings out the deeper significance of man's deeds, as the sun the colours of the landscape. It is a principle of proportion and sanity, which gives its own place both to what is small and transient and to that whose worth is great and permanent; and it is far less an affair of another world than men have usually thought. In its light men walk more securely:

> "You groped your way across my room i' the dear dark dead of night,
> At each fresh step a stumble was: but, once your lamp alight,
> Easy and plain you walked again: so soon all wrong grew right."
>
> Browning: *Shah Abbas.*

But man's life in modern times has attained a vast compass. Its interests are multifarious, and each of these interests has not only a wider reach, but is more strongly entrenched within itself than it was when human society was more simple. Never was it more easy for men to be the servants of one-sided causes, or the victims of class ideas. The task of religion, which is to see life singly and show it whole, is therefore much more difficult than it was in the past; and, in one respect at least, religion is itself less fitted for its task. Its spirit has outgrown its forms. Its views of the relation of man to man and to God are more generous far, but their outlines are dim and indefinite. The need is great for the master-spirit who shall articulate our thoughts and direct our practical aims, "setting to music the tune that is haunting millions of ears."

But the disposition of the age is by no means unfavourable to religion. Its spirit is not secular nor negative —what it negates is only the supernatural. Its very scepticism is half-religious. The dogmatic denial of the middle of last century has given way to a confession of ignorance, to an Agnosticism which leaves room for the "grand Perhaps." Many people divine, and to most of the more thoughtful it is as certain as mathematics, that the issues of the present life do not all lie on the sensible surface. Hedonism in ethics, Deism in religion, Individualism in social practice satisfy us no more. Man's duty to man is duty to God, and there is no higher way of obeying God than that of serving man. "Inasmuch as ye have done it unto one of the least of these my brethren, ye have done it unto Me." "Religion is being moralised, and morality is being socialised."

Many causes have concurred to bring about this fundamental change of attitude towards life and its problems; and that change, as yet, is more a new disposition of the heart and leaning of the mind than a formulated creed. The Church has helped to produce it, but to do so was not amongst its conscious purposes. The new times have come unobserved, and there was none to cry "Lo here," or "Lo there." But the Church *feels* the change. Its sympathies have become wider and its task has grown in its hands. It knows that its own destiny hangs upon its power to grasp and guide the moral and social tendencies which have appeared amongst us. But its understanding of them is imperfect. It believes that the problems of society are, in the last resort, problems of character, and, in that sense, spiritual[1] problems. They can be solved only by a spiritual agency, by the associated will of good men, which is what the "Church" ought to mean. Only

[1] "Character" is a spiritual fact. But the word "spiritual" has to be relieved more completely of supernatural associations. Nothing is spiritual except that which "spirit" is and does, and spirit is that and that alone which thinks, feels, and wills. It is the best word we have for that which performs all these functions.

the Church can save society, and only by saving society can it save itself. But the Church can do this by no mere warmth of feeling or emotional enthusiasm, although it can do nothing without them. These have done harm in the past, they are doing harm to-day, and they will do harm to-morrow, so far as there goes not with them some comprehension of the conditions under which human character is formed. And of all these conditions, there are none which signify so much for men as those which bind them together in society. What we call "the social environment" envelopes individual character more closely than aught else. It penetrates man's life more intimately, and sustains it more vitally than any physical circumstance, which, indeed, can be interpreted by him only through its medium. It is a power within man as well as without him. And no one will deny that to understand this social environment is a condition of its proper use, or that in seeking to do so those who have come to serve man are engaged in their proper business. It is the most urgent practical task of the day for good men.

I wish I could tell you how to go about it. But the problems of social life are so complex, and the principles that should contain their solution are so uncertain and obscure, as to make the attitude of a teacher in this field inept and absurd. Where no one knows, all must inquire, if the subject of inquiry is sufficiently important. And the field of social life is emphatically, if not uniquely, one in which the inquiry must be conducted by many minds. Plato tells us that justice and reverence, the virtues on which human society rests, have been differently distributed amongst men from the arts. Skill in the latter has been given only to the favoured few,—"one skilled individual having enough of medicine, or of any other art, for many unskilled ones." But reverence and justice must be given to all. "I should like them all to have a share," said Zeus; "for cities cannot exist if a few only share in the virtues, as in the arts."[1] "The growing good of the world," says George Eliot, speaking in the same spirit as Plato, "is partly dependent on unhistoric acts; and that things are not so ill with you and me as they might have been is half owing to the number who lived faithfully a hidden life, and rest in unvisited tombs." It has taken us all to build the social edifice; it will take us all to comprehend it.

It has ever been a mark of the successful worker in the social field that he has a living sense of this truth. He does not merely contemplate his fellows in the mass, nor employ the "method of averages" when he seeks to help or understand them. He knows that every individual of them all has his own internal life, intensely real and significant to *him*; and society is not to him a general term, but a system of personalities, every one of them unique. And he has the gift of sympathetic imagination, to construct their experience from within. The distinction between right and wrong is plain for him and firmly drawn, and every other distinction is of comparatively little account; for it is to men of an ardent ethical spirit that the problems of social life appeal most strongly. But he is not intolerant; he has no fixed prejudices or rigid standards. He is sensitive to the worth of institutions, of ways of life and of types of character different from his own. He knows that the good takes many forms, and that God fulfils Himself in many ways. He is like the

[1] Plato's *Protagoras*, 322.

student of nature who recognises one life in all the scale of plants and animals, from the hyssop and the rue to the forest trees, and from the protozoon to man, and yet lovingly notes the things in which they differ. The rational life that builds society we also know to be one ; but so vast is the latent wealth of that one life that it requires nothing less than the inexhaustible variety of human character, shaped under all kinds of natural conditions and spiritual climates, in order to express itself.

And, chiefly, the true social reformer realises the supreme value of it all. To him there is nothing common or unclean. He is quick to discern the touch of good that lives in every man, and makes him live. His wisdom is not that of the man-of-the-world, who interprets things by their meanest aspects, and therefore *mis*-interprets them. By the insight of sympathy, he gets near the facts of human character, to the confused and obscure struggle for something believed to be good, which, after all, is the ultimate reason of any human act.

Aristotle demanded good character of the student of ethics ; and following him, we may say that if a man's equipment of sympathy is scanty, his study should not be men in their mutual relations, nor that system of services we call society, but something else. We can understand the needs and wrongs of men only if we feel them, and we can remedy them only by atoning for them in our own lives. The reformer who has not this working faith in his fellow-men, who only blames them and attacks their institutions, has not learnt the alphabet of his science. Hard judgments of human character and human institutions are generally false, and always shallow. The helper of mankind recognises the good in that which he would change, and finds room for it in the greater good which he would bring into the world.

Insight into the needs of men, a high opinion of human nature, strong trust in the good which is already working in the world and which has brought it thus far on its way —these are cardinal constituents of the reformer's practical faith. But along with these must go another, and possibly in these days, a quality more rare. Looking round at the social life of this country, there seems to me to be one need more imperious than any other: it is the need of clear light upon the broad principles of social well-being.

"The great defect of Mr. Mill's later writings," says Mr. Fitzjames Stephen, "seems to me to be that he has formed too favourable an estimate of human nature." Should I be committing the same most pardonable error as Mr. Mill if I were to say of the British people of to-day that what they lack in this matter of social reform is not so much the will as the way? Many and urgent are the problems that confront us. "How," we ask, "shall we house the poor, provide for needy age, teach sobriety and thrift to a thoughtless and wasteful nation, dispense our charities so as to raise the recipients: how shall we find employment for empty and willing hands, prevent the exhaustion of the best wealth of the nation, which is its manhood, and hinder the deterioration of the physique of the people by the migration of the country population into the towns: how shall we reconcile capital and labour, the rights of the individual and those of the state: how far shall we regulate unions and trusts: where shall we draw the limits of municipal and national enterprise, and determine which, if any, of the ideals of socialism can be safely realised?" What is it that blocks our way to these reforms? How is it that, while we have tried to handle a few of these problems in a most timid and tentative way, most of them neither party in the state has dared even to touch? It is not that we do not desire these and similar reforms. It is not selfishness only, nor even primarily, that arrests our efforts and paralyses the will for good. Who would not wish to see the inequalities of wealth levelled, and levelled upwards—which is economically not impossible; the collision of interests, all known to be necessary to each other, mitigated; individual and social activity growing together; a nation that is sober; its workers better housed; its children and its youths better educated; its aged poor spending the evening of their laborious day in some ease and comfort?

The answer is plain: We do not see our way to these ends. The reforms we all desire, more or less vividly, seem to us, and indeed veritably are, for the most part impracticable. But they are not intrinsically impracticable; they are, we believe, only impracticable at the present time; and they are made so by our ignorance. We acknowledge the social evils, but we know no remedy, or we dare not apply it. Such is the magnitude of the issues involved and the complexity of the texture of modern social life, that we are afraid of the unknown perils of dislocating our accustomed ways; we prefer to endure the evils we know. In this region of moral and social phenomena we are not able to trace the incidence of our acts, nor follow the lines of antecedents and consequents. As a rule, practical men engaged in municipal and other social work have no theory on these matters; and such is the state of popular ignorance that they are probably better without it. Nevertheless, the wider the experience of these men and the greater their responsibilities, the more they long for some less spendthrift way of seeking the public good than that of blind empiricism, which can distinguish the right methods from the wrong only by trying both. Indeed, no one who is interested in the social well-being of the people will deny that amongst the deepest needs of our times is the need of clear light upon the broad principles of social well-being; —the need, in short, of *A science of social life.*

But where is such a science to be found; or what prospects are there that it can ever be established? The very suggestion of such a science seems incompatible with sobriety of judgment. There can be no science save where broad general laws colligate, or rather constitute, the facts; and what laws which are not so general as to be well-nigh meaningless hold in this region of human life? Is not human nature plastic, and are not the forms which it has taken endlessly varied? Does it not express itself in individuals and is not every one of these, in each detailed deed, free? Amongst the characteristics of our times is its distrust of theory. We are most apt to be Agnostics, except as to things which we can touch and see, deeming true causes to be beyond our reach, and our knowledge to be only of their outward show; and we are not aware that our Agnosticism is due to a sense of a world more sane and stable, which is just the product of our widening knowledge. Even the natural sciences are found to be defective. Their results, it is averred, are proximate generalisations, their bases are hypothetical, their very facts are only phenomena. Our knowledge gives us something of the use of things, and is in that respect not vain. We can gain such truth as serves our occasion, and define objects by reference to our own ends. But what these objects veritably are we do not know. Truth, in the old sense, we should not seek, it is said: it is the unattainable ideal of the Intellectualist. And the Intellectualist is the apathetic looker-on at life, the bloodless remnant of man which deals with abstractions, and does nothing to help the world. Let us be modest and Pragmatists—if the combination is possible.

Now, I do not consider that this diffidence is of much practical consequence so far as research into the truths of nature is concerned. The faith that the physical world is a cosmos, and that its great uniformities can be discovered by patient inquiry, is too profound to be disturbed by such academic doubts. There is no evidence that men of science are about to change their methods, so as to interpret facts in the light of their own needs, or to will them into accord with their desires. If they seek theories that "work," they mean by "working" the production of effects which are intelligible, accordant at once with the nature of things and the nature of mind.

But this sceptical prejudice touches inquiry into the phenomena of the social, moral, and religious life much more deeply. In this region the faith in the objective order is feeble and comparatively new. Religion, indeed, teaches it; for religion is an optimist. It is a theoretical and practical faith that what is best must be real. Poetry also maintains it, and most of all have the greater modern poets, from Wordsworth to Tennyson and Browning, taught that God dwells in the mind of man and rules the caprice of human history. But there is a long and difficult way to travel from the inspired insight of religion and poetry to the reasoned conviction of philosophy and science. The former gain the highest by first leap; the latter move painfully along the links of intermediate causes, testing each fact as they go, as a blind man feels his way with his staff. Belief in an invariable and unerring social order is ours only during moments of passionate exaltation. And that belief is rebuked, and seems to be convicted of rashness and sentimental enthusiasm, when reason enters and throws its cold light on the contingencies and complexities of human life—the caprice of man and the chance of circumstance, which make up his history.

For is not man the most unintelligible of all beings? Even as an animal he gathers into himself the complex forces which have evolved him. And as to his conscious life, is it not the reflex image and ideal rendering of all the world he knows, and is he not therefore the résumé of all its problems? Above all, the moralist—if he has not distinguished between caprice and freedom—sees in the very conception of an inviolable social order a principle which is fatal to the moral life, which undoubtedly does demand that man shall choose his own acts and be responsible for his destiny.

Now, it seems to me to be idle to deny the force of these objections. Undoubtedly, the last object which man will explain will be man himself, and his spirit must brood long over the deeps of social life before the order of its laws will emerge. Nevertheless, it does not seem to me to be possible to deny the existence of these laws, or to aver that all knowledge of them—the tentative, proximate, but growing knowledge characteristic of man—entirely transcends his powers. And inasmuch as it is certain that men will not act with confidence amidst unknown forces, and that they will not inquire with any constancy of purpose into what they believe to be unintelligible, the first task of the social reformer is to confront this doubt which paralyses social theory and makes the advocacy of far-reaching social enterprises the monopoly of the rash.

A full discussion of the sceptic's objections would lead us very far afield, and I must spare you that enterprise. A shorter way, and possibly enough a more secure way at present, would be to appeal from the social theory of the sceptic to his own social life: for, like other men, he is sometimes better than his creed, and apt to be more significant than he knows. It seems to me that in all his intercourse with his fellows—which constitutes his social life, which really is his *whole* life—he presumes the reality of that order and uniformity which he denies in theory. He draws inferences, as Hume has pointed out, concerning his own and his neighbours' actions; and he cannot help doing so if he is to act at all. In total ignorance of consequences, under the conviction that there is utter discontinuity between motive, will, and act, and that there exists the equal possibility of any or of no results, he would act at his peril, or rather he would not dare to act, nor have any reason for either acting or not acting. In a society where there were no permanences, there would be no expectations; no pact or promise could be either broken or kept; for where everything is unstable or incalculable, no pact or promise could be made. And hence the sceptic's argument destroys the object it deals with: for, to show that there are no obligations, is to show that there is no human society, which is just a system of obligations.

I find in the denial of the laws of the social order that singular lack of imagination which is characteristic of scepticism. I do not mean the unbridled imagination which runs away from facts, but that saner power which is the light of much of our seeing, because it can anticipate facts, and forecast the consequences that flow from general principles. The social sceptic is a dealer in generalities, and his thinking is much too facile. He sees the collision of purposes in human society, and the wrongs and suffering and disorder which spring therefrom. But he does not see that these are the offspring, on the one side, of the very faith in law which he condemns as an illusion. On his theory, no purpose would be foiled and no strife of purposes would arise, no expectation could be disappointed and no failure experienced; for the pursuit of ends would be impossible. To loosen the bonds of society is not merely to dissolve it into the dust and powder of individual units, but to destroy these units themselves—for man is a rational being only in virtue of society.

The source of this error lies in the view that is taken of the nature of universals: they are regarded as the results of inference. It is the same error as brands physical laws as mere generalisations invented by abstract thought—things useful for explanation, or at least for intercommunication, but having no existence in the realm of the real. On this view the idea of necessary law, whether physical or social, is one of the late products of reflective thought. In truth, however, it is not so much a product of thought as it is a postulate and constitutive principle of thinking, which necessarily manifests its presence in every rational act. The housewife, though all unconscious, assumes the uniformity of nature when she places the kettle over the fire, and she postulates the stable order of society in ordering goods from her grocer. In one sense it is true that the uniformity of nature is only a hypothesis, and a hypothesis imperfectly established, for there are sequences we cannot trace; and this is still more manifestly true of social uniformities. But, on the other hand, at whatever point we deny the truth of these hypotheses, there knowledge and action cease. Their truth is as wide as our rational life, and is a condition of that life.

But it may be answered: Granted that man never acts except with a view to results, and that the most ardent missionary of social chaos does not expect to gather grapes from thorns or figs from thistles; granted that man cannot live in society, and that there cannot be a society, except under the conception of the uniformity of connection between antecedent and consequent, between desire and will, and will and act; and granted, even, that what we must conceive as real is as good as real for us—it still does not follow that we can discover these laws.

To this objection I shall proffer only one answer,—an answer, moreover, that comes from man's experience, and not merely from theories of that experience. It is, that there are some experiments in social well-being which will be tried no more by any civilised people. There are consequences which we would pronounce impossible beforehand, not because our procedure is *a priori*, but because the judgment of history lies behind it and sustains it.

Mankind has not only experienced much since it housed itself in caves, but has learned much from its experience. Distances we cannot measure separate the earliest life of man, the crude societies of the clan and tribe, the civic states of Greece, the iron imperialism of Rome, and the modern states of Europe. During this long history men have sought their private ends, fulfilled the duties of narrow stations, thinking little of society. But they have constructed society all the same: the complex modern state stands to-day as their accumulated wisdom, made incarnate in its manifestly stable customs and institutions.

Like a vast primaeval forest, the civilised modern state, which is the highest form so far achieved by human society, is a thing self-sown, renewing its immortality from age to age. No one has planned and no one has planted it. But it has its laws of growth all the same, and its own grave grandeur. Every individual within it, struggling for his own life, and reaching up towards the sunlight, contributes not only to the variety but to the vast unity of the whole. The statesman, the philosopher, the artist, the preacher, the legislator, the judge, the soldier, the maker of tools, the tiller of the soil; the wise and good in every degree, nay, the foolish and wicked, by their negative experiments, have for successive generations shed their lives like forest leaves to make the black soil on which our social institutions grow.

But society differs from the native forest. Its structure is spiritual. It is the product, in every part, of the rational nature of man, and by far the most glorious exhibition of his powers. We call the reason that has compacted it "unconscious" when we wish to indicate that, taken as a whole, the construction of society was never the deliberate ideal of a single human mind, or that in bringing it about men built better than they knew. But, in strictness of speech, the reason that built society was never unconscious. Not one step was taken, large or small, in the advance or retreat of its history, which was not guided by the conception of some good to be attained, and which did not rest on the presupposition that consequent follows antecedent and necessary law. "Unconscious reason" is only a general term, to which no real thing corresponds. The conception it is meant to signify is that of reason operating in a vast multitude of persons, each of whom seeks and achieves ends by conscious methods, but none of whom reflected on these methods, or was even aware of them. And society is the interrelation of these ends, not one of which can exist for itself alone, but only in vital interaction with all the rest.

Now, what follows from all this? Evidently, it seems to me, that society, which is the product of reason, or spirit, is the exhibition of the nature of reason, and therefore itself rational, and capable, so far as its intrinsic character is concerned, of rational interpretation. And there follows, further, the fact, so often overlooked, that the philosopher who attempts to discover the laws of social life, and to reveal the broad principles that should guide the effort after social reform, is not engaged on any new or unheard-of enterprise. Social reflection did not begin with him any more than moral life began with the moral philosopher. Every act that has gone to the building of society has implied someone's attempt to interpret his social environment in relation to his own needs and ends. The philosopher has only to continue the reflection exercised by the simplest of men when he tries to determine his own duties and to live his own life. The philosopher's reflection may range wider, and deal with broader issues and problems more profound; but, in the last resort, he does not stand apart from his fellow-men. For philosophy is only the common consciousness seeking to do justice to all the facts and to think more persistently. The greatest interpreter of his times is the truest child of his times, and all his wisdom he gets by inheritance. He "moves *with* the larger march of human destiny."

I do not deny that the realm of man's history is intricate, nor assert that the laws that make the life of human society one marvellous evolution are simple or on the surface. A fixed and determinate science of its phenomena we shall never have.[1] Indeed, a fixed social science would be false, for the phenomenon it would explain is a growing, and therefore an ever-changing, fact. Simple prediction cannot be had in this region, as in that of physical facts. Nevertheless, growth has its laws, even though they are the laws of change, and it implies an ever-living, self-enriching identity: the reason and will for good which have created society have their great uniformities as well as the stars and planets. And these laws are being discovered. As in the field of natural science, theory and practice, abstract speculation and practical invention, have gone hand in hand, inciting and aiding each other to advance, so in the moral and social sphere do the theory and practice of life reflect light upon one another. Social life is an experiment on which all men are engaged and on which every man throws some light.

But the sad and amazing fact is, that our pursuit of truth in this realm proceeds without method. We recognise the vital importance of social problems; we know that here, if anywhere, the intellect of man should summon

[1] I do not say this because I share the view, not even yet quite extinct, that at the core of character there lies hid an insulated self, or at the core of the self an incalculable will. Such a self, or such a will, is supposed to be a condition of freedom. But it would be either undetermined, that is, it would be a self or a will which could do nothing whatsoever; or it would be determined by chance, which is not only necessity, but irrational necessity.

all its powers into the field ; and yet we commit the charge of this most complex and delicate structure in the world, this force that makes most momentously for man's weal or woe and is most within his power to make or mar, into the hands of men whose natural gifts of mind and heart may indeed be great, but who have no other resource or trust than common usage and tradition, and no guide save generous sentiment and honest purpose, and the perilous contingency of uninstructed thought.

In our dealings with our physical environment we act otherwise. We do not look for the discoveries that change the conditions of our outer life to mere good-will and commonsense, indispensable as these always are. We seek and we secure more. No labour of research is too severe, no training is too prolonged, no equipment is too costly, no endowment is too generous, no inquiry is too remote from all visible practical purposes—provided only that they are concerned with natural objects. And this is well: no national investment has brought a greater return than that which flows from what we have sunk in the sciences. But the study of the spiritual, mind-made environment which we call "Society," and which is the inmost content as well as the supreme outer condition of man's rational life—where is it methodically pursued? It is less in evidence in our universities than the study of algae or protozoa.

Were it not well that where there are so many "sitting by their studious lamps, musing, searching, revolving new notions and ideas," there should be some striving to comprehend actual living society? The study of the history of the past is valuable, we need its light; the discovery of economic laws is desirable, for man is a maker and consumer of wealth ; the ethical sciences are still more indispensable, for the forces that rule the destiny of society are moral. But while all these have their contributory uses, none of them deal directly with the nature of society as it stands, or with the problems which confront the social reformer when he takes up his task as a citizen. For want of a philosophy of political or social life we let the politician loose upon the world, the victim, if he counts more than his vote, either of the obstructive prejudices of mere common usage, or of a rash enthusiasm for untried and impossible ways of social life.

The schools of learning, it is true, cannot make social reformers any more than they can make poets. But they can foster them. The Universities reveal to the students of literature something of the treasures of classic thought, they make their appreciation of beauty more generous and discipline their taste. Above all, they can send them out into the world prepared to learn, and apprenticed to the lifelong service of a great art. And it seems to me evident, that although the art of life is even more subtle than that of poetry, and our knowledge of its deeper principles is quite inadequate, our Universities could nevertheless win for it the interest of many of their alumni, awaken and enlighten and discipline their social conscience, train them to observe history-in-the-making, and make them sensitive to the prejudices as well as to the wrongs which burden civilisation and keep back the happiness of mankind. In one word, they could launch them upon life "prepared to learn"; neither clinging with the stubborn strength of stupidity and ignorance to ways of life outworn, nor rashly blind to the complexity of modern society, and the delicacy of the equipoise of its many institutions. The youths that left them year by year would enter upon the privileges and responsibilities of practical life, which is the citizen's life, made aware of the perseverance, the wisdom, and the patience of the will for good which has built the state; and it is reasonable to believe that they would prove to be "more considerate builders, more wise in spiritual architecture," than their fathers have been.

In a word, it is time that we should methodise our inquiry into social life, and give to the Political Sciences their due place amongst our studies. The danger of trusting exclusively to social instinct and the sporadic insight of uninstructed empiricism was never so great as it is at the present time. For our ways are in many respects untried. The very structure of human society has changed, even though the fundamental passions of mankind remain the same from age to age. For society no longer consists of petty rural or urban units, each leading its own secluded life, speaking its own dialect, cherishing its own particular customs, meeting its own peculiar wants. Modern society is one tumultuous whole. The powers that bring the success or the failure of the individual merchant or maker of goods travel from afar; all the lines of social life go out through all the earth. Society is stratified into classes, and the impact of their collision shakes the state. While the state itself is now an empire so vast that we may well do what in us lies to discipline the mind and train the public conscience of those upon whom its responsibilities must rest: and these, in the last resort, are *all* its citizens.

Even the growth of social sympathy, which is so characteristic of our times, brings its dangers if it be not chastened by a sense of the past and disciplined by science.

Brought for the first time into contact with the merciless forces of economic competition, and the physical misery and moral wretchedness of much of modern city life, the more generous youths, nurtured on the ideals of Christianity, are naturally, nay, almost inevitably, led to condemn the whole social system which produces these evils. No remedy seems to them to be possible short of a general overturn; and they dream of some new social beginning upon some entirely new basis of common brotherhood and common possessions, where greed and injustice can find no foothold. The strong ethical temperament is always prone to impatience with the evil of the world, and to cry, "How long, O Lord, how long?"

Nor can we measure our debt to these moral enthusiasts, who shake the torpor from our social creeds and disturb the complacency with which we suffer the customary evils of others. But they may be bringers of mischief all the same, and society may have a perfect right to defend itself against them. Every society wrongs itself if it yields to anything except to *its own* better condition; and it can accept no service except that which is continuous with the social forces that have brought it thus far on its way. And this means that the world can be helped only by those who link themselves to the good that is already present within it and warring with its wrongs. It is an axiom of fruitful research and a postulate of real reform that their starting-point shall be in things as they are. The wiser our social work, the more we shall believe in reform, and the less we shall trust in revolution; and the better we understand revolutions, the clearer we shall see that, so far as they have had lasting value, they were simply evolution, with its steps somewhat hastened.

This was the truth which, in trying times, Edmund Burke enforced with many strong arguments and illumined with all the splendour of his eloquence. It is a truth generally urged in the interests of social and political conservatism. I press it, rather, in the interests of reform. The consciousness of the good embodied in our social life is not so much needed by those who would leave things as they are, as by others who would lay their hands upon its complex relations in order to change them. Burke pled for reverence towards the state. He would deal with its evils as with a father's wounds. And even in the presence of evils that may seem to be accumulating, of a public life that is in danger of forgetting its ethical foundations in the ardour of its pursuit of material good, and of a legislative assembly that seems at times to be spendthrift of its own dignity, I should counsel the same spirit. The reform of the state, and of the social life within it, must be based on loyalty ; loyalty must rest on reverence, and we can revere only that which we believe to be in some ways great and good.

Now, it may seem a paradox to say that this reverence can be best learnt, not from the writings of great men who have projected ideal states, but from observing the practical life of the world as it is. But such is my experience. Among the deepest impressions left upon me after visiting the worst plague-spots of the great city in which I dwell (where I saw only what has been often described) was their comparatively limited area. Pitiful beyond speech and most repulsive was the scene of their dissoluteness and vice. But I could not help contrasting it with the vast extent of respectable, decent, commonplace, but well-doing life, which, during the obscure hours when wickedness was awake, lay resting all around throughout the quiet miles of streets, recuperating its strength for the duties of the morrow. And not less impressive was the completeness of the control of the city authorities over these evil centres. The officers of the law and the criminals knew each other as familiarly as opponents in a game of chess, and were on not less friendly terms. And the rules of the game were thoroughly understood on both sides. There were some evils for which the law had little remedy; but in almost every case these were evils for which legal coercion was not the proper method, or in which the crude powers of legal justice could not be applied without invading legitimate rights and endangering the public welfare in wider ways. The law seemed to me to have crept in after vice into every crevice, and to press upon it constantly on all sides, like the waters of the sea on an indented shore. I came away with my mind filled with the sense of the vastness of the wise labour of good men during many generations, devoted in unobtrusive ways to the social service. And there seemed to me to be very little room for the mere innovator.

Now, I am not prepared to say the same of all the aspects of our social life. Crime is a direct menace to society and a direct challenge to its forces; and, on the whole, society has learnt how to protect itself against it. But the misery that comes from sheer misfortune and incompetence, from the personal feebleness that lacks the energy which goes to crime is a more insidious evil. The problem of the outcast poor, of the occasionally innocent and always helpless victims of a society that is not cleansed of the methods of barbarism, is far larger and more difficult; and the same serious and systematic thought has not been applied to its solution. The work that remains to be done in this respect is very great. But still it seems to me to lie, in by far the greater part, along the lines of the old endeavour. The effective reformer, even in these comparatively neglected fields, will, in the first instance at least, realise the value of the work already done, and seek simply to continue it. He must find his fulcrum for raising society in things as they are. He must live within the world if he is to make it better, and arm himself with its powers in order to conquer it.

Few things have entailed such waste of ethical force, which is man's very life-blood, as the neglect of this simple practical maxim. It is exemplified in many ways. We seek, for instance, to engraft straightway the elevated thoughts of the Christian religion upon crude and barbarous civilisations; or we would introduce amongst ourselves ideal ways of life for which neither our disposition nor our habits nor our institutions are prepared. In doing so we ignore the most elementary and cardinal of all the truths we know of human experience, namely, that it must be continuous; that neither in theory nor in practice can anything new be introduced except that which the old can assimilate. Morality, whether personal or social, can be acquired only step by step. There is a scale of ascending ideals along which, in due order, man must travel to the Good. As well expect to solve the problems of higher mathematics before we have learnt to add or subtract, as hope to attain, or even to recognise, great ideals when character is crude or social life rudimentary. Human history seems, no doubt, to present society as subject to sudden conversions; and history verily has its greater moods. But these conversions are never so sudden as they seem ; the most abrupt changes have their gradual causes. Their explanation lies in the wondrous capacity of human character for storing up its experience. For it is questionable if anything is really lost. It is certain that a constant, silent, for the most part unconscious, accumulation of inwrought tendencies takes place. And, given certain personal or social temperaments and a certain conjunction of circumstance, the accumulated force breaks its barriers in ways that astound. The whole process of social change is continuous and law-sustained ; and the social earthquake comes as naturally as the falling dew.

Trust in the good that is in the world, loyalty towards the society he would raise to a higher level of well-being, seem to me, therefore, to be cardinal qualities of the reformer's faith. His attitude towards society is never negative or denunciatory. The great reformer comes to fulfil, not to destroy. He is no visionary who prophesies a new world, and he does not mean to overturn. What most distinguishes him from the futile enthusiast is that his aims are positive and concrete, and that his touch with things as they are is immediate. He enters upon his task seeking to remove some particular wrong which has become intolerable, or to bring back some old and obvious truth that has been forgotten ; and it is in dealing with these, often enough to his own dismay, that revolution comes. For the particular wrong or old error is found to have other wrongs and errors clinging to it, and to be really the dead husk of what once was true. It has worked itself into the structure of institutions, and become a part of the texture of the mind and habits of the times. Hence it cannot be removed without violence, and consequences follow the assaults against it of which the reformer had not dreamed. The forces of the past and of the future, the good that was and the good that ought to be, range themselves in opposition; passion awakes, and the reformer is caught up amongst powers which are greater than he knew and which he cannot control. The characteristic that marks him as a hero is that his courage mounts with the call that is made upon him, and his ideas widen as he moves. He dares more and more. But all his daring is obedience to the demand of moving circumstance. There is nothing *a priori* in his procedure; and he brings to his task, not distant ideals, not fair Utopias, but the intelligence to interpret what everyone sees, and the heart to dare what many desire. His work for mankind is, in fact, due to the contact of times that are ripe with a spirit that is great enough to understand and to obey them; and he himself is, in a sense, little more than their instrument.

It is not, however, from the fear of speculation that I thus urge reverence for the past and loyalty to the existing institutions of the state, but from distrust of the shallow, abstract, mischievous thought that is not in touch with facts. If the reformer plants his feet well upon actual experience, devoting to the understanding of it a mind trained to the severe, impersonal, disinterested methods of science which alone can bring him to the facts, he can then be as speculative as he pleases—at least in this country. For, of all the people in the world, the least likely to suffer from excessive speculation in social and political matters is the English. Their tendency is to see no evil till they stumble over it. Distrust of ideas is in their blood. They are not an unheroic people, but their heroism is the persistence of a semi-conscious force which wears down public wrongs by constant attrition. And it is quite certain that those who desire to lead the English people to better ways of life and a richer common good must respect its temperament. They must possess ideals, but these ideals must be the inner essence, the truth which is at the same time the reality, of the facts of their social experience. And that truth is not easily attained. Prejudices intervene between us and social facts, passions distort them; the serene and open mind comes not without a severe and prolonged discipline to which our present untutored ways are foreign; and, above all, in this instance the object of criticism fashions the critic. But these are matters which I must deal with in my next essay.

# THE WORKING FAITH OF THE SOCIAL REFORMER

## II

## THE MISUSE OF METAPHORS IN THE HUMAN SCIENCES

MAN must interpret unfamiliar objects in the light of things already known; hence he is prone to think in Metaphors, and has sought to employ physical categories to explain social facts. Dominant categories: their nature and succession. The application of irrelevant categories and how it gives rise to insoluble problems and to the despair of knowledge.

The metaphorical use of physical and biological categories and its distortion of the facts in Logic, Epistemology, and Ethics: "the foundation" of knowledge.

The application of physical categories to social problems illustrated by reference to the dispute as to the relative significance of "Character" and "Environment." The discussion proceeds on a false assumption: character and environment are two names for the same thing. The self and the world imply and even *are* each other; and the growth of both is concurrent.

Results of the adoption of this view in the practical reform of society, and how they correspond to the results of actual experience. When the character is formed, that is, when the self has internalized its environment, attempts to reform it fail; for a vitiated character turns all opportunities into its own substance. The methods that society must employ when a vicious character is already formed. Society must employ different methods when character is not yet fixed, and attempt to do more. How biological metaphors have prevented social action in relation to the children of its useless or criminal parents. That vicious propensities are not hereditary: and that the risks of State interference are not so great as is assumed and are worth the running.

II

## THE MISUSE OF METAPHORS IN THE HUMAN SCIENCES

In my last article I tried to show that the social reformer must have faith in the world as it is, if he is to make it better. His ideals will prove impracticable unless they are implicit in the facts he would change. The world must "tend" towards the reformer's ends. His efficiency as a reformer is measured by his power to apprehend and use this tendency, which, like an unconscious purpose, is the essential significance of his facts.

But it is not easy to discern it. Even in the case of a simple life we cannot predict; we must wait and observe how its interaction with circumstances brings forth its characters one by one. But the social organism is incomparably complex, and it has many forms, all of them unique in fundamental ways. There has been no other society or State quite like our own; and in every age of its history it reveals new features as well as confronts new tasks. The laws of social growth on which we might rely in trying to discover its future possibilities are very general; and the conditions of its growth are very intricate, for social life consists in the complex interaction of many mutually implicated human wills.

Besides, society touches us very nearly. We are ourselves caught within its meshes and entangled in its traditions. Prejudices intervene between us and the facts, passion distorts, and the serene spirit of science, with its purely objective ardour, is hard to attain. Society moulds the individual long before he thinks of criticising it. He *is* his society individuated, so far as he is an individual at all; hence social criticism is the most difficult of all criticism, for it is self-criticism. And the criticism is conducted by any individual from the particular angle of his station in life and in the flaring light of his personal interests.

But all these obstacles in the way of a science of the facts of social life are obvious. I shall dwell in this article on another difficulty, which is at once much more subtle and much more powerful. It springs from our very way of knowing, or, at least, from our way of knowing anything new.

"Ordinary knowledge," said the late Professor Wallace, "consists in referring an object to a class of objects; that is, to a generalised image with which we are already acquainted. It is not so much cognition as re-cognition. . . . Once we have referred the new individual to a familiar category or convenient metaphor, once we have given it a name, and introduced it into the society of our mental drawing-room, we are satisfied." Now, scientific thought breaks up these crude classifications of ordinary consciousness, and generally brings under the same principles objects that have few superficial or sensible similarities. But neither scientific nor philosophic thought escapes from the law which binds us, in the first place, to interpret new objects in the light of others more familiar.

And it follows that even these more rigorous kinds of knowledge are apt to be the victims of analogy. They play with conceptions as ordinary thought does with mental pictures, and apply old principles to facts without inquiring whether they fit them or not. Man never knows how metaphorical he is.

These considerations apply with great force to all the sciences of human life, but especially to that of human society. Both the psychology of the individual and the history of thought on the large scale of its philosophical systems show that man thinks of himself, and of the products and activities of his own spirit, last of all. His coming to himself is always a return from the world. It follows, therefore, that he seeks to interpret himself in the light of the world.[1] He contemplates the order of human relations through the medium of the more obvious and familiar order of the physical cosmos. He applies to the former categories of thought that have assisted him to comprehend the latter. He thus thinks in metaphors, and is not aware that he does so. And, consequently, the sciences of man, and especially of human society, are "the playground of analogies." These unconscious analogies, in the next place, are allowed to fill the part of scientific hypotheses; and the power of a hypothesis of explaining facts, if it is true, or of falsifying facts, if it is false, is not easily measured. Hypotheses are constructive, and not merely colligating, conceptions. We live under their

[1] It is quite true that man interprets the world in terms of his self, and that not only religious, but all knowledge is anthropomorphical. But it is also true that only by rational interaction with the world is man a self at all. A man's world and a man's living experience, which is his self, are two names for the same thing. A self separated from the world, and a world separated from the self are abstract unrealities.

dominion even when we do not know that they exist ; and their authority over us is all the greater because it is not suspected.

Our own times exemplify these truths. Our thinking, we all recognize, is ruled by the idea of Evolution. We should find it difficult to say how we came to adopt it. We may not be able to say precisely what it means. But we employ it all the same, and employ it in different senses, much to the detriment of many of our discussions, especially in morals and theology. And such has been its power that it has transfigured the world. All the sciences have been transformed by it—Geology, Biology, Physiology, Psychology, Logic, and Metaphysics. Even Theology, which, unlike all other sciences, is prone to look backwards for its truths, has not been exempt from its influence. Beneath the constructive conceptions proper to each of these sciences, taken severally, there has been this wider hypothesis, directing the method of knowing of the whole age, making all the sciences move together, and giving to the thought of our times a certain unity of direction and of purpose.

The history of human thought in the past is the story of the succession of these great dominant conceptions ; and that succession marks the true stages of human civilisation, dividing it into distinct epochs. There is no event in the life of the race comparable in significance to the transition from one of these dominant conceptions to another ; for it means a change in all its ways of thinking and acting.

Now, it might seem that if man is always under the sway of some one or other of these conceptions, which thus fill his whole sky and colour his whole world, he cannot know facts as they are. He must apparently observe them through a disturbing medium. But such a sceptical and despairing conclusion does not necessarily follow. It depends itself on an assumption, and indeed on a visual metaphor. This assumption, too rarely examined, is that what is not altogether true must be altogether false; and that the succession of categories is the aimless substitution of one dominant error for another. But there may be degrees in knowledge as there are grades in goodness; and it is possible that although we only know in part we *do* know in part. The "medium," instead of intervening between us and the facts, converting them into phenomena, may be a principle which so far interprets the facts. And the succession of such media, the substitution of one general hypothesis for another, may not be accidental, but may follow some deeper law which secures that the movement of human thought shall be continuous, rational, and self-enriching. It may be the gradual self-manifestation of the principle in virtue of which the world subsists.

Whether this be verily the fact or not can be seen only by an analysis of the relation of the successive categories, and of their successive embodiments in systems of thought. We cannot enter upon this fundamental question here.[1] But we may learn something useful for the science of human society if we examine briefly how such transitions are brought about. The attempt may reveal the part which metaphors play in our thinking—a matter which social theorists and social reformers have to lay to heart much more deeply than they do at present.

The unsatisfactory character of any earlier hypothesis

[1] This was the task which Hegel attempted; and, whether his success in it was great or small, it is a task which philosophy cannot avoid, least of all if the world is spiritual and the idea of evolution holds.

reveals itself by the fact that it is not only inadequate to the matter which it professes to explain, but that the explanation which it proffers is self-contradictory. It reveals truths which seem necessary, but which cannot be held together. That is to say, the facts investigated somehow combine aspects which the *thought* of the facts cannot reconcile. Hence arise controversies that are interminable. They are interminable because each of the conflicting doctrines carries within it an aspect of the truth, and, as it takes that aspect for the *whole* truth, it is obliged to endeavour to refute its opposite, which is not possible, for truth is a spirit which cannot be laid.

The impartial observer, the mind which is sufficiently open to admit the truth from both sides, is tempted under such circumstances to despair of human thought. It is held to be inadequate to facts. It is by its very nature condemned to choose without reasonable cause between exclusive alternatives.[1] But mind ceases to be mind when it seeks to *rest* amongst contradictions. To do so it must give up its own nature, which is to organise its content into a systematic unity. Absolute scepticism—that is, distrust of the intellect as such—is not an attitude possible for the intellect. It is itself contradictory.[2]

The intelligence is thus thrown back upon itself, or, what is the same thing, it is thrown back upon the facts.

[1] Such, for instance, was the view of Sir William Hamilton and Herbert Spencer; and it lies at the root of positivism and other forms of that incomplete scepticism which we call agnosticism.

[2] For it denies the possibility of all knowledge and at the same time asserts the validity of its own knowledge and of its own criterion of it. A genuinely absolute scepticism would neither assert nor deny anything; that is, it is not an attitude of thought at all.

And the result which ensues is that on examining itself it discovers that it is employing, whichever of the contradicting truths it adopts, an unjustified and even an unsuspected hypothesis; and on examining the facts that their opposing aspects are, both alike, phases of a deeper unity. And these hypotheses prove, I believe invariably, to be metaphors. The object which is investigated has been observed through the medium of a familiar conception which was serviceable in the interpretation of other facts, but is not applicable to it. For metaphors cannot give the truth, any more than analogies can prove. Metaphors are not metaphors except when they omit something relevant and introduce something irrelevant. But facts have their individual rights, and will not submit to vicarious treatment. And no science can ever set forth on a progressive path till its regulative hypothesis and method of inquiry are determined for it by the facts it investigates, and not merely by some other facts with which the investigator happens to be better acquainted.

Now, modern theories of society have been passing through precisely this process. They began by endeavouring to explain man, and his social manifestation of his rational nature, by means of the categories which had proved effective in the explanation of the natural world. *It was taken for granted* that subjects are related to each other as objects are. The interaction of their wills in society was an instance of stress and strain, of attraction and repulsion and external collision. Society was a mechanism; its elements were compacted together coercively.

But this view led to an endless controversy in both social theory and social practice. It was impossible—if I may refer to one instance—to see how, from this point of view, the welfare of one individual can contribute to the welfare of another, or how social order and effective individual freedom can grow together, which they undoubtedly do. Then it was discovered that the social science was based on a metaphor. It was speculating about man in terms of Physics.

After that, recourse was had to the biological categories. The social philosopher conceived that he was dealing with an "organism," and, with a suspicious facility, spoke of "natural selection," "struggle for existence," "survival of the fittest," and so forth. And, for a time, social science, if we can dignify the inquiry with that name, fared better. The biological idea does admit the possibility of the mutual welfare of the parts, and indicates that a certain independence and variety of functions is compatible with the unity of the whole. It left much unexplained, but it explained many things which from the mechanical point of view were unintelligible and impossible. Society may not be an animal, but, at the worst, it is more like an animal than a machine.

Still, society is not an animal. And the attempt to treat it as an animal led to new contradictions. Human society contains both physical and biological elements, but its *basis* is neither physical nor biological. Its basis is the rational nature of man. The physical and biological elements in it, its *natural* life, are organic to, and therefore transmuted by, their relation to a rational principle. Society is the product of conscious ends; it is generated in the course of the attempt of its members to realise good things conceived and willed. And this conscious, purposive element, which is the active and fundamental agent in the matter, cannot be explained by biology. Biology leaves it out of account. "Acting, living society," says Professor Bosanquet, "is an infinitely higher thing than a steam-engine, plant, or animal; and the best of our ideas are not too good to be employed in analysing it." Society is the product of self-consciousness, in fact, and we must employ the idea of self-consciousness as a category in order to explain it. Man, man as rational, is the only key to the nature of society.

Now, I believe that the attempt to explain man in the light of the physical, the biological, or any other category than self-consciousness, is the main reason for the unsatisfactory condition of the sciences of man—I mean of Psychology, Logic, Ethics, Sociology, and so forth—and is the chief cause of the confusion in Metaphysics and Theology. This is why these sciences are infected with insoluble problems which have brought discredit upon them, prevented them from partaking in the sure advance of the physical sciences, and even rendered suspect the validity of all human knowledge.

The importance of the matter demands that we should dwell upon it and illustrate further this metaphorical use of conceptions, before coming to the social problems with which we are most directly concerned. There is no lesson which the student of human nature must be so careful to learn as this of detecting and guarding himself against the unconscious use of metaphors. And he may learn this lesson from the history of any one of the human sciences. Logic, for instance, has long endeavoured to explain such ordinary processes of thought as judgment and reasoning by means of mechanical categories. But, in their light, it was not possible to account for the unity *in* difference which is *the* characteristic feature of both of them. We were left the choice between an Inductive and a Deductive Logic, both of which are false, because they are abstract. Psychology has been in a condition of utter confusion from the same cause. In its theory of the "Association of Ideas," for example, ideas were treated like objects in space and time, mutually external, separate, isolated, awaiting connection by means of relations. But no ideas could be found without relations, nor relations without ideas. Nor could ideas be resolved into relations, for relations can only exist *between* ideas—"they must have points on which to hang." But there are no such "points": if there were, they would have no meaning; and it is not possible to relate the meaningless. The difficulties, in short, are insoluble, and they arise from the application of the metaphors of mechanism to mental facts.[1]

Perhaps, however, the best illustration of the confusion which metaphors introduce into the theory of knowledge is furnished in the common notion that a science or philosophy, or any systematic body of truths, is a kind of "edifice." Being an edifice, it must, of course, rest on some "foundation." Hence, to find such a foundation is the first and most important business of the investigator. Unless *it* is sure, the whole body of doctrine is untrustworthy; but once it is found, the erection of the superstructure will go on apace, new facts being added to the old by means of observation and logic.

[1] An even more instructive illustration is furnished by psychologists. With great unanimity they reject the mechanical notion of a mind made up of externally inter-acting faculties; but they bring back as "elements," or "factors," what they have rejected as "faculties," and they discuss their relative priority, and expound their inter-action!

The discovery of this foundation for human knowledge is regarded as being especially the task of the philosopher; and the philosopher has undertaken it, sometimes in a highly picturesque way, as in the case of Descartes. Having discovered the insecurity of ordinary opinion and found that even the sciences are based on hypotheses, and being unwilling "to lean upon principles which he has taken on trust," he sets himself to pull down the "edifice" of experience, never staying his hands till he finds some truth that is valid in its own right. Descartes thought that his *Cogito, ergo sum* was such a truth. Doubt itself had to assume it; and that being the case, his *Cogito, ergo sum* offered a foundation for knowledge which was ultimate and could not be shaken. But his successors, on analysing it, discovered that it was full of implications. It consisted of only three terms, but every one of them was complex, and stood in need of vindication. Hence they must dig deeper in order to find a safe "foundation." They must find some simple truth, some sensation, impression, intuition, axiom, dictum of common-sense, *a priori* principle of knowledge which is valid in its own exclusive right. But the result has invariably been the same. No idea could be found which did not imply another idea, and which did not lose its meaning and become useless if it was divested of these implications. The search was intrinsically futile. It was a search after what does not exist.

Then followed, as usual, the distrust of human reason itself. Man's thought was called relative: its doom is to go back from condition to condition in an endless regress, and to hang its chain of knowledge upon nothingness. Or should not philosophy take to working miracles, and base knowledge on the unknowable with Herbert Spencer —which is about the maddest of all the projects propounded to suffering mankind?

But it is easier and more profitable to examine our assumptions than to work miracles, and, in particular, to see whether some metaphor has not been playing us false. Perhaps knowledge is not an edifice; perhaps it is not built by the external addition of idea to idea; nay, perhaps it has no "foundation." There are things in the world which have no "foundations." The roots of a plant are not precisely its "foundations," nor the feet of an animal. Plants and animals are organisms, and every part of them both rests upon and sustains every other part. Perhaps there is no elephant to hold up the world of ideas, and no tortoise to support the elephant. Knowledge may be like the solar system—an equipoise of elements which sustain one another. Ideas may have meaning only in their relation to each other, and relativity may not be a defect. The realm of relations may be the native element of human reason. Reason may not need a ποῦ στῶ. In its own thought-element it may rest on its wings, like the albatross.

Such, in fact, is the most significant of all the discoveries of modern Epistemology—that an idea is an idea, and a judgment is true or false, in virtue of their relation to a *system* of ideas or judgments; that their certainty rests not in themselves, but in the system of knowledge of which they are a part; and that their certainty grows as the system of knowledge expands. The truth of this view is illustrated in any ordinary discussion, or whenever the validity of any idea is challenged. Do we not at once bring up some other idea to the defence of that which is challenged, and still another to support the second? "Deny A," we say, "and you must deny B; deny B and you must deny C; deny C and you must deny D, the truth of which you yourself admit, and which, therefore, you cannot deny without stultifying your very thought, and bringing down the whole system of experience in incoherent ruins." The strength of the whole body of an organised system of ideas, such as a science, or a philosophic or theological doctrine, belongs to every element within it; to deny the element is to discredit the principle to which it is related; and to discredit the principle of the system is to demand the re-interpretation of every part of it. Knowledge, in fact, is in this respect analogous to the cosmos of reality which it is meant to represent; it is held up by itself; it is the equipoise of its own constituents, and built to the sound of its own music.

The discovery of the organic (or hyper-organic) nature of knowledge involves epistemological consequences not even yet worked out—so far do they reach, and so long a task is it to reinterpret the phenomena confused by the use of the mechanical metaphor which for long ages has mis-directed the endeavour of human thought. And the theory of human *conduct* has fared even worse at the hands of the same metaphor. Even yet the idea of *natural* cause is applied to the relation of man to his environment, with the result that the futile controversy between determinism and indeterminism goes on as merrily as ever, and that the problem of human freedom is called insoluble—*as usual.* As usual, too, the confusion is due to a material metaphor. For "natural cause" is as inapplicable to the relations in which man as a rational being stands to *anything*, as is the idea of colour to the virtues. Mind is never either mere antecedent or mere consequent. It trammels up its before and after, and even its environment is potentially within itself, an object of *its* thought and an element in *its* volition. Similar confusion marks our treatment of motives, purposes, the relation of the will to the intelligence, and so forth. Man's moral nature, which is in its essence a movement, a transition, a becoming, is treated from a static point of view. It is asked whether he is rational or irrational, free or bond, good or bad, as if he ever were "either" the one "or" the other of these. But "either," "or," the reflective categories, cannot explain a process; and man *is* a process, his very life is a constant reproduction of itself, a dying-to-live both in knowledge and in conduct. Ethics is also "the playground of analogies."

And now we come to social science, prepared, if my attempts have not been in vain, to find in this field also the distortion of facts into unintelligible enigmata, and the endless controversies and confusion which mark the presence and activity of metaphorical hypotheses.

I propose in what remains of this paper to take up one of these controversies—one which affects in no superficial way the working faith of the social reformer. I refer to that which turns on the relative significance of "Character" and "Environment." How far, it is asked, are the evils of society capable of being remedied by state or civic enactments which affect the outward circumstances of life? Or, how far [1] must all such changes remain futile and the

[1] It may be worth observing in passing that the question "How far"? is really as much out of place in philosophy as it is in mathematics. Prudence is the most worldly of all the virtues, and is often given to count the cost of being good. In philosophy it is a vice.

effort of the reformer be directed upon raising the level of the people's character? The answers usually given are as follows:

1. Change the outer conditions of life, equalise property, or abolish property so far as it is private, give to every one opportunities of service and reward him according to his needs, take away the occasion for greed, competition and the collision of private wills, and all will go well.

2. Do all these things and more, pull down the rookeries, give their denizens clean homes and clear air, place them in palaces, provide them with work—they will turn the palaces into hovels and styes, they will refuse to work, and be greedy only for its rewards. The change must come from within, for the determining element is there. Their environment will take care of itself if you teach them industry, sobriety, and thrift, and make them lovers of what is fair.

Such is the controversy waged on every occasion of social reform. It divides reformers on every social problem, such as charity, temperance, housing, and so forth; the one school desiring, the other deprecating, the extension of state or municipal action—both from the best motives. Solution is sought by compromise, the compromise being contingent on the counting of heads. Social reform stumbles along the rough road of blind experiment, and we "muddle through."

Is there no better way of solving our social difficulties? None, I should answer, on the usual lines of thought; for we are dealing with a problem whose conditions are falsely stated. We are seeking a solution in terms of merely natural causation where merely natural cause does not exist.

We are thinking in metaphors and passing counters for true coin. It is assumed that character and environment are separate things, acting and reacting upon each other like impinging natural objects. The relation between man and his world is treated precisely as if it were a relation between two physical things, in spite of all the accent that modern thought has laid on the fact that man is a *subject*, that his self and his world exist only in their mutual relation, and that they interpenetrate so as to constitute in truth but one fact. In a word, the old error persists in this new science. It is not realised that nothing which man does can be explained from the point of view of "either," "or,"—not the making of a simple judgment, such as "The grass is green," far less the building of character, or of society, which is the greatest and most complex of his achievements.

The truth is that man does nothing by himself; for he *is* nothing by himself. He is, in fact, only another name for his world. What we call character from one point of view, we call environment from another. Character and environment are not even separate elements, far less are they independent, isolated, externally interacting objects.

Now, such a doctrine may seem to be a mere paradox, and merely to confuse differences: it is the Hegelian "theory of the altogetherness of everything." For is it not evident that the "self" is here, and the "world" there, and is not the distinction between them the deepest known? And does not the obliteration of this distinction destroy the very principle of freedom on which the possibility of character rests? What remains on such a view except either the naturalisation of man or the spiritualisation of nature?

And in either case is not man degraded into a mere element of a larger whole?[1]

"Undoubtedly," I reply, "if unity shuts out difference, or difference unity"; or—to apply ourselves to the matter immediately in hand—"if man in focussing his environment within his personality destroys it." But this is the point at issue. It is the use of these *exclusive* categories that we would question.

Let us, then, go back to the facts, and put the matter to the test. Take up any self or character and examine its history and its content. Will you find his history at any stage to be anything else than the simultaneous building up of his self and his world? Will you find any shred or item of his content which is not also his environment? Modern psychology answers clearly in the negative. Investigate the "personality" of a farm labourer, or a college tutor, or a country parson. You will find that he is born of certain parents, and that he may carry within him, as breeders say, "strains from both sides." The qualities he inherits are probably not the same as if he had been born in the stone age, or from lake-dwellers; for into the very constitution of his parents, and therefore into his own, there has entered something of the results of the customs of civilised life. And even if acquired aptitudes are not inherited, he is born into a very different world from that of the lake-dwellers; and that world "leaves him not a moment alone, but continually tampers with him." "The

[1] What does it matter, it has been asked, whether the machine of which man is a part is a physical machine or a spiritual machine? He is still a part of a machine, and carried round in its revolutions. A most cogent objection, I should reply, provided we do not ask what either "a machine" or "spirit" means.

tender care that receives and guides him is impressing on him habits . . . the icy chains of universal custom are hardening themselves round his cradled life." Watch his growth on the hearth, in the school, in the pursuit of his avocation. "He learns to speak, and here he appropriates the common heritage of his race; the tongue that he makes his own is his country's language, it is (or it should be) the same that others speak, and it carries into his mind the needs and sentiments of the race (over this I need not stay) and stamps them in indelibly. He grows up in an atmosphere of example and general custom, his life widens out from one little world to other and higher worlds, and he apprehends through successive stations the whole in which he lives and in which he has lived."[1] He appears before us at last as a formed character, a distinct personality, who confronts the world in his own fashion, and bears on his own shoulders the weight of the responsibilities of his station in life and its duties. His history teaches us that his self, or character, and his world have grown together, and that they are not merely counterparts of each other, but the same thing looked at in different ways. The process began at a point where there was neither a self nor a world, but the indistinct, inarticulate, blurred possibilities of both.[2] The process ends, on the one hand, with a character formed, which can face the world and even condemn

[1] Bradley's *Ethical Studies*.

[2] And it does not matter whether we call him, or his world, "a manifold," after Kant, or an "undifferentiated *continuum*," after Dr. Ward, for both are equally false. It is not possible to proceed either from mere difference to unity or from mere unity to difference. We require both in their relation; that is, we must assume that the crudest experience, as well as the crudest fact of experience, is already a "*system*."

its ways and rise above them ; and, on the other hand, with a world which limits and resists the caprice of the self, and in the very act of doing so guides it to wider views and larger ways of life.

The same result appears if we adopt a negative method. Take away from "the world" of any individual all that is due to his attention and interest, his observation and purpose, his distinguishing and organising activities—there will remain a tumultuous something pressing upon his senses, which has neither meaning nor order. Take away, again, from "the individual" all that he has borrowed from his world—there will remain something that can think no specific thoughts, form no purpose, seek no good, speak no language. We can give no name to such empty, impotent residua.

Hence we cannot tear a man and his world asunder without destroying both ; nor can we say that this is his soul, and that is his environment. "The soul within him is saturated, is filled, is qualified by, it has assimilated, has got its substance, has built itself up from, it *is* one and the same life with the universal life, and if he turns against this he turns against himself ; if he thrusts it from him, he tears his own vitals ; if he attacks it he sets his weapon against his own heart. He has found his life in the life of the whole ; he lives that in himself ; 'he is a pulse-beat of the whole system,' and himself the whole system."[1]

As we can nowhere find a man who, having been born and nurtured amongst savages, exhibits either the virtues or the vices of a man bred in a civilised country ; so we can nowhere find a civilised world of social usages, traditions, customs, mutual obligations and services, which is not

[1] Bradley's *Ethical Studies*.

sustained by the right-thinking and the right-doing of the individuals which constitute it. The relation between man and his world is not that of mutual exclusion nor even of mutual interaction. It is that of *mutual inclusion.* A cross section of any individual character, at any stage of its development, would show that its tissue is his social world; a cross section of any social world would show that its cells and fibres are the rational activities of its component individuals.

Let us now observe what light this view throws upon the working faith of the social reformer. It would seem that, as character is simply environment, he can almost mould it as he pleases; and that as environment is character, and character is always an inward and private possession, he can do almost nothing. The doctrine both encourages and rebukes his efforts. But it does more—it indicates the direction which social action should take, and the point of attack for the social reformer.

What we have been describing is *a process*: a process by which the outer world is formed anew within the individual's mind and will, or by which the individual forms himself through taking the world into himself as his own content, and becomes a person with powers, rights, and duties. At the beginning of the process the individual and the world are only potentially one; the world beats against a mind that is not opened, and the good in it finds little response in his blind and undisciplined will. The individual is, as it were, an empty form, feeble in his powers both of reception and reaction. And his world has just as little order or meaning. But as we follow his history, he both borrows and gives to it significance. He absorbs the truth of his environment more and more into himself, and at the same time builds up its truth over against himself into a rational objective system. The outward element is not abolished as it becomes an inner content. It becomes a life whose power of resistance and reaction is ever on the increase, until in the later stages nothing can withstand its alchemy. The individual is armed with his world, and entrenched within an established order of opinions, interests, likings and dislikings; so that ultimately nothing can enter into him except by being subdued into conformity with these. His self is like a consuming fire which converts all things alike into fuel for its flame.

And the practical conclusion which follows for the social reformer is manifest; it is, indeed, that to which his own work amongst the social wreckage generally leads him. While character is still in the making he can do well-nigh everything to bring out its latent powers; for the environment which is to be its content is within his reach. When character has been formed he is well-nigh powerless to affect it; for the environment is not only within the individual he would reform, out of his reach, but within him as an active power that admits only what is kin to it and gives to everything that it admits its own qualities. We might even omit the qualifying phrase "well-nigh," were it not that we can never quite go back on the one side to the bare individual in a state of *mere* potency, nor go forward on the other side to the stage where absolute senility has been reached, spontaneity is quite extinguished and character is unalterably fixed. In the first case "character" has not been born, in the other it is dead.

Herein lies the reason for the distressing and socially disastrous fact that schemes of reform applied to depraved men and women not only fail, but aggravate the conditions which they are intended to ameliorate. Our charities corrupt them ; the work we proffer them only proves that they are unemployable ; shorter hours of labour and increased wages merely give them new opportunities for self-indulgence. We pull down the rookeries and disperse their denizens, but we only scatter the seeds of ill-doing wider and bring down the level of life in new districts. We build night-shelters for the homeless, and thereby increase the facilities for a homeless life. We care for their children, and their vicious parents neglect them the more. In short, our best laid plans seem only to relieve such men and women of the pressure that tends to compel some forethought and to teach them that if they are to live in civilised society they must in some degree fit themselves for civilised life. But all these results are perfectly natural : for a vitiated will must, as a matter of course, convert new circumstances into instruments of the old life, and a weakened, dissipated will must fail to appropriate the good that lies in its environment. The same law holds, of course, in the case of the virtuous will. The spirit made strong in the service of the right finds, even in adverse circumstances, opportunities for moral heroism.

> "Why comes temptation but for man to meet
> And master, and make crouch beneath his foot
> And so be pedestalled in triumph ?"

If it be said that men's lives are too various to permit us to infer such a universal law, and that we exaggerate the power of environment over character if we deny either the lapse of good men into evil ways or the conversion of the evil into good ways, I should reply that in a sense this is true. But I should examine the alleged exceptions, and I should expect to find that when the forces of evil have taken the citadel of the soul there was a traitor within who had been holding secret parley with the enemy without; and, on the other hand, that where there was the conversion of an adult vicious character to the ways of virtue there had been a good upbringing—there were old memories and associations, remnants of good intentions and virtuous effort to which appeal could be made. The mere force of circumstance, taken by itself, has no potency once the character is formed. And the substantial truth remains that if society allows any of its members to entrench themselves in their inner world of character as enemies of the public weal, it cannot add to the opportunities of their environment without degrading them further.

I am not urging these considerations as an excuse for doing nothing to assist our less fortunate fellows, but rather as a reason for doing more and especially for doing it in a different way. They seem to indicate a principle which should guide effort. It is: that the succour which is given is justified only if it promises to restore the individual into social relations that will sustain whatever of good remains in him; and, if that be impossible, that methods of coercion must be employed, both for the sake of the individual and for the sake of society. For the vitiated nature, carrying its environment within, lives in its own stifling atmosphere, sees and selects only what corrupts it further: it must therefore be placed where it cannot pervert and denaturalise its social medium. And, in this regard, labour-colonies and other therapeutic methods seem to me to have a far larger use than is as yet recognised either by the people or by the Parliament of this country.

But the main interest of the practical reformer is in the other aspect of this truth. As life is a process of internalising the world, and the environment is the potential content of character, the power of society over unformed childhood is indefinitely great, and it must be turned more deliberately and systematically in this direction of developing the character, more especially in the cases where the home-influences are evil. We are entitled to hope more from such action, and bound to attempt more than we do. And we should probably do so, were we not as much misled by notions of the fixity of character in childhood, which are as false as those of its fluidity in later life.

Judging from my own observation, I should say that biological metaphors, and especially the argument from heredity, have something to answer for in this context. They conceal the fact that rational life implies stronger powers of reaction, and is always nearer being a new beginning or a potential reincarnation of the world as a whole, than animal life is. The notion that the children of dissolute parents carry with them a definite predisposition towards vice has had much to do with paralysing social effort on their behalf. The adoption of children left by their parents in circumstances where a strong and virtuous manhood cannot grow without a miracle, would be more general were it not for this fear. But is this fear justified? Biological science has investigated with great thoroughness the problem of the transmission to offspring of the *acquired* characters of parents; and its verdict is "Not proven." Nevertheless in our social practice the truth of this doubtful hypothesis is taken for granted. It is assumed that the children of depraved parents are not only physically inferior to others and afflicted with an unstable nervous disposition (which is probably true as a rule), but also that they are charged with definite propensities towards a degraded life.

This view, however, is not endorsed by those social reformers who have had most to do with placing ill-treated and neglected children in happier surroundings. The Poor Law Inspector in Glasgow, Mr. J. R. Motion, sends every year to Kirkcudbrightshire in the south of Scotland, to Ross-shire and Inverness-shire in the North, and to the remote islands of Iona and Islay, numbers of little children found in the streets, "picked up selling newspapers between the knees of drunkards in public-houses." On being asked by the writer how far these children, born almost invariably of the worst parents, suffered from their inheritance, his startling reply was, "Provided you get them young enough, they cannot be said to suffer at all from that cause." He supported his conclusion by statistics which showed that out of some 630 children sent out by him and kept under close observation for years, only some 23 turned out bad. "A smaller proportion," it was playfully added, "than if they had been the sons of ministers or professors."

"Thraw the willow when it's green,
Between three and thirteen,"

says an old Scotch educational maxim. Mr. Motion would have the child in his hands earlier: "At any age from a fortnight to ten years: after ten, unless the child has had one, at least, decent parent, the results are long in coming and uncertain."

I have no doubt that the risks of a tainted heritage are exaggerated. So also, I believe, are the dangers of lowering the sense of parental responsibility amongst the poor.

The obligations of parentage will not be loosened on the hearths of the respectable poor by any state regulations. A working man's son may well believe that these obligations are usually felt to be closer on such hearths than on any others. The children of the poor are not made over to the care of nurses, nor sent from home in order to be educated. They are brought up around the mother's knees, and learn early to bear their share in the daily cares of the home, and to brighten it with their sunshine; and they are apt on that account to mean the more for their father and mother. On the other hand, wherever the obligations of the parents *are* easily loosened the conditions are already so bad that it is time for the state to interfere on behalf of its coming citizens.

But even if the danger of State-interference were considerable I should still say, after Plato and Aristotle, that the first, the paramount care of the State, is to educate its citizens, and that the State itself is, in the last resort, an educational institution; and I should give to "Education" their wide meaning. In performing this function towards the children, it can afford to run risks, for *these* risks are run in a great cause.

# THE WORKING FAITH OF THE SOCIAL REFORMER

## III

## THE METAPHYSICAL BASIS—MINE AND THINE

THE conclusions already reached: that Society is the product and the expression of beings who are by nature rational or spiritual, and that no rational relations are external or exclusive. The great value of the achievement of Idealism in that it has proved the dependence of the object upon the subject of knowledge, or, in other words, that the real must be ideal. The tendency of Idealism to dissolve the former in the latter and thereby to become a purely subjective doctrine. Two forms of this one-sided Idealism examined—Dr. Ward's abstract Pluralism, and Mr. Bradley's abstract Monism. How both theories indicate the need of accentuating the self-differentiating movement of spirit. The way in which spirit sets up its own necessary order of objects as against itself illustrated in *Knowledge*, which progressively represents reality as an independent system; in *Morality*, where the practical reason represents the moral laws as categorical, and obedience to them as nevertheless free; in the *Family* where every member is both subject and sovereign.

That the same twofold movement of spirit is manifested in Social life. How the Biological view of Society fails to recognize, and the Economic view recognizes only indirectly the fundamental principle that spirit preserves its opposite, and itself through its opposite. The application of ethical categories to Society, and its concurrent realization of the private and the common good.

III

# THE METAPHYSICAL BASIS—MINE AND THINE

If we wish to reform society, we must strive to comprehend it; if we wish to comprehend it, we must not allow metaphors to rule our thought, but contemplate it in the light of its own constitutive principle.

Human society is rationally constituted. It is, without doubt, the product and expression of the rational activities of knowing, willing, and feeling. It may be, nay, it is, physically conditioned, but its principle is spiritual. It may be in some way a continuation, upon a higher level, of physical forces; but in any case, whatever its origin or history, it is *now* a spiritual phenomenon. It is a rationally compacted system of interacting personalities. Its essence is reason—the concrete reason, or "spirit," which feels, wills, and knows. Hence, reason, spirit, or self-consciousness furnishes the only clue to the real nature of society, and the only point of view for the solution of the problems of social life.

Such is the first of the main conclusions to which our inquiry has led.

The second conclusion reached was concerned with the

kind of relation which subsists between rational facts. Physical phenomena are mutually exclusive, although even here the exclusion is not absolute; spiritual facts, strange as the expression may sound, are mutually inclusive. We can say of the former, "Lo here," or "Lo there," for relatively they shut each other out, as do the parts of space, the moments of time, the succession of causes and effects. But reason or self-consciousness identifies its content so closely with itself that all its elements interpenetrate and subsist only *through* one another. The categories of exclusion and alternation do not hold in this region. The world in which man lives as a rational being is not merely an outward fact, but itself lives in him. *Its* phenomena are *his* thoughts. Rational life *consists* in internalising its environment. It constitutes, or at lowest converts, it into a subjective, personal possession. The world is the content of knowledge for the intelligence, it is the content of purpose for the will, and for feeling it acquires personal value. It is no exaggeration to say that in apprehending the world we appropriate and transmute it into personal *character*—almost as a living tree converts everything it assimilates into wood. But not quite in that way; the analogy is not too strong but too weak. It expresses neither the range nor the intensity of the transmuting power of spirit. For there are things in the world which organic life cannot assimilate, and which it must simply exclude; and what it does assimilate it does not identify completely with itself,—for which reason it has not a "self" in the full sense of the term. But there is nothing in the world which is not the potential content of spirit—the raw material, as it were, of the intelligence and the purposive will. And this content spirit appropriates and internalises so completely that it finds its *self* in every part of it.

This is a very great truth. The discovery of it may be regarded as the one significant result of the long labour of Idealism from the days of Kant to our own. I have already indicated, though only by reference to a single example, how this truth affects social theory. It closes the idle discussion, and puts an end to the confusion which springs from taking character and environment as two independent things acting externally on one another. It does much more. It furnishes the only intelligible ground of the possibility of any rational life, whether individual or social. It contains the refutation of the Materialism which paralyses morality and religion, and also of Dualism and all its Agnostic offspring. For it makes the relation to self-consciousness a *constitutive* principle of reality. It spiritualises the world. Hence, man can no longer be deemed to have been placed in a purely natural or alien setting. Nor does the world repel reason: it invites and informs it. It is not an obstacle to the moral life, as Huxley thought, nor indifferent to it, as Arnold believed. On the contrary, it is the means whereby man acquires knowledge and learns goodness; it is his partner in the great enterprise of morality and truth. In short, Idealism shows us that spirit, even when dealing with facts in the material world, is still moving under its own sky and breathing its own atmosphere.

It is not possible to exaggerate the value of this principle of the spiritual nature of reality which Idealism has, I believe, rendered secure. Nevertheless, the task of Idealism is only begun. Nay, I must try to show in this article that, as held by many of its exponents, a radical imperfection—the ruinous imperfection of possessing only a half-truth—infects its results. It is not merely that there remains before it the difficult and long enterprise of applying its spiritual hypothesis to facts. It is giving an abstract, and therefore erroneous, interpretation of its own primary principle. Idealism is itself the victim of physical metaphors which it has done more than any other theory to expose; for it still sets unity against difference, it still employs the categories of exclusion.[1] And until it escapes from the domination of such categories it cannot furnish the clue to the nature nor the key to the problems of social life.

This is a matter of cardinal importance; for to misinterpret the main hypothesis of a science is to distort, or to render unintelligible, all the facts that fall within its scope. I must first indicate in a few words what Idealism has done, what truth it has discovered. Then I shall indicate in what ways I consider its truth to be only a half-truth. And lastly, I shall try to show how its half-truth turns in the hands of some of its best exponents into opposite errors. The discussion must be philosophical; but at no less cost can we deal with the fundamental principles on which social theory must rest, and in the comprehension of which alone lies the possibility of progressive social evolution.

Idealism has proved that every object, actual or possible, physical or spiritual, is essentially implicated in the subject, and that spirit gives subjective form to its content, or possesses it in what I may call a personal way. It has detected the ideal nature of all reality; it has revealed its

[1] This defect is less characteristic of Hegel's theory than of the version of it usually given by his disciples. Hegel is the most objective of all modern Idealists.

spiritual trend and marked its self-revelation in self-consciousness. Idealists, with a unanimity of assent which is most rarely found in the history of philosophy, aver that "Reality *is* Experience." This is a great and permanently valuable achievement.

Nevertheless, Idealism has adequately grasped only one aspect of reality, and only one moment of the activity of self-conscious spirit. It has demonstrated the Unity of Nature and Spirit, but not their difference. It has proved that the real must be ideal, but it has not shown how the ideal can be veritably real. It has shown how Spirit subsumes the world as its own, but it has not reinstated the world as its object and opposite. On the contrary, in relating objects to self-consciousness, it has robbed them of all their characters save those which are directly ideal. In order to demonstrate the unity of Nature with Spirit, it has reduced Nature into a mere shadow of spirit. It has set the unity *against* the differences; and, in consequence, it is constrained either to represent the unity as less real than the differences, or the differences as less real than the unity. In one word, within Idealism itself, there is a tendency, which in our day is well-nigh universal, either towards an abstract Monism which has no real content, or towards a Dualism (or rather a Pluralism) whose content is unintelligible and chaotic.

I shall now proceed to substantiate this charge, so far as space permits; and I shall try to do so by reference to two Idealists to whose trenchant thinking the present age owes a deep debt, and each of whom may, without injustice to others, be regarded as one of the leaders of his school.

Dr. Ward, like all other Idealists, has learnt the lesson taught by Kant. For him the object is essentially related to the subject. But, owing to a timid, and, I believe, treacherous care for the moral freedom of man, he would fain not implicate the subject in the object—in this also, as might be shown, following Kant. He will not permit the world to participate genuinely in the intrinsic activities of the individual spirit. In the last resort the process by which the individual shapes his world—attends to this item rather than that, breaks up the objective *continuum*, selects certain elements and rejects others, binds them together into objects—is a purely private process. Every rational being, at the inmost heart of him, appears in Dr. Ward's theory as an isolated, monadic entity, spontaneously radiating out its own activities. Nay, every minutest thing has its own secret, impermeable core, which sits lonely amidst its qualities and operates outwards.

Now, at first sight, this looks like breaking up the world into fragments, and endowing each fragment with its own separate as well as distinct soul. "The only *things* of which we have positive knowledge are subjects with intrinsic qualities. . . . . Again, the only *causes* of which we have positive knowledge are minds."[1] But Dr. Ward gets these independent minds to interact. This "interaction of mind with mind is," he believes, "what we know best, and must be the basis of our interpretation if we are to understand at all."[2] The result, or the manifestation, of this interaction, is a relation between the individuals. "The intercourse, the co-operation or conflict, actual or possible, of the individuals themselves is their relation. The passion and action of things must take the place of relation. . . . There are no objective relations other than this living action and passion."[3]

[1] *Naturalism and Agnosticism*, ii. 279. [2] *Ibid.* [3] *Ibid.*, pp. 279-280.

Dr. Ward explains his view further in his account of the relation of Individual and Universal Experience, and of the supposed transition from the former to the latter. Each Ego—L, M, or N—is originally shut up in its own peculiar, particular world; every self has for its object its own private not-self. L has non-L; M has non-M; N has non-N.[1] These particular selves are to emerge somehow from their particular exclusive worlds and to build up one world, which is the object of a Universal or a Common Experience. And thus the unity of the real is to be restored.

I have only one word to say on this matter: it is, that the emergence of such independent selves from such originally separate worlds is impossible. Human society cannot arise among such beings: indeed, they themselves would not be human. But Dr. Ward *assumes* that a part of their several experiences is common to them. "The most, then, that L can indicate or communicate to M of any part of his own experience is so much of it as is common to the experience of both."[2] On the other hand he also assumes that there is nothing "common" to more than one experience till intercourse has taken place. Hence follows the awkward conclusion that there cannot be anything common or universal till there has been intercourse, and that there cannot be intercourse except where something common or universal already exists.

Again, let us look for a moment at the nature of these unities or common elements, which universal experience contains, and which, in Dr. Ward's hands, serve to make the world into an orderly universe. These universals are thoughts, conceptions, general ideas; and they are the

[1] *Naturalism and Agnosticism*, ii. 167 ff. [2] *Ibid.*, ii. 167.

products of thinking—regarded as a special faculty which, compared with experience, deals only with abstractions. They are nothing but thoughts. Against attributing to them any kind of existential reality, Dr. Ward offers the most uncompromising opposition. It is, he believes, a cardinal error of Natural Science, to assert, for instance, that Laws of Nature exist; or that they have a place among, or above, real things, and their particular, incessantly repeated activities. "Laws of Nature" are only general ideas invented by scientific men for the purposes of explanation. It is on the unreality or pure ideality of Universals, that Dr. Ward relies in order to free the moral and religious consciousness from the fear of inexorable law and mechanical necessity. For why should we fear them when they are only the products of our own thought?

But are these universal thoughts merely false ideas? Are the necessary relations which reason must have if its experience is not to be purely contingent and chaotic, mere fictitious creatures of our minds? No! replies Dr. Ward. They are not *true* in the sense that universal thoughts point to, or stand for, universal entities; or that things-in-general actually exist, and correspond to general ideas. All reality consists of particular things and their particular activities. Nevertheless, although these universal ideas are not *true*, they are "valid." Although they are "necessary truths," they are not truths of fact, but "truths of reason."[1]

Nothing, it seems to me, indicates more clearly the straits in which this theory finds itself than this attempt to distinguish between true ideas and valid ideas. And to say

[1] *Naturalism and Agnosticism*, p. 283.

that there are "necessary truths" which are not "truths of fact," is to sever the intelligence from its object, in such a way as to grant to utter scepticism all that it can require. What conclusion can be drawn from this except that "thought" is a blunder, and that its explanatory ideas do not explain?

And even if we granted to Dr. Ward this ambiguous realm of thoughts which are neither true nor false but "valid," it will not serve his turn, nor heal the divisions of his broken universe. For how can general ideas unite particular things? The former are in the ideal world of Epistemology, the latter are in the real world of Ontology. Real things have no universal side, or element, or character; thoughts have no particular side. Yet these opposites and exclusives are put into opposite and exclusive regions, and then required to constitute somehow that concrete "one in the many," that orderly and yet varied universe, the reality of which is the one postulate which reason demands, and which it is the object of every intellectual endeavour to demonstrate. Dr. Ward himself requires unity no less than difference; but having excluded it from his original premisses, he can re-introduce it only on condition of its not being real.

The whole force of this theory lies in its criticism of existential universals. And this criticism is unanswerable. For it is quite true that the real world contains none of these abstract, general entities; and that the world is not made up of things *plus* relations, of facts and events *plus* universal laws. But it is not less true that the world contains no particulars, and that it is as impossible to find a thing out of all relation as to find a relation existing by itself. A genuine particular, as Aristotle has shown once for all, would so occupy, or rather fail to occupy, its instantaneous "now" and "here," as not to be one *even with itself.*

But no one is interested either in pure particulars or in mere universals, or in the impossible adventure of bringing these two kinds of fictions together, except those who are the victims of the mechanical metaphors which set unity against difference. Universal and particular exist only as elements in a system, and disappear when separated. The universe is such a system, nay, it is a system of systems. Every item within it "in each tense fibre feels the one all-conquering lure." Hence we require something better than the see-saw categories of exclusion in order to interpret the world, and we cannot afford to make its unities or universals less real or less true, in any sense, than its particulars and differences.

But no more can we afford to make the differences less real than the unity, which is the opposite error into which, as I believe, Mr. Bradley has fallen. This is an error which Idealism has always found it difficult to escape. For the main mission of Idealism has been to insist upon the internalising, subjectivising process by which reality comes to be apprehended in the form of experience. In proving that self-consciousness must unite all things, or find all things to be united, in itself; in destroying dualism, whether of nature and spirit, or of thing and thought, or of real and ideal, or of subject and object, it most easily falls into abstract Monism.

Such an abstract Monism is implied, it seems to me, in the phrase "*Reality is Experience*," as it is understood by the great body of modern Idealists. As a rule, they do not tell us what they mean by "Experience," and I am inclined to say that their best refuge lies in obscurity. They seem to have substituted this vague term "Experience" for the word "Thought," into which, as they believe, Hegel had evaporated reality. "Reality is richer than thought," they say; and "this reality, richer than thought, is experience."[1] Thought is abstract, general, the manifestation of only one aspect, and that a secondary aspect, of mind. It contains neither feeling nor volition, and it satisfies no one except the bloodless "Intellectualist." But "Experience" comprehends thought and more. It is original and all-inclusive. Thought produces at best a mere image of reality, a solemn shadow-land of interconnected notions, a still, dead world of mere ideas. But experience is concrete, living. It is an activity, and an activity that has emotional value and active purpose as well as meaning. Experience is adequate to reality: reality is experience.

With this indefinite and figurative contrast between "thought" and "experience" most Idealists are content. But Mr. Bradley has no faith in obscurity, and brings his conclusions to the open. He tells us what he means by the "Experience" with which he identifies "Reality." "Experience means something much the same as given and present fact. We perceive, on reflection, that to be real, or even barely to exist, must be to fall within sentience. Sentient experience, in short, is reality, and what is not this is not real. We may say, in other words, that there is no being or fact outside of that which is commonly called psychical existence. Feeling, thought and volition (any groups under which we class psychical phenomena) are all the material of existence. And there is no other material

[1] *Naturalism and Agnosticism*, p. 282.

actual, or even possible."[1] "Being and reality are, in brief, one thing with sentience; they can neither be opposed to, nor even in the end, distinguished from it."[2]

I do not think that any comment or paraphrase of mine could add either clearness or emphasis to Mr. Bradley's language. I take it that he asks us to believe that time, space, matter, spirit, sticks, stones, selves, human society, any object whatsoever which we can feel, think, or will, is itself just feeling, or thought, or volition, or some combination of them; that the objects of consciousness are themselves consciousness. Ordinarily, feelings are viewed as the result of feeling; thoughts as the products of thinking; volitions as the consequences of willing. On Mr. Bradley's view they are the ready-furnished material of these operations; and there are no operators save themselves.

What proof does Mr. Bradley offer of a doctrine which is apparently so incongruous with the opinion not only of ordinary and scientific men, but of most philosophers? It consists in challenging us to produce or point out anything besides feelings, thoughts, or volitions, or whatever else constitutes psychical phenomena. "Find any piece of existence, take up anything that anyone could possibly call a fact, or could in any sense assert to have being, and then judge if it does not consist in sentient experience. Try to discover any sense in which you can still continue to speak of it, when all perception and feeling have been removed."[3]

This argument is unanswerable, and yet it proves nothing. The demand which Mr. Bradley makes is a self-

[1] Bradley's *Appearance and Reality*, p. 144 ff. [2] *Ibid.*, p. 146.
[3] *Ibid.*, p. 145.

contradictory demand, similar to requiring a mathematician to prove that $2 \times 2 = 21$. For Mr. Bradley requires us to "find," "take up," "assert," that is, to possess as experience, what, at the same time, must not be experience. It is impossible to do so; but that tells us nothing as to the nature of experience. A dualist might quite well acknowledge that he can "find," "take up," "assert," "speak of" nothing but experience, and still try to maintain that experience consists of utterly disparate elements. That we cannot go beyond experience, that "we can conceive only the experienced," does not prove that experience consists of mere unity, nor of mere difference, nor does it throw any light whatsoever upon its constitution.

Neither does the fact that "nothing remains when all perception and feeling are removed" prove that nothing exists except perception and feeling. It is an old fallacy, exposed by Mr. Bradley himself, to conclude that because the removal of one element in a whole destroys the whole, therefore that one element *is* the whole. Pleasure may be an essential element of the good, but there may be other essential elements in it as well, the removal of any one of which would destroy it.

Neither of these arguments proves that "reality is experience"; or that it consists, on both its subjective and objective aspects, of feelings, thought, or volitions. They show that the object is relative to the subject, and that subject and object are indiscerptible elements of experience; but not that they are so indistinguishably one that knowledge knows knowledge, feeling feels feelings, volition wills volitions.

Indeed, Mr. Bradley does not aim at any such insipid iteration, nor does he need to be told that unity implies difference, and difference unity—any more than does Dr. Ward. His Absolute is to contain, combine, transmute, nay, *be* all finite things.[1] The Absolute "*is* its appearances, all and every one of them." In a similar way Dr. Ward's God is to be "the living unity of all."[2] An abstract pantheistic Monism is as repugnant to the one as a polytheistic aristocracy of Monads is to the other. But Mr. Bradley's logic is inexorable. His premisses are such that differences must not merely be reconciled or harmonised, and relations not merely be surmounted, but *eliminated.*

First, he can admit distinctions, but not divisions: "What we discover is a whole in which distinctions can be made, but in which divisions do not exist."[3] Then the distinctions must be quantitative only, not qualitative: there are differences of *degrees* of reality, and no other differences. But even these, like every other distinction, are mind-made, like Dr. Ward's universals. And because mind makes them, both they and mind are appearances; that is to say, they are self-contradictory. All the rational functions of man—his thought, his will, his feeling—aim at compelling distinctions to disappear. "The theoretic object moves towards a consummation in which all distinction and all ideality must be suppressed."[4] The same must be said of the object of the practical and of the æsthetic activities of mind. They seek "to transcend the opposition of idea to existence, and to surmount and rise beyond the relational consciousness."[5]

They cannot attain their end. If they did, "if the ideal and the existing were made one, the relations between them

[1] *Appearance and Reality*, p. 486. [2] *Naturalism and Agnosticism*, p. 280.
[3] *Appearance and Reality*, p. 146. [4] *Ibid.*, p. 462. [5] *Ibid.*, p. 463.

would have disappeared"[1]—*for it is assumed that where there is oneness there are no relations, and where there are relations there is not oneness.* And rather than question this assumption, or the assumption that thought, will, and feeling aim at rising to a region where there are no relations, Mr. Bradley first calls these functions failures, and then constitutes their failure into the sole ground of their existence. For if they made the ideal and the existing one—in the sense, that is, of an abstract one which excludes all difference—they would undoubtedly cease to exist, and so would their object. We should have blank Nihilism; a universal collapse into abstract sameness. Knowledge would be no more, nor morality nor art any more; and not even their transmutation in the Absolute would avail, unless that transmutation still left to them the differences in which alone they find their existence, that is, unless even the Absolute kept them from attaining their end.

Now, when a theory is at war with the whole universe and can be maintained only by depriving it of all content, or by merging it in an incognisable Absolute, it may be considered to have completed its task. It has revealed, if it has proceeded consistently, the abstract character of its fundamental hypothesis.

I believe that this, in the last resort, constitutes the crowning merit of Mr. Bradley's great work. Ever since the time of Kant, Idealism—especially in so far as it has not set due value upon the self-differentiating moment of spirit which Hegel accentuated—has been intent upon the unity of the subject and object, and on the ideal aspect of reality. Mr. Bradley has pushed this tendency home.

[1] *Appearance and Reality*, p. 463.

He takes the dictum that "Reality is Experience" literally and earnestly: he interprets experience as psychical existence, and psychical existence as thought, feeling, volition; he will spare no remnant of dualism, no division, no difference, no distinction, no relation; he will "overcome," "surmount," "rise above" even the distinction of ideal and real, although the thought, volition, and feeling with which he began must contradict themselves, and disappear in an Absolute which transmutes them, and defeats itself in doing so. For if it transmutes them so as to leave the difference standing, the object of the transmutation is lost, and their hurt is not healed; and if it transmutes them so as *not* to leave their difference standing, it itself collapses into nothingness.

By his more stringent logic he makes it more evident than even Dr. Ward has done that Idealism has yet its greater task before it. Without abating its enthusiasm for the ideal nature of reality, it must, somehow, do better justice to the real aspect of ideality. It must restore the differences it has sought to expunge.

Let me illustrate my meaning. If we accept Mr. Bradley's result, the only science that will ultimately remain is the science of feeling, thought, and volition, that is, the science of Psychology. Mathematics, Physics, Chemistry, Biology, and so on, must be shown to be not only incomplete, but false. They must be convicted not only of omitting to consider the relation of their object to mind—which they do; but of having no vocation left to them once they admit that relation. For it is assumed that the relation of object to object, namely, the relation of externality, ceases to exist when objects are known in their truth, that is, in their relation to self-consciousness.

But is it not possible that self-consciousness, through which objects are related to one another, instead of abolishing, maintains the mutual externality of things in space and time? Spirit may be as vitally interested in difference as it is in unity.[1] Under-reaching or subsuming the successive moments of time, the self-exclusion of extended space and of cause and effect, and the alternation of the forms of a constantly transmuting physical energy, spirit may still leave the distinctions, the differences standing, and even give them fuller play. The not-self through which alone the self builds up its life may, after all, not be vain show, and the self may not be condemned to realise itself by reference to its own shadowy products.

We might learn from Natural Biology to look everywhere for a double movement in natural life; for differentiation and integration advance together. But Idealism, in dealing with the higher life of reason, has been intent merely upon the affinity of all objects with spirit.[2] It is still occupied in endeavouring to reduce all things into spirit: it is trying to show that every natural object, and every atomic part of every natural object, and, I suppose, every point in space and every instant of time, if they are real, must be spiritual realities, that is, conscious or feeling centres.[3] It is *assumed* that only in this way can the world

[1] In a similar way evolution is as vitally interested in maintaining the variety of the manifestations of life as it is in maintaining its unity: a truth apt to be overlooked "when the accent falls on 'the survival of the fittest.'"

[2] It had to refute Materialism: a task in which it would appear it has been completely successful.

[3] The reader will find in Lotze's account of space, and of distance an instructive instance of the attempt to reduce all "*realia*" into feeling points.

be proved to be spiritual and the last dualism be overcome. And it is certainly not realised that if Idealism succeeded in this enterprise and reduced all things into feeling, it would then be obliged either to content itself with a world without distinctions, or to evolve out of feeling the differences it had deleted. In fact, this abstract Idealism is not explaining the world of objects, but explaining it away. And its spiritualisation of it will remain barren—as barren as the otiose acknowledgment of a secular-minded man that God exists—until it reinstates the variety of real being, which it has melted down into the dismal sameness of mere feeling.

Philosophy, it seems to me, is crying aloud for a more objective expression of the truth. Having proved that the real world is ideal, it must prove that the ideal world is real: that space is real, and time is real, and matter is real, and that the self-exclusive relations of natural objects hold *just because* they are all manifestations of spirit. For rational life also has its double movement. Spirit also scatters as well as gathers. It surpasses natural life in the intensity of its oneness, for it is *all* in every part; it is itself the essence of all its elements. But it surpasses it, too, in the variety of its content, in the depth of the differences it comprises, and the independent significance with which it endows them. Rational beings, just in the degree to which their spiritual nature is realised, possess a private intensity of distinct individuality, an impermeable internality of intellectual life, an undivided exclusiveness of moral responsibility, a repellent force against, and an uncompromising antagonism to all mere "otherness," of which natural objects are not capable. And yet, in virtue of this, they are under an intrinsic necessity of mutual interpenetration, of binding their very essence in a single universal life to whose oneness a natural organism offers but the faintest parallel.

Until this double movement is recognised Idealism will only misinterpret spirit; and its ruling hypothesis, being itself misunderstood, will explain nothing. It will certainly not explain that unity in variety; that order through liberty and liberty through order; that intense communion *and* independence; that one mind, one will, one life in a matured society which is yet the mind, the will, the life of each of its members; that deepest of all unities in the deepest of all differences which constitutes the essence and marvel of the civilised State. And spirit or self-consciousness *is* misunderstood so long as its outgoing, self-differentiating, self-negating movement is practically ignored, as it is at the present time.

In what remains of this and the succeeding article I shall endeavour to indicate what I mean by this outgoing moment. To exhibit its full significance, as it shows itself in all the great domains of spirit—in knowledge, in art, in morality, in human society, in religion—will be the task of Idealism for a long time to come. I can, of course, at the very best, do little more than suggest the main direction which, I believe, it must follow. In doing so, I shall begin with a brief reference to knowledge, proceed thence to morality, and end by applying our hypothesis to one or two of the more fundamental problems of social life and social reform.

First, then, as to Knowledge. We have learnt, perhaps more especially through the advance of natural science, two apparently opposed truths regarding the world: the inexhaustible multiplicity of its content, and the solemn stateliness of its single, immutable order. It seems that knowledge can deepen endlessly downwards in its analysis of any minutest object, and that, so far from exhausting its content, it ever finds itself in the presence of that which has significance and which is therefore not purely simple; and yet, in doing so, it is only revealing a more concrete *One*, bringing to clearer light the uniformity of law, the *concrete* identity of principles which connect every atom with all being, and maintain for them their own place and significance within a cosmos that is the expression of "one law, one element."

Ordinarily, it is assumed that while science must discover its universals, the particulars are presented to it for its passive acceptance. They are said to be "given." I wish to point out that the order of nature is not more the discovery or product of human thought than is its variety. The world for the ancients, as compared with our own, was as shallow in content and barren of differences as it was insecure in its order and unity, and subject to the caprice of the gods. The enterprise of knowledge has had a double aspect. Man's thought has not only proved the affinity of the world with the subject, and its dependence thereon for all its meaning; it has also, and by the same act, distinguished objects from each other and from the self, recognised it more and more fully as a system of elements interlocked in an order which *gives the law* to the investigating mind. In possessing the world, knowledge has been engaged in establishing the world in its own rights. With every advance the objects which thought discovers limit its caprice, rebuke its wilfulness, oust its prejudices, dictate its modes of inquiry, expel the irresponsible imagination, demand the complete submission of reason.

The discovery of the qualities and relations of objects, of their differences and their unity and the construction of the whole architecture of the objective order, is the work of the intelligence. But on that very account the objective order attains rights *over* the intelligence; and man, as he learns, obeys ever the more implicitly the work of his own hands. The day on which modern science was born was the day on which man learnt to stoop in order to conquer, to give up dictating to nature his *a priori* notions, and to sit listening at her feet. And all knowledge grows by the same method. Every object, in the degree in which it is known is found to possess qualities of its own, and in the degree in which it is understood takes its place in a necessary order. The mind can deny neither the distinct qualities nor the necessary connection without doing violence to itself. They are *its* manifestations as the one-sided subjective Idealism of the day recognises; but they are also the manifestations of its objective, outgoing moment which Idealism ignores. Their necessary inter-relation is the expression of its free enterprise; and it is because their concrete being and necessary relations are the work of mind that the mind must respect them.

To overlook this outgoing movement of spirit, to reduce all things into thoughts, feelings, volitions, is not to show that "Reality is Experience," but that it is only one aspect of Experience; for experience never consisted of this barren assertion of sameness, nor was its trend ever *merely* inward.

On the side of the human will, in the realm of morality, the outgoing, self-negating movement is still more evident. Man starts from caprice. "When thou wast young, thou girdedst thyself, and walkedst whither thou wouldest; but when thou shalt be old thou shalt stretch forth thy hands, and another shall gird thee." As man learns goodness he gradually builds up around himself a system of obligations, an unbroken ring of duties, whose imperatives are categorical and still free. They are built up by himself, against himself. When the obligation is complete it commands his heart as well as his will, and becomes an enthusiasm. As his individual purposes become more sane and effective, that is, as his practical personality deepens, he finds his will more and more closely linked to the trend of things. His recognition that he has come not to be served but to serve is ever the more gladsome, and his will ever the more invincible, for it is more at one with the will of the whole.

Thus, then, both on the theoretical and on the practical side, there is the same double movement. As a man possesses the truth and learns goodness, he finds the world, more and more, to be just the content of *his* intelligence and the means of *his* moral realisation. This is the subjective side which Idealism has rightly accentuated, and which means that man finds everywhere nothing but his own experience. But in the very same process man is enriching his world. For he is bringing into light an objective order, natural and moral, a not-self whose authority over him is ever growing more complete. That objective order is his ideal; it is the larger reason of the world to which his subjection is the more full, the wiser and the better he grows. And the subjection, being the subjection of reason to reason, is free. This is the objective side of the movement to which Idealism has on the whole done so little justice.

There is not harm but good in insisting upon the possession of the world by the finite spirit. It is quite true, as the Pragmatists or Personal Idealists aver, that our purposes define the meaning of things. But it is only a preliminary and partial truth, only a fresh accentuation of the subjective aspect of reality and of experience. Behind this truth lies the history of our purposes, and beyond it altogether remains the fact that our purposes are valid and effective only in the degree to which they are expressions of the wider and wiser purpose written in the nature of things.[1] For, as soon as purpose or personality begins to signify anything, it is found to be the medium, the active, co-operative medium, through which the world translates itself into ideality.

> "It is all triumphant art, but art in obedience to laws."[2]

The significance of personality is objective. The substance of our life is in the whole, and our life *has* substance only for that reason.[3]

But perhaps the simplest example of this double movement of spirit is presented by family life. *There* both "Mine" and "Thine" grow together, and exclusive alternatives disappear. Where wedded life is sound, and the love of husband and wife is mutual, there is, on both sides, a sense of complete possession. Each is means, and is glad to be the means and mere material of the other's life. Subjectivity has its complete sway in this sphere—the reduction of the "other" into the self. But this is

[1] The Pragmatist himself insists that a theory must "work," if it is true; but, so far, he has not asked what is meant by "working."

[2] Browning's *Abt Vogler*.

[3] This raises the question not only of the relation of psychology to metaphysics but of the possibility of the science of psychology.

plainly only one half of the truth. For each is end to the other also. The fuller of insight is the affection, the more is its object valued for its own sole sake. The husband respects the independence of the wife, the wife that of the husband. Each finds the rule of conduct in the other, who reigns with applauded sway, sovereign no less than subject.

It is precisely in the coexistence of the two sides, both of them built up by rational love, that family life attains perfection, and shows itself the most beautiful ethical being on earth, and fittest emblem of the "Kingdom of God." There individual rights are accorded to the full, and are found not to clash, but to combine in a fuller life for each of the members. The several voices are unrestrained, full-throated, free; and yet these independent units enter harmoniously into a single, *new* fact in which the beauty of each is transfigured and enhanced.[1]

This example of the way in which self-consciousness both possesses its object and builds it up against itself in the family suggests a principle which we can carry with us, as a lit lamp into the more intricate depths of the larger social world. That world, with its many interests and institutions, differs from the family in many respects. Nevertheless, just as in the last resort there is only one way of knowing, so there is only one way of building up or maintaining the social fabric. It is not that of subduing others to the self, or the self to others. It is the way of

[1] "And I know not if, save in this, such gift be allowed to man,
That out of three sounds he frame, not a fourth sound, but a star."

Browning has detected the alchemy in musical harmony. It exists not less in every product of art, of knowledge, and of the moral life.

concurrent endowment, of saying not "either," "or," but "*both.*"

This is the characteristic way of spirit, and nothing but spirit can perform this feat of making everything an element in its own life, and deepening its reality and enriching its objective worth at the same time. Animal life consumes its material and does not reinstate it. It not only uses but uses up. And it is on this account that biological metaphors when applied to the State are misleading. "Struggle for existence," "Survival of the fittest," can apply only when every individual lives at the expense of his neighbour, and finds his strength in his weakness. Such a biological "State" is, in fact, not possible.

For a similar reason, the economic view of society also fails; though it is as much more adequate than the biological view, as the biological is than the purely mechanical or individualistic. In the economic sphere the need of preserving the "other" just begins to make itself felt. For what we have in this region, in the last resort, is an *exchange* of utilities.[1] Nevertheless "the other," the purchasing, selling, the producing and consuming rival, whether an individual or a community, though no longer a mere opponent to be destroyed, is still mere means. The altruistic reference is present, but it is indirect. In a purely economic state neighbours would tolerate one another, but each would find his end in himself. Hence the economic view, respecting, as it does, only natural necessities, can never account for the State. For this we

[1] This is the truth which Protectionists forget: for they would sell and not buy, which is a very difficult transaction and has to reckon with "the nature of things."

require ethical categories—and not even such pseudo-ethical categories as those of Utilitarianism will serve.

But the very essence of the ethical attitude is the union and concurrent realisation of self and not-self, of the good that is personal with the good that is common. In the next article I shall exemplify this truth by reference to private property, and to the general relations of Individualism and Socialism.

# THE WORKING FAITH OF THE SOCIAL REFORMER

## IV

### THE COMING OF SOCIALISM

THE concrete idea of Spirit applied to social questions, and first to the idea of private property. Ownership in material things and in "things of the mind" distinguished. The assumption that private property may be a purely material fact at the basis of the controversy of individualism and socialism. The assumption examined and the controversy defined. That private property implies spiritual elements: the idea of possession by *right*, in an object which has *utility* and is therefore relative to personality, and comes by social institution and as the result of self-renunciation on the part of the State. Private property is, therefore, a sphere of social activities, and is at once essential to the individual and to the State.

Socialism as the extension of communal activity. Socialism in this sense not only coming, but has already come. But does the extension of State and civic enterprise involve what the socialist wants or the individualist fears? Or is it possible that the function of the State and that of the individual may grow together? Private ownership in State undertakings: *Mine* on the part of the State implies more than *Not Thine* on the part of its members. Legitimate State and civic enterprises imply not elimination but organization of private wills, and deprives the citizen not of his freedom, but of his caprice. How many of the enterprises now conducted by the State or municipality would by consent of the citizens be committed back to private companies?

Every proposed increase of corporate enterprise should be carefully scrutinized. The rights of the individual absolute, but only because of their identification with the wider good of society. The essence of society is moral, and the supreme duty of the reformer is to moralise the social relations as they stand.

IV

## THE COMING OF SOCIALISM

THE progress of social reform must be slow and uncertain, so long as the nature of society is not understood; and society can not be understood till the methods of science are substituted for the empiricism which distinguishes the right way from the wrong only by trying both.

This was the subject of our first Article.

Even science must fail to interpret society unless it adopts as its regulative hypothesis the principle which has produced society. It must, therefore, cease to employ the mechanical metaphors derived from "Nature," and seek in the conception of rational spirit its only clue.

This was the theme of our second Article.

But spirit itself has been mechanically understood, even by many Idealists; for they have opposed the activities by which spirit unites its objects with itself to those by which it asserts and establishes facts against itself. They have proved that the real world is ideal, but not that the ideal world is real. They have shown that spirit makes all things into elements in its own life, but not that in doing so it deepens and enriches their independent objective significance.

This was shown in our third Article.

In the present Article I shall first test the truth of this view of the concurrent realisation of the self and the not-self by reference to Private Property, and then illustrate the significance of it by applying it to the general relations of Individualism and Socialism.

Private property manifestly provides a crucial instance for testing the truth of our principle. Here, if anywhere, the concurrent realisation of the self and the not-self is impossible; for the very essence of private property appears to be an unmitigated assertion of exclusive rights. Surely, it will be said, what is mine is not another's, and what is another's is not mine. The privacy of property disappears when it is made common; its community when it is made private.

The only exception, the only property which can be both mine and another's is "spiritual" property, if the term can be allowed. Men may share the *same* opinions, seek and secure the *same* moral or social ends, and each grow richer thereby. The share of each in spiritual spoils grows with their distribution. No individual becomes ignorant by teaching others; nor do the wills which unite in the pursuit of a common good lose either their privacy or their spontaneity.

But *material* property seems to have nothing of this character. Gold or land cannot be mine unless it is not another's, nor another's unless it is not mine. It can become another's only if I relinquish it or am deprived of it. Nor does it matter whether that "other" be another individual, or a civic community, or a State.

In this contrast between material property, such as land or gold, and spiritual property, such as knowledge or virtue, we come once more upon the essential distinction between spirit and nature. Physical nature is always self-resistant; its parts are held together as a whole by the mechanical strain of mutual exclusion, and by the dependence which is necessity. But spirit can have no genuine "other." It must be universal, un-divided or individual, penetrate its object, and therefore be *itself* in its opposite.

Hence, if self-exclusion, the mutual repulsion of parts and elements, be the last word about material things, and if property be purely a material thing, then the assertion of one economic will against another, the "struggle for existence," the brute force of competition, in which the individual not only strengthens himself but weakens his neighbour, are ultimate facts of social life. The individual will, so far as it asserts itself in material property, must therefore be expelled, if social ends are to be harmoniously sought.

But Idealism, in asserting the relation of the object to the subject, has denied the utter or complete materiality of any object whatsoever. And it is precisely this assumption—that "property" is at any time, or in any object, a *merely* material fact—which I desire to question. I must question it the more closely because it is the source of some of the most stubborn obstacles to practical progress in social matters and of some of the most difficult social problems. I refer, in particular, to such problems as the extension and limits of communal or State enterprise in manufacturing and trading, the rights of the State to prohibit or regulate trusts, combinations and unions, and, in general, the apparent antagonism of socialistic and individualistic ends, of private and social rights.

Let us first make the assumption clear. If we take public opinion as it stands to-day, we shall find it well-nigh unanimous on one point. Both those who advocate and those who resist the extension of the business functions of a municipality or State consider that such extension can be effected only by limiting the range of individual enterprise. It seems too obvious for discussion that the more the organised community undertakes to possess, or control, or do, the narrower the sphere of individual activity, enterprise, and ownership. But, while Socialists and Individualists agree as to the effects of the extension of the communal powers, they differ as to their practical value. The former welcome the extension on the ground that it would limit the individual's opportunity for doing wrong; the latter oppose it on the ground that it must limit the individual's opportunity for doing right.

Public ownership of the means of production is advocated, not merely or primarily because the community would show greater enterprise, or be economically a more efficient producer than the private person, but because it seems to be the only means within our power of avoiding the manifold evils which spring from the cupidity that comes of irresponsible private ownership. The word "State," we are told, has taken to itself new connotations —"the State idea has changed its content. Whatever State control may have meant fifty years ago, it never meant hostility to private property as such. Now, for us, and for as far ahead as we can see, it means this and little else."[1]

Public ownership is resisted on the same ground. The individualist insists, sometimes wrongly and sometimes rightly, that communal production is wasteful and economically inefficient. But his real objection to it does

[1] *Fabian Essays*, p. 208.

not spring from that cause. On the contrary, he objects to it whether it be wasteful or not, and objects to it more vigorously even if it is *not* wasteful, for in that case it invades the province of individual rights more successfully, commits a wrong without bringing immediate retribution, and therefore, in the long run, brings the greater social danger. For he, too, sees in communal appropriation "hostility to private property," and in State and municipal trading the competition of the whole with its own members.

Full agreement as to the *exclusive* relation of the private and the public will, and the direct antagonism of private and public rights of ownership—such is the attitude of both Individualists and Socialists.

It follows that this social problem is material or economical only on the surface. In its deeper bearings it is ethical: it is the question of the rights of personality. And questions of right are always fundamental; for rights are ultimate, and involve the person. A nation or individual which is fighting for its rights is fighting for its life. It is as a right that the Individualist would limit the enterprises of the State or municipality; it is as a right that the Socialist would extend them. And to do them justice we must admit that "rights" are sacred to both alike. No Socialist would advocate the violation of a citizen's *rights*: but he does not admit that the citizen has rights of property against the State. All property, he believes, belongs to the State; it is held by the individual as a loan or trust; and the State can resume its borrowed property whenever, in peace or war, it sees occasion. The Individualist, on the other hand, believes that the rights of the individual are final. Even if they did emanate originally from social relations, and the State has given them as well as helped to maintain them, still the gift is a veritable gift, made once for all. If the State in national straits has to resume them, its resumption is only a borrowing from the individual, to be repaid with interest when once the crisis is over.

The collision of views between the Individualist and Socialist is thus direct. The opponents stand on the same ground: for both assume that individual *and* social rights in the *same* objects are incompatible, and that the rights in each case are fundamental. Hence any compromise necessitated by the exigencies of social life is deplored as a wrong; and it is effected only after a severe struggle between the parties. The equilibrium thus secured is essentially unstable, and it is disturbed whenever a new exigency arises.

This is one of the main causes both of the present social unrest and of the helpless empiricism of our social methods. Nor is there any hope of better ways except in examining the ground from which the antagonism springs. And this can be done with the better prospect of success inasmuch as the assumption made by both sides has been examined by neither, nor has either side realised the significance of its own negation. The controversy persists, in fact, just because both the defence and the attack have lacked uncompromising thoroughness.

The Individualist can prove that the utter denial of all rights of private property will destroy the State, on whose behalf it is made, by destroying the individuality of its members. Let the individual own nothing but himself, and he will not have a self to own. Having no foothold whatsoever in the outer world, he would live only on sufferance; having no right to impress his own will on any object he would not be able to express himself in any act: he would have no sphere for his activities, no trust or responsibilities, no duties, and, therefore, no opportunity of realising his personality or learning virtue.

The State—if, indeed, such a community of mere dependants could be called a State—might be benevolent to him, feeding, clothing, and housing him, satisfying every want as it arose, or forestalling them like a mother with her babe. But as man reaches manhood he develops other wants than these. He wants to rule his own life, to exercise his own powers, to pursue his own ends. The State might engage him; but it would be in labour not his "own," upon objects not his own, and in the service of purposes not his own; for the State has said of all things, "Not Thine, but Mine." In short, if Socialism is verily the extinction of all individual property, men would be reduced into things. This result is concealed from the advocate of such extinction by the fact that he unconsciously retains the sense and rights of individual ownership. Indeed, he makes every citizen heir to the good of the whole State. But this is either to reinstate Individualism in an aggravated form, or it is to rise above the distinction of "Mine and Thine" from which the whole controversy has originated. Private property may, as is alleged, give occasion for cupidity, competition, aggression, the untold miseries of extreme poverty, and the no less tragedy of unjust, profligate, and irresponsible wealth. Nevertheless it is the condition of the opposite virtues—of loyal service, of justice, of generosity, of manhood itself. The means of doing what is right are the same as the means of doing wrong. There must be choice between them, and the choice must be real; and that is not possible unless personality has its own sphere and inalienable station in the outer world. The remedy does not lie, as the Socialist believes, in removing the *occasion* of cupidity and the other evils, but in putting the occasion to a better use. The Individualist is right in insisting upon private property as unconditionally necessary both for the individual and the State.

But to acknowledge this exclusive side of property and even of self-hood, and to acknowledge it in a full and unqualified way, is, after all, to admit only one half of the truth.

If we examine the conception of private property more closely, we shall find that it means more than mere possession by one person to the exclusion of others. Mere possession and exclusion does not exhaust the significance or express the sacredness of private property. It does not account for the *right*, which is the essential element. A man may possess a thing which he does not own; he may hold it against others, like a robber his booty. To convert it into *property* requires more than his private will to own it himself and to exclude others. In the first place, property must be regarded as an instrument of utility. A claim to a thing which a man can never use, either directly or by exchange, is a claim to an encumbrance. In owning such a thing he owns less than nothing. Property incapable of use is really not property but dead matter, and matter out of place. To make it property is to make it the possible instrument of a will; and anything which doubles or halves its use, doubles or halves the property. It is relation to man's desires and will, that is, it is the spiritual aspect of a thing which makes it property.

In the next place, property implies not only utility to the owner, but the *recognition of the ownership* by the society in which he lives. It is true that I must be able to say of an object that it is mine, and mine as means of possible personal ends; but I must also be able to add that it is mine *by right.* And in order that I may say this, society must be a partner in my act of appropriation. The purely individual or isolated will cannot constitute a right, for a right is an essentially social matter. To my statement, "It is Mine," Society must add, "It is Thine, and Thine by my enactment."

An important principle lies here, which it will be well to illustrate. When I say that a thing is mine by right, I mean that my possession of it *ought* to be recognised by others. My possession implies a social obligation on my fellows. I consider that they must refrain of their own accord from appropriating or injuring my property. Their recognition of my ownership is not an act of grace on their part, but a claim I have upon them. I consider myself wronged if I must protect my property by force, as if I were a robber. The most individualistic of private owners, the most strenuous in asserting that he can do as he likes with his own and that his property is the mere instrument and creation of his own private will, is usually the first to call upon the State to assert and make good his rights. But he is not aware that, in doing so, he is acknowledging that his property is an expression of the social will; that his ownership, whenever it becomes a right, is due not alone nor primarily to his having said *Mine*, but to the State having said *Thine*.

He is calling the State to ratify not his will, but its own.

Hence we can condemn the mere Individualist from his own mouth. In his claim for the acknowledgment and defence of his property as a right, he is admitting that his property is an institution of the State. His demand that the State shall throw its ægis over his property means that the State, in protecting him, is only making good its own decrees.

Hence, further, the property of an individual is a symbol of renunciation on the part of society. Property is an ethical fact, implying, on the part of society, the recognition of a restraining and binding though self-imposed law. Indeed, the essence of private property is that it is the result of an act whereby society endows its individual members with rights against itself. Merely private self-assertion can never of itself create property; that can be done only by the affirmation of the social will. The individual's rights are therefore not individual in the isolating sense, but social. They are rights because they are *not* merely private. The more private they are the more they tend to vanish as rights, and the more the property becomes a mere possession held by force. On the other hand, the more full and sacred the rights the more they embody the mind of society, and are endowed and endorsed by the social will.

We arrive thus at a conclusion which is as important as it is interesting. We took up the conception of private property for analysis because it seemed *prima facie* to contradict our main thesis, namely, that spirit, in breaking down all final antagonism to itself and abolishing every exclusive "other," nevertheless did not absorb that other or nullify its opposition to itself, but rather fortified its opposite against itself by putting *itself* into it. But instead of contradicting, it illustrates our main principle, exhibiting the same phenomena as we have already observed in knowledge and in morals. If, in knowing, reason does away with the dualism of spirit and nature, it at the same time establishes the order of nature as a reality (though no longer an unspiritual reality), which gives the rule to reason and stands as the ideal of the whole process of knowing. If, in action, spirit negates the rights of the passions to war against reason, it at the same time gives them new rights and a new freedom and range of utterance as the instruments of reason, and even as its elements and self-expression.

In a similar way, as private property is really property only when it is an instrument which the individual can use, or when it is means of his self-realisation through action, it implies, and indeed is, a social fact. Property is a sphere of activities, a "station and its duties," a system of obligations set up by the individual against himself. On the other hand, as private property is more than individual appropriation, as it is rightful ownership, it means the recognition by society of a law which imposes restraints on its own caprice, and a system of obligations which it must observe, and observe the more scrupulously, regard as the more binding, because they are expressions of its own will. Private property, in a word, is an institution wherein the individual finds a rule of action in society and society a rule of action in the individual.

With the progress of civilisation the rights which the individual on the one side or the State on the other establishes within its "other" become at once more wide and various and more sacred. The more highly developed an individual's morality, that is, the more his will is socialised, the more his property and person find their use and function in social activities. And, on the other hand, a developed society accords more independence to its members than any other. It recognizes more of their rights, and it is more strenuous in their defence. So complete is the self-alienation of the State, that it will maintain the rights of its citizen against itself. He can confront its actions with its laws by help of the laws; and, by constitutional means, he can arraign the State-that-is before the State-that-ought-to-be. In short, in the right that it accords its citizens, the State gives a convincing example of the evolution of spiritual subjects by fortifying their opposites against themselves; for it plants *itself* in its own members. Even "private property" illustrates the concurrent growth of both the subjective and objective aspects of spirit.

I must now endeavour to apply our principle to one of the gravest social problems of our time.

Amongst the social changes most desired and most feared in our times is that interference with individual rights, or that extension of communal activity, implied in the word "Socialism." Both those who desire and those who fear this change are prone to regard it as inevitable, and as taking place with an accelerating velocity. The new economic conditions arising from industrial combinations, the vastness and compactness of the organisations both of capital and labour, and the shock of their impact when they collide, seem to many reflective people to threaten both the freedom of the individual and the stability of the State. It is concluded, and often unwillingly concluded, that the State must put forth more powers; must control, or buy out, or appropriate, or socialise by some method or other the means of production. If it does not, it will either become the victim of the will of the Capitalist, or fall into the hands of United Labour, which is hindered from seizing the reins of the State only because, as yet, it is not fully awake to its own powers.

Nay, we are told that Socialism is already come. "Step by step the political power and political organisation of the country have been used for individual ends, until to-day the largest employer of labour is one of the ministers of the Crown (the Postmaster-General), and almost every conceivable trade is, somewhere or other, carried on by parish, municipality, or the National Government itself, without the intervention of any middleman or capitalist. . . . Besides our international relations, and the army, navy, police, and the courts of justice, the community now carries on for itself, in some part or other of these islands, the post-office, telegraphs, carriage of small commodities, coinage, surveys, the regulation of the currency and note issue, the provision of weights and measures, the making, sweeping, lighting, and repairing of streets, roads, and bridges, life insurance, the grant of annuities, shipbuilding, stockbroking, banking, farming, and money-lending. It provides for many thousands of us from birth to burial—midwifery, nursery, education, board and lodging, vaccination, medical attendance, medicine, public worship, amusements, and interment. It furnishes and maintains its own museums, parks, art-galleries, libraries, concert-halls . . . markets, slaughter-houses, fire-engines, lighthouses, pilots, ferries, surf-boats

. . . public baths, wash-houses . . . cow meadows, etc., etc.

"Besides its direct supersession of private enterprise, the State now registers, inspects, and controls nearly all the industrial functions which it has not yet absorbed."[1]

Then follows another significant list, concluding with the words: "Even the kind of package in which some articles shall be sold is duly prescribed, so that the individual capitalist shall take no advantage of his position. On every side he is being registered, inspected, controlled, and eventually superseded by the community; and in the meantime he is compelled to cede for public purposes an ever-increasing share of his rent and interest. Even in the fields still abandoned to private enterprise, its operations are thus every day more closely limited, in order that the anarchic competition of private greed . . . may not utterly destroy the State. All this has been done by 'practical' men, ignorant, that is to say, of any scientific sociology, believing Socialism to be the most foolish of dreams."[2]

Now what are we to say of this picture? That it is partly the effect of rhetorical grouping? And that where operations are so various and so extensive in scale as they are in a great State, skilful grouping may bring out almost any result? Not merely so, I believe. The facts are in the main accurately set forth, and the general tendency of the times is not in the least doubtful. The manifold industries now conducted by public bodies were all "at one time left to private individuals, and were a source of legitimate investment and capital." Social industrial functions have

[1] See *Fabian Essays*, pp. 47–48.

[2] *Ibid.*, pp. 49, 50.

enormously increased, and they have all been assumed through the dispossession of individuals.

But before we take the side of the Socialist in rejoicing at this fact, or with the Individualist in bewailing it—before we take sides, if take sides we must—it will be well to ask a question which both have practically overlooked. There is no doubt that State and civic enterprise have increased, but has private enterprise contracted? Can the former increase only at the expense of the latter? Are the two spheres mutually exclusive, or is it possible that the general law of the growth of spiritual subjects, whether individual or social, holds here too, and that each in developing may strengthen its opposite?

Let us look once more at the facts of the case—the facts cited by the Socialist to prove that "every day they limit private enterprise more closely, and by eliminating private ownership remove the anarchic competition of private greed." What do we see when we look abroad at the commercial and industrial community of to-day? Is it a mammoth State, a Leviathan, gradually absorbing its citizens into itself, annihilating their private wills and all the good and evil which spring therefrom, and reducing them first into mere employees and then into mere tools? Or is it a country whose people are more free, whose private wealth is greater, whose individual enterprises are more far-reaching, whose persons are more effective in their command of the material conditions of life than at any other period in its history? And is competition less keen, and the race for wealth no longer run, except by the few? We are told by those who are engaged in business, whether its scale be great or small, that competition is daily becoming more sharp, and that the weak and incompetent are being eliminated with more and more automatic certainty and less and less mercy. And is private greed disappearing under the new régime? What does the moralist fear more, or with better reasons to-day, than that the new industrial conditions will absorb the mind of the nation to a degree that imperils the deeper foundations of its welfare?

The contention that "Socialism is already upon us" is true, if by that is meant that the method of organised communal enterprise is more in use; but it is not true if it means that the individual's sphere of action, or his power to extract utilities, that is, wealth, out of his material environment has been limited. It is being overlooked that the displacement of the individual is but the first step in his re-instalment; and that what is represented as the "Coming of Socialism" may, with equal truth, be called the "Coming of Individualism." *The functions of the State and City on the one side and those of the individual on the other, have grown together.* Both private and communal enterprise have enormously increased during the last century, and, account for it as we may, they are both still increasing. Hence it is possible that here, once more, the principle is illustrated according to which the realisation of the self, whether on the part of the individual or of the State, is at the same time the realisation of the self's opposite. It is possible that the State as a single organism grows in power, even as its citizens acquire freedom; and that the more free and enterprising the citizens, the more sure the order and the more extensive the operations of the State. The antagonism of the State and the citizen is one of those things, taken for granted without being examined, which have done most mischief in social matters. It is possible, at least, that by its regulation of industries the State while limiting caprice has enlarged freedom; that in appropriating industrial enterprises it has liberated the economic power of its citizens—nay, that it has multiplied owners, and increased for them the utilities of wealth, which is to increase wealth itself.

If we judged things solely by their first appearances, the conclusion is inevitable that appropriation by the State means the expropriation of the citizen, and nothing further. Did the State not carry our letters, it is certain that private enterprise would do so, and reap the profits. And yet I can conceive no one, from the king to the beggar, who would take the carrying of letters from the hands of the State. Everyone recognises that by the present method his private purposes are being realised better than they could by any other. And the publicity of the means in nowise militates against the privacy of the communications. Nor does the use of that means by all diminish their value for each. On the contrary, through the combined desires of the many the desires of each are met with greater facility and efficiency.

We must, therefore, take into account not only the displacement of the individual capitalist who might have run the penny post, but also the productive use of the capital of the vast multitude who employ the penny post. The actual result of this State invention is to make us all shareholders in a vast enterprise whose services and utilities are greater to each because they are open to all—or to all who can buy stamps. The State in this undertaking has indeed prevented the individual from saying "*Not Thine*" to his neighbours; but it has also enabled its citizens to say "*Mine*," with new significance over a wider range of utilities. And the essence and value of property do not lie in exclusion, in saying "*Not Thine*," as the unsocialised and unmoralised agent believes, but in its inclusion, in widening and deepening the meaning of "*Mine*."

But this aspect of the truth is ignored by the Socialist. He sees in this instance only the supersession of the one private capitalist, and he ignores the creation of the millions of active shareholders. He sees the displacement, but overlooks the re-instalment. He overlooks the fact that the State only holds the capital for its members, that it gives back the profits in utilities, and that it makes itself the instrument of the individual will, and thereby indefinitely enlarges its powers. For the State, after all, acts for the individual, and by means of the individual in this matter; it organises the powers of its citizens, but it does not annul them.

We should reach the same results, on the whole, if we examined other State and Civic undertakings. And although I am by no means prepared to say that there is no limit or rule to State and Civic enterprises, I may claim that both the abstract opposition to, and the abstract advocacy of, State or municipal action, on the ground that it is an encroachment on individual enterprise and nothing else, are radically unintelligent and false. They rest on categories of mere exclusion, which in the sphere of rational activities are never true.

All legitimate State or Civic enterprise means the organisation rather than the elimination of individual wills; and this, in turn, means not only more united action on the part of the whole, but more efficient action and a deeper individuality on the part of the members.

Organisation no doubt carries with it limitation. When we become members of a club, or church, or a body of college fellows, or a business concern, we give up something of our own will. In this respect all social usages, traditions, institutions, and laws, are what Rousseau thought them—bonds and chains; and the free man would be the man who ran wild in woods, enjoyed the liberty of the consistent Individualist, and of the wild ass. But, precisely in the degree to which the purposes of the society are rational and it attains these purposes, what is limited for the individual is not his freedom but his caprice, not his power to do right but his inclination to do wrong.

And such, on the whole, are the so-called "interferences with the individual," which are implied in the restrictions, the control, the activities of the State and the city. Either by explicit ordinances, or by a recognised code of usages, customs and manners, we are limited in a thousand ways. We cannot ramble whither we will over meadow and through forest as our blue-painted ancestors could; we must keep to the paths and roads. We cannot be judges in our own cause, nor right our own wrongs. We cannot even make any bargains we please, nor do quite as we like with our own. We cannot employ women in pits though they be willing, nor little children in factories, nor men in foul air and unwholesome premises.

But the good citizen and the intelligent capitalist does not desire to do these things. What the legislature has done, on the whole, is to limit the will to do what is wrong and stupid. It is only the pseudo-freedom of irrational caprice which has been limited. Nor has the State invaded any rights in such action ; for the liberty to do wrong is not a right, but the perversion of a right and its negation ; and the elimination of caprice is no loss to any one : it is one of the ends of all moral and social development.

But there is much more than this negation and limitation of the individual's caprice involved in his organisation into society. A good law, or social institution, is, at bottom, not negative but positive. It apportions rights, and gives the individual a more effective personality. In taking from the individual the right to be judge of his own cause, and avenger of his own wrongs, it re-instates it on a better basis. Though at the moment of contention we might desire to take the law into our own hands, we recognise that our neighbour would also desire it, and that on the whole the State can do this business better for both. The State does not annul the will for justice of either party, but puts an instrument in their hands for the better realisation of that will.

Now I believe this reinstatement of the individual will on a more effective basis takes place in nearly all of the matters which the State and the city undertake to perform. At least, it is a striking fact that, in this country at least, in spite of its purely empirical and unscientific social methods, there has been very little disposition to withdraw from the city or the State any industrial or other undertakings which have been once committed to them. It is not merely that it is difficult to do so, that private enterprise cannot enter into the arena or hold its own against a trading municipality or State, but that, except in the rarest instances, the reversion to private enterprise is not desired.

The reason is that, in spite of displacement, the individual has received from State and Civic organisation a vast accession of strength. The organisation of modern activities, of which the State is only the supreme instance, has placed in the hands of private persons the means of conceiving and carrying out enterprises that were beyond the dreams of the richest of capitalists in the past. The merchant in his office, the employer in his yard, can command far wider and more varied services, and make their will felt to the ends of the earth. The imperial post, the telegraphic system, the civic lighting and cleansing of the streets—what are they except most powerful instruments of the individual will? The State and the city have appropriated these undertakings and many more, but it makes over their utilities to the citizen, liberates his will for other purposes, and multiplies its power a thousandfold. More men can now say "Mine" of more things. Citizens have been drawn into the activities of the State, for their good has been identified with it in new ways; and enterprises which in previous times were outside the range of their lives are now within it. We can say "*Ours*" of parks, tramways, bridges, art-galleries, public libraries and museums; and if we are worthy of membership in this organism of many functions, we would as soon impair or destroy these common goods as squander our "private" wealth. No doubt in all these cases we must say "*Thine*" as well as "*Mine*," for the utilities are common. The negative aspect of property is becoming more contracted, but that is no loss to anyone, not even to the jealous and unsocialised unit, if he would only believe it.

Once it is clearly seen that the essence of property is

the ownership of utilities, the exclusion of others becomes a secondary matter. It is quite true that common ownership and common enterprises turn us into limited proprietors; but they make us limited proprietors of indefinitely large utilities. Through the common use of public means to meet individual wants, the real possessions and power of every one are enlarged. Break up the common use, and the use for each by himself will be less. Take the individual out of the organised state, disentangle his life from that of his neighbours, give him "the freedom of the wild ass," make him king of an empire of savages, and he will be as naked and poor and powerless as the lowest of his subjects—except, perhaps, for some extra plumes and shells.

Thus we return once more to our main principle; in the mechanical sphere equilibrium implies exclusion and resistance; in the sphere of life, and especially of rational life, mutual exclusion gives way to mutual inclusion. State and citizen live and develop only in and through each other. It is the unmoralised community and the unsocialised individual which follow methods of resistance and mutual exclusion. As they grow in strength—that is, in the power to conceive wider ends and to carry them out—State and citizen enter more deeply the one into the other. If the State owns the citizen the citizen also owns the State; each finds in the other the means of its power and the defence of its rights. So that the Individualist might well desire more "State interference" and the socialist more "private rights"; for the best means of producing strong men is a highly organised State, and the only way of producing a strong State is to make the citizens own so much, care for so much, be responsible for so much, that each can say, without injury to his neighbour, "The State is mine."

This concurrent evolution of social and individual rights, duties, and powers is inconceivable on the ordinary view. But history teaches it. I am not sure that the growth of civilisation teaches anything else of equal importance. The civic States of Greece, first experiments as they were in corporate freedom, both gave more freedom to their citizens and performed more functions themselves than the earlier despotisms. But if we contrast the Greek with modern States and municipalities we shall find that their service to their citizens was as much less varied and effective as the recognition of their private rights was more limited. Life was not so safe on the streets of Athens as it is in London, nor were the conditions of public health or the means of satisfying so many wants so fully or securely provided. Athens did far less for its citizens. On the other hand, it is not necessary to add that it respected their rights much less.

It is the inspiring spectacle of all men caring better for each, and each caring more for all, that the evolution of human society presents. That this is the conscious purpose and set aim of either men or States in general may be impossible to maintain. But the principles of life operate when they are not observed: men reason without knowing logic, and social motives operate when they are not watched. Indeed, the human spirit is never completely conscious of itself, and the ends attained both by men and States are often greater than their aims. Men set forth to realise private ends, to seek their private welfare, and they find that in doing so they have helped to realise the social order. And the same truth holds of

States: in seeking the well-being of the citizens, which is becoming more and more their ruling purpose, they not only enlarge their own functions, but strengthen and secure themselves. So that, taking both sides together, and viewing both aspects of the truth, the process shows itself to be both a more intense integration and a more diverse articulation of the moral cosmos. It is synthesis and analysis at one stroke; it is the growth of society as an active unity with an ever-increasing number of obligations and variety of services to the individual, and also the deepening of the individuality of the citizens as free and efficient personalities.

If this be true, we are entitled to look to the future not without confidence. No doubt the creation of ever new and more powerful combinations within the State brings difficulties. They can neither be let alone nor "regulated" or "annulled" rashly. And in our dealings with them we cannot lean on the experience of the race, for in this respect our times are untried. Nevertheless these combinations, whether of labour or capital, and the regulation or assumption of their functions by the State, are not things to be in themselves deplored. Organisation is economy and power, and never the *mere* negation and displacement of the private will. It is not, therefore, to be resisted and retarded as a matter of course. It is possible for order and liberty to grow together: it is certain that they cannot grow apart.

But, it will be asked, does this mean that we are to welcome any and every municipal or State activity? Is all increase of corporate enterprise a liberation of the individual's force? By no means, I would answer. There are many reasons why every new departure should be carefully scrutinised, and tried by every test. The dislocation of private enterprises is not to be lightly entered upon: probably never, if the good results which accrue terminate in a class and do not raise the State as a whole, or if private combination can serve the purpose with equal efficiency. The entrance of a municipality or State into the competitive field is not in all respects on a par with the entrance of a private competitor. And, above all, the range of the activities of the State or municipality varies with its intellectual capacity and moral strength. There is hardly too narrow a limit to the functions of a weak State or a corrupt city, or too wide a limit for the intelligent and strong.

The essential point, however, is this—that the limits are not to be fixed by any conception of the abstract antagonism of society and the individual: for each of these is true to itself precisely in the degree to which it is faithful to its opposite. The criterion of the action of the State is the effective freedom of its citizens. There remains in the moral life of the citizens an intensely individual element which the State must never over-ride. The rights of personality can be wisely sacrificed to nothing, nor its good postponed to either city or State or humanity. But, on the other hand, the sovereignty of the individual's will and all its sacredness come from its identification with a wider will. His rights are rooted in the rights of others; and all the rights alike draw their life-sap from the moral law, the universal good, the *objective* rightness, of which no jot or tittle can pass away. Hence, the individual can resist the will of the community or the extension of the functions of his city or State only when he has identified his own will with a will that is more universal, more concrete, and the source of higher imperatives than either. And this means that he can resist the State only for the good of the State, and never *merely* for his own profit. The content of the authoritative will must always be the common good, and the common good must always assume a personal form.

In a word, the essence of society is moral. It is only on moral grounds that we can determine the nature and limits of its functions. And the social reformer who comprehends this fact, so far from either welcoming or resisting the increase of social enterprises as a matter of course, will seek for only one supreme innovation, namely, that *of moralising our social relations as they stand.* And the need for this is paramount. We have been teaching rights: henceforth we have by practice and precept to teach duties; and of all these duties, most of all the duty of sanctifying our daily sphere of ordinary labour. We have been teaching Charity; but charity must become justice yet—not in the way of partitioning goods, but of rightly appraising services. To both master and man the social reformer must teach that every industry in the land is meant to be a school of virtue.

We must come back to ourselves, or rather reach forward to ourselves; for we ourselves are the roots of all our problems, and in ourselves alone is their solution to be found. *We must moralise our social relations as they stand*, and every other reform will come as a thing of course.

V

## THE MORAL ASPECT OF THE FISCAL QUESTION

It is a universal belief that material gain must not be sought by methods which are detrimental to public morals: yet it is assumed that the State has no moral function, least of all in its international relations. That the State cannot make its citizens good, but can foster morality by furnishing the conditions for its exercise. Hence the State is never a merely secular force; and any change in industrial or commercial conditions has moral significance for its citizens.

The problem of Fiscal Reform is being wrongly stated, for a main factor of material progress is left out. The economic value of human qualities illustrated. The State is a moral agent: Burke's view of it. Its significance to the individual. The perversion of its powers to private uses. "Our Trade, our Politics" a fundamentally immoral maxim. Illustrations of its operation.

The Fiscal Policy and international relations. Every State rightly tries to be self-sufficient; and all States are natural rivals. But is the welfare of the one opposed to the welfare of the others? The question illustrated by reference to the controversy between the individualist and the socialist. The difference between the numerous and concrete relations of a citizen to his State and the abstract and unarticulated relations of independent States. Nevertheless, the conditions of their welfare is the same, and they are never exclusive. Protection, and Retaliation are "methods of barbarism," and not in the line of progress, which is progress in interchange of advantages, and in the realisation of the conception of a good for each that is a good for all.

## V

## THE MORAL ASPECT OF THE FISCAL QUESTION

It is a common if not a universal belief that there is a very strong case against any action of government which comes into conflict with public morality. Any political gain secured at the expense of the national character we should consider to be too dear at the price; and, however much we desire the material prosperity of our country, we are not willing to seek it by methods which are detrimental to public morals.

Nevertheless, when a new policy is projected comparatively little is heard, either in Parliament or elsewhere, of its moral aspects. There are many reasons for this, but probably the most potent of them all is the opinion that many, if not most, of the actions of government have little to do with morality, at least directly. The function of the legislator is to conduct the business of the nation; the aim of government is to protect the persons and property of the citizens; and the State itself is merely an organ of secular force, and a pledge of lawful dealing between man and man. It has no directly moral or religious function. It cannot undertake to inculcate morality by direct enactment, nor employ compulsory powers to make the people religious, without both travelling beyond its province and defeating its own aims. For morality and religion cannot come by constraint. The *rôle* of the state stops short of the inner life of its citizens, and ends in securing for them a free field and favourable circumstances for the practice of the virtues.

Owing to these opinions, the practical man is very reluctant to subject political projects to moral criteria. Ethical considerations, weighty as they are in their own proper province, are deemed to be somewhat remote from the ordinary business of Parliament. It is not thought desirable that our statesmen should complicate their task by raising moral problems. If they are contemplating a change of our fiscal policy, for instance, their duty is simply to discover the system which conduces most to the industrial and commercial prosperity of the country. Morality will take care of itself; and, in any case, it is a concern of the people themselves rather than of their political representatives. The national character is lost or won on the broad arena of public life, and not on the floors of the Houses of Parliament.

Nor is the task of the politician the only one that is held to be pursued without raising moral questions. "Business is business everywhere," we say—meaning by this, not that the business man recognises no moral restraints, but that business has its own province, maxims, and methods, which, though they must not be immoral, have nevertheless no moral purpose. Artists say something similar regarding art, and the scientific man or the philosopher regarding knowledge. Moral considerations are thought to be irrelevant to these provinces. A work of art must be judged by the canons of beauty and not by the laws of morality, and a mathematician or physicist does not ask what are the ethical aspects of a problem in geometry or of Kepler's laws.

In the last resort it will be admitted, no doubt, that all these different provinces may be found to touch upon that of the moralist; for the world is one, and so is the human soul which deals with it. Other things being equal, a good man, whose powers are well in hand, will perform any work he undertakes better than a man whose will is weak, whose aims are low, and whose life is confused and distracted by warring passions. But this is all that can be said. And if the moralist seeks to interfere beyond this, and introduces theories as to the ethical aspects of such work, there is no option but to take him reverently by the hand and lead him out of court as a most respectable but irrelevant witness.

Now, this view is regarded as holding in a pre-eminent degree of international business. Considerations enter here which remove this province still further from that of ordinary morality. For States are not considered to be moral agents, and in their relations to each other the ordinary moral maxims are supposed not to hold. Statesmen, while engaged upon international business, must neither act nor be judged in the same way as when they are occupied upon their private concerns. "Lying, indifference to human suffering, rapacity, cruelty," says Lord Lytton (in his Rectorial Address in Glasgow in 1888), "do not lose their essential character because they are incidental to public actions. And yet we are not, I think, to judge statesmen as we should judge private persons." He maintains that, as between nations, the sixth and the eighth commandments do not hold, at least in the same way; that self-sacrifice, which, in some circumstances, is the duty of an individual, is never the duty of a State; that a State is both entitled and bound to be more selfish in its relation to other States than is morally permissible to individuals; and that *national* selfishness ceases to be selfishness in any proper sense of the word, and becomes patriotism.

Indeed, when patriotic considerations enter, problems seem to change their aspect even for the ordinary citizen. The love of humanity must not be allowed to obscure his duties to his own country. "I address you," says one of our political leaders, "as Britons, and address you as patriots." Other "great nations consider, and rightly consider, their own interests first. . . . I want that Britons, all over the world, should learn the lesson that they should treat each other better than they treat anyone else."

Now, what is to be said of this view? That it is easily caricatured is obvious. We have only to say that great statesmen may act like kings and think like emperors, leaving the minor moralities to the minor prophets and the little men; and that there is room enough for affection on our own national hearth, and time enough for philanthropy out of business hours. But this does not dispose of the truth that lies in the doctrine. For it *is* true that business is business; that patriotism has its obligations as well as its privileges; that statesmen must not be judged in their public capacity precisely as when they are engaged upon their private affairs. Nay, we may state the fact quite generally, and say that every one of the different relations between men demands a different response. We should be neither wise nor good if we behaved in the same way amongst our children and amongst our clerks, on the charitable board and in the council chamber, in the pulpit and in the senate.

We may concede further that some relations in life lend themselves more naturally and easily to moral purposes than others do, and are fitted to call forth some of the virtues rather than others. The profession of the minister or physician, for instance, naturally gives more scope for the benevolent virtues than the trade of the retail dealer. It is probably easier for a professor to tell the truth than it is for a politician—even though he should be a professor of Political Economy. He has nothing else to do except to find and to tell the truth; his constituency cannot throw him off, nor his party leaders call him to account; and the public applause is not likely to turn his head.

But to allow that some walks of life are more favourable to the exercise of the virtues than others, is very different from admitting that there are some circumstances in life which call for the exercise of none of the virtues. It does not follow that we can divide the trades and professions into two classes, and call some of them moral and some of them immoral or non-moral, placing the ministry, say, in the former, and politics and international statesmanship—and horse-couping—in the latter.

The truth is that no province of life, no form of occupation, has *in itself* any ethical character. A man's station in life furnishes him with the *opportunity* of doing right and wrong, but it does nothing more; and it can do nothing more. That opportunity he may either use or throw away; and his profession derives its moral character entirely from the way in which it is handled, and the personality he throws into it. Intrinsically there is no legitimate business of any kind which is moral or immoral, and none which is not capable of being made either the one or the other.

Hence, so far from regarding the province of politics, national or international, as having no ethical significance, I should say that, like all occupations, down to that of selling tape, it *furnishes the means* of both learning and teaching goodness. The only difference between the business of the statesman and that of his humbler neighbour is that it gives him opportunities of doing right and wrong on a larger scale. The consequences of his actions reach illimitably further: the welfare of a whole people may lie in his hands, and the destiny of nations hang upon his lips. There is here more call than anywhere else for the wise mind to conceive, and the resolute will to realise great ends. It may be more difficult for the statesman to recognise the good he should strive to do; for duties collide and obligations are frequently inconsistent, and his wisdom and rectitude are more sorely tried. But that right and wrong are irrelevant, that morality does not count, that the nation is not safer in the hands of the wise and good than in those of clever tricksters whom moral considerations do not bind nor moral ideals inspire, is certainly not true. Men, placed in such situations, stand for a nation's character as well as for a nation's might; and an enlightened people will not separate the two, nor willingly see either the one or the other betrayed.

But great as are the consequences that may flow from a statesman's action, and vast as are the possibilities of good and evil at his command, he still cannot directly touch the nation's inner life. He cannot *make* it righteous, any more than a father can *make* his children good; for moral character is a peculiarly individual possession, and must be built up entirely from within. In this respect the statesman's function, like that of every individual, is entirely secular: he can touch, not life, but its outer environment.

On the other hand, however, there is an environment which is favourable to a good life and an environment that is unfavourable. There are circumstances which provoke the rectitude of a people and circumstances which provoke the opposite. And these the statesman can affect, making it easier for his people to be good or bad. Indeed, he cannot avoid affecting them; and, in this respect, there is no act of statesmanship which has not its moral meaning. Every law inscribed upon the statute-book alters the conditions under which someone lives; it establishes rights, defines duties, and creates opportunities of a better life, or places obstacles in its way. That the State does not directly inculcate morality, or cannot compel the people to pray,—that it can best serve both religion and morality by letting them alone,—does not touch the truth that it ought to foster the conditions favourable to the good life.

In so far as the State is progressive and its legislative action wise, it can hardly be said to be doing anything else; for it is only by fostering such conditions that it can provide for the larger and freer life of its citizens. But to do this is to act as a moral agent; and no private individual can do more. Hence it is a wrong to the State to regard it as a mere organ of secular force, and its policy as having no ethical character. It never is a mere secular force, and its might, in reference to its own citizens, is always measured by its moral right; for it itself is nothing else than the embodied conscience of the people.

It is the story of a moral agent, ameliorating the conditions of a worthy life for its citizens, that we read in the history of our own country. "A state," says Professor A. C. Bradley, "which, in however slight a degree, supports science, art, learning, and religion; which enforces education, and compels the well-to-do to maintain the helpless; which, for the good of the poor and the weak, interferes with the 'natural' relations of employer and employed, and regulates, only too laxly, a traffic which joins gigantic evil to its somewhat scanty good; . . . a state which does all this, and much more of the same kind, cannot, without an unnatural straining of language, be denied to exercise, in the broad sense, a moral function. It will seek not merely 'life,' but good life. It is still, within the sphere appropriate to force, a spiritual power,—not only the guardian of the peace and a security for the free pursuit of private ends, but the armed conscience of the community." [1]

Our statesmen have been building better than they knew. Amidst the turmoil of debate and the strife of parties they have been engaged upon a great moral enterprise. By legal enactments that often seemed, even to themselves, to be merely secular in character and to affect the mere material environment within which we live, they have diminished the opportunities of doing wrong and increased the opportunities of doing right; they have made straight the paths, filled the valleys, brought low the hills and mountains, and made the rough ways smooth for the feet of those whom they govern. And the one question we have now to answer is, not whether, at this supposed crisis of our history, the purposes of our legislators have an ethical meaning, or are out of touch

[1] *Hellenica*, pp. 242, 243.

with right and wrong, but whether they tend in the same progressive direction. Moral significance those things *must* have which propose to change the fundamental conditions of our industrial and commercial life, and to alter the relation of Britain both to its colonies and to foreign states. The question is what *is* their moral significance: Is it favourable or is it unfavourable to the better life of the nation?

It has been necessary to dwell at some length upon this apparently preliminary matter. For, judging from the great mass of opinions expressed in the present controversy, two assumptions of cardinal importance have been tacitly made: first, that moral considerations do not enter in a vital way into the question of our material prosperity; second, that the State, being an end to itself, cannot be regarded as a moral agent, nor its relations to other States be subject to moral criteria. I propose to examine these assumptions more closely, for the crux of the whole situation seems to me to lie in their truth or falsehood. And I shall try to show that, on account of these assumptions, the problem of our material prosperity has been wrongly stated, and that, in consequence, the change proposed is in some respects inadequate to secure our national welfare, and in other respects directly contradictory to it.

Now, it will be conceded at once that our national prosperity depends both upon material conditions and upon our national character. But while the first truth has been discussed in all its bearings, the second has been either overlooked altogether or treated as a matter of little weight in determining our future policy. It is no doubt true that an occasional statesman has proposed to meet the present crisis—if, indeed, crisis there be—by seeking to raise the personal efficiency of the people rather than by changing the conditions of trade. They have suggested better public education, especially on the technical side, and they have called for social reforms which shall make our lives less wasteful and more sober and simple. But their words have fallen flat upon the national ear, and the remedies which they have proposed have seemed stale, commonplace, practically insignificant and negligible. As a people, we have been behaving precisely as if moral considerations were either too remote, or too irrelevant and slight, to have any practical bearing in determining the method of averting the decline or securing the progress of the nation as a producer and distributor of wealth. We have puzzled over the increase and decrease, relative or absolute, of our exports and imports; we have traced economic causes and effects; we have accumulated statistics, true and false, just as if human qualities did not count, and as if the problem from beginning to end were purely material. And, of course, our diagnosis has dictated the remedy; the terms in which the problem has been stated have determined the character of the solution.

Now, when we turn from the business of the nation to our own, we see and recognise the value of these human qualities clearly enough,—I mean their purely economical value. What sum, for instance, would one of the great Clyde shipbuilders, harassed by the ignorance, the stupidity, the intemperance, the irregularity, and the untrustworthiness of the workmen in his employment, who keep his machinery idle, dislocate his plans, and frustrate his contracts, be willing to pay in hard cash for some magic invention, legislative or other, which secured for him, and for him alone, that every man in his yard shall henceforth be sober, intelligent, punctual, industrious, slow to assert his rights, and sensitive to his duties? I venture to say that as a practical man he would consider that such an invention would give him an inestimable advantage in the competitive struggle. And if such a change could be brought about in every yard and workshop, in every counting-house and office throughout the land, is it likely that we should need to trouble much to protect ourselves behind tariff walls? On the contrary, if this could be done in part, and even in very small part, if the level of the moral relations of masters and men were raised but a little, we should increase our industrial efficiency as a nation much more than by any meddling with our fiscal policy. And, besides, the gain of the latter method is doubtful as well as exiguous, while that of the former method is indisputably certain. But we have not thought this moral aspect of the question worthy of serious consideration.

Let us look at this matter for one moment from another point of view. It is a common saying that "Money breeds money," and I think it is a common opinion that wealth increases by spontaneous generation. But the economists tell us that wealth, whether national or personal, is maintained only by constant reproduction. Apart from that portion of our wealth which is in a relatively permanent form, such as roads, machinery, houses, cleared land, etc., we consume it all and recreate it all within the year. And we do that, of course, in virtue of our personal qualities. Deprive us of these, strike the community with a wand so as to stop its activities, or make a free gift of the business of the nation as a going concern to a rude people, and what would be left of our prosperity at the end of six months?

The wealth of a nation is the product of two factors, neither of which can be left out of account. One of them is the material means, the other is the intelligence and rectitude, the industry and the skill that employ them. And if I were forced to distinguish between these, I should say that the latter is by far the larger factor of the two. I should much prefer to share the destiny of a people which is great in the qualities of its men, even although their hands were empty, than that of a wealthy nation whose citizens had lost their manhood.

If it is urged, in reply, that these are familiar truths, I answer, "Undoubtedly. But their familiarity seems to have obscured their significance. They are, so far as our practical diagnosis and our legislative remedy are concerned, outside our thoughts; our assent to them has been merely theoretic and academic." We have stated the problem of our national prosperity with one of the supreme conditions left out, and in politics, as in mathematics or science, the solution must be either impossible or wrong. The problem has to be stated over again. It is a primary requirement of the present situation, now that the question of our national ways of doing business has been raised, to state the problem with a greater breadth of outlook, and with strict fidelity to *all* the fundamental facts of the case.

This has not been done. We may admire the boldness, whatever we may think of the wisdom, of the statesman who is primarily responsible for shattering our national complacency, challenging our familiar ways, and pointing us back to discarded methods of trading. So far as he has roused the nation to self-inquiry he has done well. But the inquiry has stopped short at the surface. It has reached neither the real needs of the country nor their true remedy. By an error which is natural to a mind supremely equipped both by natural endowment and by experience for the arena of the competitive industries, but sustained and enriched by no historical or philosophical background, he has treated the State as if it were a business concern and nothing more; and he has confined the thoughts of the people, as well as his own, to the question of commercial methods. The result is that both sides of the great controversy have immensely exaggerated the significance of these methods, extending them all around our mental horizon.

The State, said the wise Burke, "ought not to be considered as nothing better than a partnership agreement in a trade of pepper and coffee, calico or tobacco, or some other such low concern, to be taken up for a little temporary interest and to be dissolved by the fancy of the parties. It is to be looked on with other reverence, because it is not a partnership in things subservient only to the gross animal existence of a temporary or perishable nature. It is a partnership in all science; a partnership in all art; a partnership in every virtue and in all perfection. As the ends of such a partnership cannot be obtained in many generations, it becomes a partnership not only between those who are living but between those who are dead and those who are to be born."[1]

Like the contemporaries of Burke, we seem to lack this larger vision and to have lost the larger courage which always inspires a progressive nation to seek prosperity by

[1] *Reflections on the Revolution in France.*

the long and hard road which leads through a reform of manners. We seem to be looking for shorter cuts to imperial welfare than that of moralising the people. And we are likely to lose our labours. For, whatever may be said of those who stir in the political waters, the better mind of the people of this country knows full well that human history, as it raises up and pulls down the nations of the world, teaches one fact plainly amidst all the confusion of its errant ways—the fact, namely, that national welfare, like individual well-being, rests in the last resort upon moral foundations, and that the value of a policy, old or new, fiscal or other, depends upon the way in which it tells upon the morals of the people. Many of the measures proposed in Parliament are such as not to involve great consequences, or to imply new departures; they continue or perfect existing conditions. In such cases disregard of the wider ethical issues is proximately harmless. But when, as in the present instance, questions are raised which, as we are told, involve our whole material welfare, our rank and place amongst civilised nations, and even the unity of the Empire, it is not good or wise statesmanship to leave out of consideration the most fundamental of all the conditions of our imperial well-being. The importance of a change in our methods of international trading is in no wise denied. For my part, I believe that to set up artificial barriers against free trade would bring deeper poverty to the poor, widen the chasm between them and the rich, bring more bitter social differences with the greater social inequalities, and complicate our relations both with our dependencies and with foreign nations. But, all the same, our ultimate destiny as a people lies not in this fiscal province. France has been prosperous under protection, and it would be prosperous were its trade free; for its people are thrifty and industrious. And I should say the same of the British Empire: it will survive its policies, if it keeps its character. But we have been forgetting the human elements in the problem, and dealing with affairs of State as if they were questions in abstract economics. The result is a distorted view of the whole situation and a change in the true perspective of things. The whole picture is false, for the focus is wrong. Imperial Britain is pictured by our orators as a fiscal unit, held together by economic bonds, pitted against other fiscal units in a competitive conflict in which what one gains the other loses. The unity of the Empire is represented as consisting of two strands—unity of sentiment and a unity which privileged commercial relations are expected to bring; good feeling *plus* sound business. But the unity of sentiment is thought of comparatively little moment, as if it were feeble and fragile as well as intangible; while all the emphasis is thrown upon the material bond, if bond it be. And, of course, the obligations of the citizens to the Empire must suffer in consequence; for the meaning of patriotism depends upon the conception we have formed of our country, and if the latter is superficial the former will be shallow.

It was this shallow, "property" view of one's country which was rebuked by the old blue-gown Edie Ochiltree, when the Antiquary suggested that he had not much to fight for. "Me, no muckle to fight for, sir!" was the reply. "Is na there the country to fight for, and the hearths of the gudewives that gie me my bit bread, and the bits o' weans that come toddlin' to play wi' me when I come about a landward town? De'il! an' I had as gude pith as I hae gudewill and a gude cause, I should gie some o' them a day's kempin'."

This homely picture of his "country" drawn by a humble patriot seems to me to imply more than kindly sentiment towards a fiscal unit—the wooden idol of our times. And grave philosophers and statesmen, in all ages of the world,—Pericles and Pitt, Plato and Aristotle, and Hegel and Burke,—agree in this with Edie Ochiltree rather than with our more modern prophet. Their conception of their country is more human, their obligations to it are more deep. For what is the individual to them apart from the State, and outside of its great social partnership? He is, in strict truth, nothing but a name. Heir to no social inheritance, sharer in the destiny of no people, his soul is blank and his hands empty; he stands refused by the moral order, without a duty to perform or the power to conceive it. For he has veritably nothing of his own which he has not borrowed. "The tongue that he makes his own is his country's language, the ideas and sentiments that make up his life are the ideas and sentiments of his race." He is, continues Mr. F. H. Bradley in one of his intense passages, "penetrated, infected, characterised by his relations with his fellows. . . . The soul within him is saturated, is filled, is qualified by, it has assimilated, has built itself up from, it *is* one and the same life with the universal life; and if he turns against this, he turns against himself; if he thrusts it from him, he tears his own vitals; if he attacks it, he sets the weapon against his own heart."[1]

The ancient philosophers recognised this inexhaustible

[1] *Ethical Studies*, pp. 155, 156.

debt of the individual to society, and especially to the highest form of human society, namely, the State. No fairer destiny was possible to man than to be a citizen of a good State, and they identified the whole duty of man with that of the citizen. The magnitude of the modern State, the stability and permanence and variety of its institutions, the multiplicity of the interests which it in some way reconciles, and the very freedom with which it has endowed its members, conceal from us the political significance of our private station and duties. The good citizen goes forth to his labour in the morning and returns at eve, and he knows not that by fulfilling the duties of his station he has been strengthening the structure of his State, and serving purposes which far outspan his own. He is a patriot unconscious of his patriotism ; for he does not realise that in fulfilling his function he has contributed his quota to the progress of his country. He does not carry with him the consciousness that his good is its good, and that its good is his good ; nor does he consider that he is a sharer in its common life, that he has no other life, and that no other purposes beat like a pulse in his veins. But the fact is as undeniable in the modern imperial State as it was in the Athens of Pericles.

It is thus no matter for wonder that the dissolution of the State has always proved to be the ultimate tragedy of human life. The decay of the Greek municipal States, the decline and disintegration of the Roman Empire, the Revolution in France, all show the same spectacle. When a State "crumbles asunder and is disconnected into the dust and powder of individuality," the bonds of private morality themselves are loosened, and man is deprived of his very humanity. The wise, during periods of great political corruption, have sought a refuge in a noble inner life; but that inner life itself is a gift of social institutions, and, severed from them, falls into inevitable decay. Even Christianity, with all its sublime ardour for the spiritual life of the individual, contributed to the corruption of the ancient world in so far as it released its adherents from the obligations of citizenship. For in a man's relations to his neighbours in the State lie the conditions of all the virtues.

But there is a deeper wrong to the State than even this disregard of the obligations of citizenship. It is that of turning the privileges of citizenship against the principle from which they have sprung, and perverting the powers of the State to private uses. And this, unfortunately, is a wrong not unknown in our own day and country. From direct corruption and misappropriation of the criminal kind we are now happily free, at least in comparison with other times. But men will do in the interests of their class what they would scorn to do directly in their own. Sustained by the consciousness of the common ends of a class, men otherwise estimable in the eyes of their neighbours become unconscious enemies of the public weal. Disregarding the fact that the State is the common guardian of all just interests, and that its stability and strength depend upon its power to reconcile those interests in one harmonious whole, seeing no wrongs except those of their own industrial or religious sect, and devoted to no other rights, they press these blindly upon the State. In doing so they strike at the heart of the common good, no matter who aims the blow, nor for what abstract cause. For when we see a class of men, be they the aristocracy or the common people, capitalists or working men, or the blind devotees of a religious sect or social cause, employing the powers granted them by the State in order to gain one-sided ends, without respect to others, we see them engaged upon an enterprise which, if it succeeded, would bring the State in ruins about their heads.

It is true, no doubt, that the legislature must always seek particular forms of the common good, removing now this and now that inequality, and advancing step by step in establishing rights. Nevertheless, in so far as statesmanship is wise it aims at the good of the whole in seeking that of the part, and maintains the social equilibrium. And similarly the desires of the good citizen are always checked and chastened by wider and more generous conceptions than those of his class and sect. To him there are few mottoes which rank in moral turpitude with that with which one of the most powerful organisations within the State has disgraced the standard under which it fights—all too successfully—and which reads, "Our Trade, our Politics."

And it is here that the policy of protection, in all its forms, stands utterly condemned. For, in spite of all the reckless assertions and negations of these days, one finds no one who has had the hardihood to assert that this policy would further public rectitude. On the contrary, it is too plain that, by something like natural necessity, it would lead thousands more to inscribe upon their banner the badge of social wrong-doing, "Our Trade, our Politics." Artificial tariffs, amongst a people endowed with the genius for combination, like our own, and keen in its pursuit of wealth by organised methods, would convert the lobbies of the Houses of Parliament into an arena where trusts and combines contend for their conflicting interests. Such a course of action is degrading to those engaged upon it, and its indirect moral and political results are deplorable. The guardians of the State, in whose probity lies the immediate security for our social well-being, would be distracted from their high duty by the "lobbying" industrial potentates. And who will dare to assert that they might not be torn away from it; or that from the high places of the nation's social will the waves of corruption would not roll back upon the nation itself?

Our social needs are many in these times, and some of them are grave and urgent; but, amongst these, I cannot reckon the need of creating larger opportunities and greater temptations to political and industrial corruption. And whether we should succumb to these temptations or not, it is certainly no wise statesmanship that calls them forth. We may be losing our commercial and industrial pre-eminence,—it is not proved; we may be on the way to national poverty,—I do not believe it; but we are certainly not, as yet, at that point in the game where we must throw our national character amongst the stakes.

It is not relevant to say that our neighbours have done this. The question is, have they done it without loss? And there is only one answer to the question, and that answer is so well known and certain as to make detailed proof supererogatory. To the mass of evidence we already possess I shall add only that of one witness—the testimony of an American citizen, a leading lawyer and financier, who has been president of a large railway company, and concerned in other large business operations. "If Chamberlain's opponents," he says, "would only study the American results of protection, and the inevitable consequences of creating an artificial profit by misuse of taxation, bringing a feverish desire in the business world to get by legislation an advantage over other trades, they could present such a picture as would save England from following him. . . . You *must* win, or civilisation takes a backward step. No body of legislators, from Parliament down to city councils and boards of select-men in towns, can be safely trusted to use the powers of taxation for any other purpose than that of merely raising money to cover the expenses of government. Throughout the political structure in America to-day, shrewd people everywhere struggle to legislate in some way money out of their neighbours' pockets into their own, and this feverish desire is the real source of the municipal corruption which pervades all our civic organisations. . . . Protection in America is the mother of corruption; and to fight Chamberlain is simply to fight for common honesty."

These are strong words, but I doubt if it is possible to say that they pass beyond the truth. That the motives of Mr. Chamberlain, and of those who have supported him, may be as pure as his effort has been strenuous, I do not doubt. Great efforts for great causes are hardly ever inspired or sustained by selfish motives. But neither ardent patriotism nor the generous dream of a greater empire has saved him from committing himself and his followers to a political method which, if applied, would put a strain upon the private morality and the political honour of British citizens and upon the rectitude of their representatives, from which we have all inherited the right to be free.

But the prospects are not really alarming. We shall not barter our political purity for the promised millions. Just for the moment, the mind of the multitude may be confused and dazed. But once quiet comes, and more sober reflection on the larger and forgotten issues, the dust of the battle will settle down and we shall see with a new clearness and pronounce with a new conviction that no dreams of gain shall lead us to risk our loyalty to those permanent conditions of our welfare which lie in the national character. Our present methods have, amongst other causes, been instrumental in extending the Empire beyond the dreams of patriotism ; and yet the accumulated responsibilities have not broken our strength, nor left us bankrupt at home. As yet, at least, we hold a place of honour amongst the great nations of the earth ; and though we should stand alone for years yet to come in guarding by the freedom of our marts and our open ports the purity and strength of our political life, we shall hold it no cause for shame nor source of weakness.

But I must pass on to the still wider question—that of the manner in which the new fiscal policy concerns the relation of the British Empire to other independent states. It is not possible for me to deal exhaustively with this aspect of our problem ; but I shall try to make clear one fact that seems to me of cardinal importance, namely, that the decisive and dominant conceptions do not belong to the province of pure, or mere, economics. If any reasons exist at all for departing from our free-trade methods, these spring from the political province.

This becomes evident when it is considered that there is no economic difference between international and any other trade. In strictness there is no such thing as international trade. All trade is between individuals (or their business equivalents), and, apart from political considerations, it is a matter of perfect indifference whether these do or do not belong to the same nation. The strongest adherents of preferential or protective tariffs do not dream of advocating interference with the freedom of interchange of goods between England and Scotland, although these countries compete with one another not less keenly, and in more ways, than with France or Germany. They tell us that, were it only practicable, they would establish free trade throughout the British Empire, and presumably, therefore, throughout the world, if all the nations formed one State. In a word, were it not for political and patriotic considerations, London would be allowed to continue to trade with Berlin, New York, and Paris as freely as with Dublin or Glasgow.

How, then, do political and patriotic considerations affect the situation, so far as it depends upon ourselves? Why should they make any difference in our method of interchanging goods? If our fiscal reformers took the trouble to examine their own presuppositions, their answer would be something of this kind:—A political State stands under peculiar obligations to its own citizens, and places them under peculiarly intimate relations to itself. In their interests it seeks and has a right to seek to enlarge its territory and strengthen itself up to the limits of its power. Ideally, a State ought to be self-sufficient, and be strong and resourceful enough to provide its own citizens with all that is required to satisfy their wants; for incompleteness implies weakness and dependence, and these carry with them insecurity for all those to whom it ought to be an adequate refuge. Hence, there is nothing to limit the self-assertion of a State, for as self-sufficient it is an end to itself; and if it recognises any restraints, they are all prudential in character. If it had the power, as it has the right and the will, it would rule the world. All that other States are and possess are simply things which, so far, it has not been able to make its own.

Now, as all States have ideally the same obligations to their citizens, and therefore the same unlimited rights, they are natural rivals; and the normal relation between them is that of mechanical strain. The expansion of the domain or the power of any one of them is a menace to its neighbours. Any increase of its industrial or commercial efficiency is secured at their expense. For it seems quite evident that, the greater the mass of goods which it is able to produce, the more restricted is the sphere of the industrial activity of the others; and the more it floods their markets with these goods, the more confined are their own markets and the less the demand for their labour.

And just as the obligations of a State to its own inhabitants are primary, so the duties of the citizen to his country must override all others. His sentiments may be cosmopolitan, but his practice must be patriotic. For as States are natural rivals, seeing that each seeks to be self-sufficient, he cannot do anything to serve other States except, directly or indirectly, at the expense of his own. In so far, for instance, as by his commercial or industrial enterprise he employs the workmen of a foreign State or otherwise contributes to its prosperity he relatively weakens his own. He ought to bewail its success and rejoice in its failure. If his own country is losing its relative pre-eminence, whether through greater prosperity abroad or through less prosperity at home, he must regard it as an evil, and, like a true patriot, look for the best methods of averting it. What other States do is work taken out of our hands; the markets they supply are shut against ourselves. Economically, as well as territorially, the different States are sections of a closed circle, and the expansion of the province of the one is an invasion of the province of the others. Hence a man cannot, at least so far as concerns material things, be a citizen of the world without neglecting, or at times violating even, his duties to his own country. We are entitled to suspect the patriotism of the humanitarian : *angel pen fford, a diawl pen pentan.* "We must distinguish between a blood relation and a business competitor. We decline to regard the colonies as coming in all matters upon exactly the same basis as foreign competitors." These words of Mr. Wyndham are indefinite, but if one is to translate and apply them to the present situation, they seem to mean that we must give to our colonies better bargains than to other countries, we must compete with them more softly—mitigating the heat for them, as some of the old theologians desired to do for lost infants. We must be less annoyed against them if they carry off our trade ; we must give them preferential tariffs ; we must tax our food and raw material for their sakes.

Whether this is not patriotism degraded into impractical sentimentalism I shall not inquire ; nor whether it be not better for our colonies and dependencies, as for ourselves, to be permitted to hold their own, rather than mix sentiment with business. Nor shall I discuss the matter from the point of view of pure economics. Otherwise I should try to show that it is not the prosperity but the poverty, not the strength of foreign countries but their weakness, that hinders and limits our trade. I should also try to prove that so long as trade exists between two countries the country which gains most from the free interchange of goods, other things being equal, is the country which is economically the weaker.

It must be admitted that, from the point of view which represents the various states as natural rivals, and sets our duty to our country against our duty to man, such results as these are not only unaccountable but impossible. *But is the point of view right or wrong?* This is the fundamental question to which we must now turn.

It is plain that this view of the nature of international relations is a particular form of a wider doctrine, which distinguishes and opposes regard for self and regard for others, egoism and altruism, private good and the public or common good. Moralists will recognise in it the familiar doctrine of Individualism (applied to States) to which Thomas Hobbes gave the classical expression. In our day we are more familiar with it as applied to the relation of individuals to society, and as illustrated in the discussions of the advocates of Individualism and Socialism. And although the problem of the relation of the individual to the State is not identical with that of the relation of independent States to each other, we shall find it profitable to dwell upon this matter for a moment.

There is one point on which Individualists and Socialists agree.[1] They all desire both the solidarity of society and the independence of the individual; they all desire the maintenance of the social order and the freedom of its members; and they all desire that both society and the individual should, each in its own province, be active and efficient. But they despair of reconciling them, except by either subordinating the one to the other, or by a mutual

[1] I have referred to this matter in another context in another essay: but perhaps its importance may excuse the repetition.

compromise which shall delimit and fix their boundaries; and they differ as to which should be end and which should be means, or as to the limits that should be set to their respective functions. The Socialist, weary of the strife and strain of competing private interests, would take away the occasion of these, so far as it lies in private property, and would restrict the possession of it. The Individualist, regarding the development of corporate social enterprise as "interference" with that of the individual, and fearing the mechanisation of society, would reduce the functions of society to the minimum. Both admit that the recent development of state and municipal activity has had the result of invading the province of individual enterprise. But they differ in that the Socialist welcomes this invasion because it limits the individual's power of doing wrong; while the Individualist bewails it because it limits his power to do right. It is tacitly assumed by both alike that individual and commercial action are antagonistic, that one can be extended only by limiting the other. For is it not plain that when the state or municipality undertakes a business it ousts individuals, and that the more the former does in an organised capacity the less room is left for private enterprise? How can it be otherwise? it is asked. How is it possible that the state or the city can do more and more for its members, and at the same time enable them to do more and more for themselves?

And yet this apparent impossibility is precisely what has taken place. The history of the growth of civilised society is one continuous illustration of the concomitant increase of social organisation and of individual freedom. The civilised state does more for its citizens than the barbarous state, and at the same time enables them to do more for themselves. A comparison between the civic States of Greece and the earlier and cruder Eastern despotisms on the one side, and the modern state or municipality on the other, shows this at once. So numerous are the functions which the latter have undertaken, that we are told that "Socialism has already come." And this is true if it means that the organised services of society have been multiplied ; but it is altogether false if it is meant to convey, as it generally is, that the individual's sphere of activity has been contracted. That he competes against society on its own lines is, of course, not true; nor can it be asserted that a state or municipality can take up a business without affecting those already engaged in it. But if it proceeds wisely, as on the whole has been done in this country, the general result is that the work is placed in the hands which can do it best, and that means general progress.

Owing to higher organisation and the enlarged functions of the modern state, the individual is a much more powerful agent than the member of a crude community. In other words, owing to the system of institutions which the state comprises and sustains, he can conceive and carry out purposes utterly beyond the reach of the latter: he is a deeper and more effective personality. The modern state is a rich treasury of resources upon which he can draw, and its organisations constitute a most powerful machinery on which he can lay his hands. It supplies him with the means of a larger life, and extends and deepens the significance of his individuality.

Now, this fact, which is illustrated in our daily lives as well as in the history of the growth of civilisation, implies that the surface view, which represents the individual and the community as rivals and their good as mutually exclusive, is radically false. Individual and social activity are coincident, and their prosperity is but two sides of the same fact; so that to limit the one for the sake of the other is absurd. Instead of seeking a fixed line of demarcation, or setting up artificial barriers, the enlightened citizen will entrust to each those enterprises which are most suited to its powers, feeling his way in doing so and learning from experience. He knows that the vital issue is that the work be well done, and that the question by whom it is done is relatively an indifferent matter. For work well done benefits all alike, there being no social good which is not an individual good, and no individual good which is not a social good.

Turning now to the relation between independent States, we must first concede that it is not in all ways identical with that of individual citizens to their own nation. It is easy to show that the individuality of a State is intrinsically much more rich, concrete, and strong than that of any private person; and, at the same time, that the larger society of mankind is a far more empty and impotent universal than any single State is in relation to its members. Hence it follows that the mutual obligations of individuals within a State are much more numerous and significant than those which States can recognise in relation to one another, or have been able to express in international laws and customs. And obligations are, of course, opportunities; duties are means of self-realisation. So that the different States, as matters are at present, can do far less for each other than individual citizens within the same State; or in other words, cosmopolitan or humanitarian ideals are far less articulated into systems of definite duties than those of patriotism.

But to represent the good of a State as antagonistic to that of humanity, or to set patriotism and cosmopolitanism against each other, is as wrong in theory and as mischievous in practice as it is to oppose the good of the individual citizen to that of his State. The attempt to do so arises from the same shallow individualism, and the same ignorance of the coincidence of private and public good. But the teaching of history is as clear in respect to the community of States as we have found it to be in the case of a community of individuals. The failure or the prosperity of a particular State has always communicated itself to its neighbours precisely in the same way. Every wrong deed on the part of an individual State is a wrong to humanity, and every action that is right and good for itself is in the last resort a contribution to the stability and prosperity of its neighbours. The British Empire, by its political and social progress, by its science and inventions and industrial enterprise, has benefited every country with which it has held intercourse. And other nations have done the same to us. Their good is ours, and ours theirs. Even in international trade, where self-seeking seems to be at the same time both most evident and most justifiable, our best neighbour is our strongest neighbour; for it buys most from us in order to supply its own needs, and sells most to us so as to supply ours. We cannot profit by its decay, nor it by ours. When Rome destroyed Carthage it destroyed a great part of its own prosperity; and any "hitting back" upon our part, if that means weakening our neighbours, weakens ourselves as well. The utmost that can be said for any such policy of retaliation is that it may conceivably lead our neighbours to mend their ways, although it must be admitted that force very rarely brings about that change of mind which we call repentance. But to justify retaliation on this ground is to concede the principle to which it is opposed. It is to admit freedom of interchange as the true end, while seeking to bring it about by the doubtful method of compulsion. It is the method of the "natural man"; in fact, it is the method of "barbarism."

But the progress which civilisation has so far achieved has consisted in abrogating the methods of the "natural man." Instead of rivalry and antagonism there has arisen, step by step, co-operation in common ends and mutual service. There exists still between States, as between individuals, that self-assertion which is one aspect of self-realisation, and there is no question in either case of a sentimental altruism which sacrifices rights. The egoistic element remains, and must remain; for the whole cannot be strengthened at the expense of the parts. But the egoism is gradually becoming an enlightened egoism, which recognises that the good which is exclusive is a false good. The antagonism is giving place to *a competition in efficiency*, to a method by which each part, whether it be an individual or a state, discovers more and more clearly its own station and round of duties, by fulfilling which it shall realise best both its own and the common good. And nowhere is this more conspicuous than in international trade, whose foundation is just the interchange of services; for nothing has ever either established or developed trade, whether between individuals or between states, except this principle of mutual help.

This progress in intercommunion has, no doubt, brought with it some disadvantages. We have lost some trades and been obliged to turn to others, and so also have other nations. But this is incidental to the process by which each discovers its own proper function; and it must not be forgotten that it liberates as well as dislocates, and brings with it the benefits of a better division of labour. International commerce has, further, made us more dependent upon our neighbours, and our neighbours upon ourselves. But interdependence is, in normal conditions, not weakness but strength, for it implies mutual utility. In abnormal conditions, as in times of war, it is, of course, mutual loss. For if war breaks out between interdependent states it tends to assume for each of the combatants alike the most dangerous of all forms, namely, that of a civil war; for the closer the tie the more fatal the rupture. But this argument tells against the comity of nations only in the same way as it does against the union of citizens, or of provinces in an individual state. The risk is worth the running, for it is only the risk naturally entailed in the establishment of social institutions and in moralising man.

The intercommunion and consequent interdependence of states may be said, further, to increase the opportunities of disagreement; for neither states nor individuals quarrel with those with whom they have nothing to do. But if they increase the opportunities of disagreement, they take away the disposition to it; for amongst interdependent states injury to one is recognised as injury to all. And besides, isolation is not amongst the practical options. Intercourse between nations there must be, and it is well that it should be. By means of it, and by means of *commercial* intercourse perhaps more than by any other, the civilised nations are gradually building up and realising the conception of a common good. And that conception, wherever it is operative, acts after the manner of a moral imperative and binds those who come under it through their own conscience, which is the only bondage that is also freedom; and it transfigures natural into moral relations, converting antagonism into competition in the arts of peace, the successful pursuit of which is at once the good of each and the good of all.

From this point of view it is difficult not to regard a policy which places obstacles in the way of the free interchange of benefits amongst nations as a crime against civilisation. And, though there may be circumstances which render such a course imperative, just as there are circumstances in which an individual must assert his rights against his country,—for the narrower and nearer loyalties sometimes come first,—still it is a wrong and a folly to invite the collision. And it is not possible to maintain that it is forced upon this country, either by its poverty or by any other unhappy fact. On the contrary, the political insight of our forefathers, and their wise regard for the welfare of their country, led them to open its ports to all the world, with advantages to itself that it is not possible to measure, and of which those which are material are not the greatest; and by a law that seems to be written in the very nature of things, its own good has spread in an ever-widening circle to other great communities, and most of all to those which share its enterprising spirit most fully and are its worthiest rivals.

To ask us to change all this is as supererogatory a task as ever an eminent politician took in hand. To change our open into restricted markets, to set up barriers against the free interchange of utilities so far as that lies in our power, to adopt methods of antagonism to other nations, to endanger our own larger patriotism by making our colonies an unwelcome burden to our citizens at home, to lay aside a powerful instrument of amity and good-will amongst the peoples of the earth, and all for the sake of a limited and still more doubtful material gain, is a wrong against humanity which we ought not to have been invited to commit. And we shall not commit it. We shall not turn back upon the methods that have made our Empire great, nor shall we weaken the moral foundations on which alone it can securely rest.

## VI

# THE CHILD AND HEREDITY

The relative significance of innate qualities and of the environment a complex problem for Biology, and a still more complex problem for Psychology and Ethics. Attempts to simplify the problem of the latter, by reserving something for the human being which is other than the natural factors of his life; and to define the limits of the Self and to isolate it. Their failure. The alternate accentuation of innate powers and external circumstance. Tendency of Biology to deny the inheritance of *acquired* characters, and to insist upon the unbroken continuity of life. That Evolution intelligently interpreted levels upwards, and assimilates nature to man rather than man to nature. Examination of the assumption that the significance of innate character and that of external circumstance are in inverse proportion. That they give meaning to each other, and that their significance grows *pari passu*. Conditions of life which are alike in being necessary need not therefore be of the same rank. Re-interpretation of the interdependence of the child and his environment. That the child does not inherit *propensities* to good or evil, and that character can not be transmitted. The influence of Society. That Society can raise the level of child life only by raising the level of its own practical conduct.

## VI

## THE CHILD AND HEREDITY

"A MAN is what he is at any period of life, first, by virtue of the original qualities which he has received from his ancestors, and, secondly, by virtue of the modifications which have been effected in his original nature by the influence of education and of the conditions of life. But what a complex composition of causes and conditions do these simple statements import!"[1] The task of determining what it is precisely which is inherited in any particular form of life, and how far and in what ways the original inheritance may be enriched or impoverished, continued in its first tendency or diverted therefrom, constitutes the main enterprise of modern Biology. And it has proved so difficult that, after many years of inquiry and discussion, biologists have hardly succeeded in laying down even general principles which they would agree in regarding as open to no further doubt.

But the problem of the nature and relative significance of inherited qualities and of the influence of surroundings with which the biologist deals, is simple as compared with that which is raised by these facts for the psychologist, the moral philosopher, and the metaphysician. For these latter

[1] Dr. Maudsley's *Pathology of Mind*, p. 87.

have to deal with the nature and the interaction of these factors within the realm of consciousness; and consciousness, however we may account for it, is a fact which must not only be acknowledged to exist, but recognized as complicating the issues of life, and indefinitely deepening their importance. We may derive consciousness from natural conditions after the manner of the Materialist, or we may attribute to it some "higher" and more mysterious origin, or we may even hesitate to seek for its origin at all, and simply accept it as a unique datum: in all cases alike it retains its own character and its own functions. These functions are what they are, whatever their history, and the problem of their nature remains the same, however they be derived.[1] Is consciousness nothing but a mirror in which man's physical activities are reflected, so that he not only lives, but carries with him a record of his life? Or is it something more than a passive mirror, and does the record which consciousness keeps of its life and its activities react upon that life and those activities, and change its inherited and environing constituents, so as to give them a new meaning and efficacy, and a place within that higher order of being which we call rational or spiritual?

On the answer that is given to these questions depends the whole meaning of heredity and of circumstance for man as a rational being. And upon the meaning that is given to heredity and circumstance depends, in turn, the very possibility of his having a rational life, with its characteristic cognitive, moral, and religious activities.

[1] The problem of the nature of a thing is not the same as that of its origin, especially if it be a thing that grows; and it is much more important. A thing that grows is, moreover, explained more fully by what it becomes than by what it arises from.

That hereditary conditions and the influence of environment somehow, and to some degree, affect human character no one will deny. But the significance of the admission is rarely seen. As a rule, the question is reduced into that of the degree or extent to which these natural elements enter into human life. For it is considered that, to make the character depend *wholly* upon these two elements, to regard it *simply* as the product of these two factors, is to deprive character of all moral or spiritual meaning. Is it not evident, it is asked, that moral character must be made by each individual for himself; that it must be the expression and manifestation of the self; and that the self disappears if it be analysed into hereditary and environing elements in their interaction?

Consequently, we find the apologist of man's spiritual or moral nature endeavouring, by means of various devices, to retain something for man, as rational, which exists over and above these natural factors. He attributes to man a will which is not inherited and not ruled by circumstance, or a self which is greater even than its own content. "The Ego is something more than the aggregate of feelings and ideas, actual and nascent." These and their natural antecedents do not exhaust the Ego or give a complete account of all its actual and possible phenomena. "When I am told, 'You *are* your own phenomena,' I reply: 'No; I *have* my own phenomena, and so far as they are active it is I that make them, and not they that make me.'"[1] The self, it is held, is something more than the whole character even. There is in it a transcendental element which character can at no moment wholly express or embody. The self is a noumenon amongst phenomena, and belongs

[1] See Martineau's *Types of Ethical Theory*, II. chap. i.

in the last resort to another order of being than these latter.

But the problem of man's rational and moral life cannot be solved in this way, nor the meaning of heredity and environment as applied to mankind be made plain. For the question is not a question of the degree in which the natural, inherited, or external elements enter into his life; but of the manner in which they enter. It matters nothing where we draw the line that distinguishes the self from the not-self, or the man from that which is before or outside of him: we may draw it between the transcendental self and the empirical self; between the self as knowing and the self as object of knowledge; between the self as noumenon and the self as phenomenon; between the self and the character; between the self and the feelings, thoughts, and volitions which are the content of character; or between the self and the physical conditions which antecede or environ it. The result is still the same. The self that we thus isolate is empty and impotent; and *the man as a whole*, whose nature is, after all, the object of discussion, is represented as a compound of extraneous and mutually repellent elements, which is in theory unintelligible, and in practice powerless for either good or evil. The natural and the spiritual, or the formal self and its extraneous content, cannot at the same time co-operate and retain their mutually exclusive characteristics.

It is for these reasons that the problem of heredity assumes in the realm of Psychology and Ethics a different character from that which it has in that of Biology. Biology could at best give only the "natural" history of man, and either his "natural" history is not his whole, or even his true history, or else his morality and religion are nothing but illusions. Either he is not the result of the action of a merely "natural" environment upon an inherited disposition, and the process of merely natural evolution does not account for him in his real inward being at all, or else his spontaneity and freedom and the moral life which springs therefrom are mere appearances. Slowly and reluctantly, but inevitably, it seems to me, the philosophers of the present time, and especially those who are idealistic in temper and who therefore will not easily let go the spiritual nature of man, are driven to choose between the naturalistic or materialistic interpretation of man on the one hand, and the spiritual interpretation of him on the other. The method of compromise, that is, of regarding man as partly natural and partly spiritual, as from one point of view a noumenon, and from another a phenomenon, as a mere subject in some respects and a mere object in others, is breaking down. It is gradually realised that *both* the natural and the spiritual method of explaining man *claim him as a whole.* Either his inmost self must fall within the natural scheme, or else that natural scheme itself must have spiritual significance. Spirit by its very nature is jealous and can brook no rival. It must be all, if it is at all. The deepest of all differences must fall within its unity with itself. Man must lapse back into nature, or he must raise nature to his own level as spiritual.

But both alternatives are difficult, and the choice between them is hard. It is hard to see in what way natural facts can be spiritualised without evaporating them into mere forms of the human consciousness; and it is not less hard for those who endeavour to look at the facts of human life as a whole to acquiesce in the reduction of morality and religion into natural things, disguised as spirit. On the other hand, the ways of Dualism and Agnosticism are easy. It is easy to make the realms of nature and of spirit into closed and exclusive systems, or into different orders of being, so that natural law terminates, and spiritual law begins at a certain point. And it is easy to postulate some incognizable unity behind nature and spirit, and to conceal their difference by making them aspects of it, or to bring in some unknowable reconciliation of them in an Absolute which surpasses knowledge. It is easier still to seek to establish man in an unexpugnable ignorance of all true being; to maintain that his science never penetrates behind appearances to the real, and is full of unverified hypotheses, which can be riddled by metaphysics; and to hold that morality and religion have even less rational cogency than his knowledge, unless we are permitted to base them upon the dogmatism of authority, or intuition, or faith. But the primrose path in philosophy leads, like others, to undesirable results.

All these methods have been attempted by the different philosophical schools of the day. But none of them has proved satisfactory or brought rest. Why should they? They merely offer as a solution a re-statement of the problem. The natural pre-determination of the child, whether through heredity, or through the power over him of external circumstance, remains to threaten his spiritual nature; and his spiritual nature remains to contradict the merely natural character of the medium within which it operates. Nor does it matter on which of these two the accent is thrown; the ideas of the fixity of inherited character in the child and of its being plastic to environment are both alike fatal to a free and rational life. The possibility of moral character, which must be of the individual's own acquisition, is destroyed in both cases; and the very conception of individual improvement and social reform is stultified. Nor is it clear, at least at first sight, in what way the operation of the two forces together can amount to anything better than a double enslavement; or how the child can be regarded otherwise than as the victim both of heredity and of physical and social environment, as of two colliding necessities.

And yet it is this latter condition that seems to be presented to us as a fact. That is to say, the child seems to be under the dominion of both. He comes into the world with powers inborn, and in great part unalterable. The whole force of circumstance can only assist him to become what, in a manner, he already is. His intercourse with the world "alters it so little and so unessentially, that we have a right to say that he remains the same." And yet, on the other hand, the influence of the environment is so great as to count for well-nigh all. Apart from it, his powers remain unrealised, for the environment is the very material out of which his character is fashioned. It determines which of his powers are stimulated and actualised, and which are atrophied and left dormant; and, apparently also, whether they shall be directed towards vice or virtue.

Owing to this double aspect of human life much confusion has ensued both in theory and practice, and we find those who are engaged either in the education of the child or in social reform involved in an endless and apparently futile discussion as to the relative significance of the inner and outer conditions of character. The emphasis is laid upon heredity and environment, or shifted from the one to the other, according to the purpose or need of the moment. From the first point of view we find it maintained that a child may inherit from vicious or dissolute parents a disposition to evil. It matters not, we are told, what influences may be brought to bear upon it, sooner or later the original strain will manifest itself in act. The vicious life breaks out in due time almost as surely as oak leaves upon an oak tree. And so strong is this conviction, so fully does it seem to be maintained by evidence gathered from all quarters of the animal kingdom, that it has been a main obstacle in the way of one of the most desirable and promising of social reforms. I refer to the adoption as members of well-doing families of the derelict waifs of the great cities. No one can deny that our sporadic and intermittent benevolences are futile for the purposes of the real moral education of such children; or that the too remote care and cool affection spent upon the children in poorhouses and other charitable institutions lack the regenerating force of a virtuous home. Nor do I believe it possible to deny that in this country and these times, where the sense of pity and of social responsibility is so much quickened, adoption might not be more general than at any other time in the history of the world. But the fear of hereditary predisposition paralyses the benevolent, and paralyses their action the more, the more they place value upon character. They cannot face the risk of twining their affections around children who may have brought with them into the world the tendencies which destroyed their parents.

Nevertheless, in other departments of personal and social reform the accent is laid upon the environment, as if heredity signified but little. Nearly all the more important public reforms are advocated from this point of view. Let but the institutions of society be changed, and it is believed all else will follow in due course. Moral disease, thinks the more militant socialist, will disappear under the new external conditions of which he dreams as surely (though perhaps more slowly) as physical diseases tend to disappear with better sanitation. Nor does this view lack some evidence to support it. There is no denying the significance of environment in moral matters, any more than in physical.

Not only are the influence of environment and the significance of heredity alternately accentuated and minimised, but these two factors of character are held to be opposed to each other. For it seems too evident to admit of dispute that the more the child brings with it into the world through the hereditary transmission of its parents' qualities, the less can external environment affect it for evil or good; and, *vice versa*, that the more there lies in the power of outward circumstance the less the significance of the inherited qualities. And it is this supposed opposition which has led to the persistent and apparently hopeless effort to determine the limits of their respective influences upon child life. What practical reformer would not prize highly the discovery of the line of compromise which would guide his endeavour and show what he may, and may not, attempt for the objects of his care?

On this account those who inquire into these matters with the dispassionate continuity of the scientific investigator listen with keen interest to the deliverances of Biology in its comparatively simpler field. It is felt, in particular, that the controversy raised, mainly perhaps by Weismann, as to the inheritance by the offspring of the *acquired* characteristics of the parent, is of profound significance. That controversy is still so far from being settled that we are not entitled to regard any conclusion as certain. But I believe that upon the whole the direction in which competent opinion strongly tends is towards the *denial* of the inheritance of such *acquired* characters. It is very doubtful if new characters can be acquired at all. Probably, as Weismann says, "Every acquired character is simply the reaction of the organism upon a certain stimulus." "No organ can be originated by exercise," says another biologist, "though an existing organ may be developed to its maximum." . . . And even, "granting that there are such things as acquired characteristics, the evidence of their transmission is unreliable."[1]

But if biological evidence tends towards denying the inheritance of *acquired* characters, it is not to be assumed that it also tends to minimise the significance of heredity. On the contrary, those who are the most strenuous in denying that acquired modifications of the parental structure can be transmitted to the offspring make the largest claims for the inheritance of other characters. Heredity, they think, can be explained only on the theory of the germ-plasm; and the theory of the germ-plasm implies, in the last resort, not only that life is continuous but that from the first it contains, in some way, the tendency towards the variations which reveal themselves in the successive stages of animal life. Outward environment only elicits or restrains, stimulates or represses, what is already present; but it can add nothing that is new.

When the environment appears to cause a change in an organism, closer investigation shows that it furnishes only the *occasion* by reference to which the living thing changes itself. "A green frog, if he is not among green leaves,

[1] Headley's *Problems of Evolution*, p. 67.

but amid dull, colourless surroundings, ceases to be bright green, and becomes a sombre grey. Put him among foliage again and his green soon returns. It cannot be said that the green foliage has caused his colour to change. It is more correct to say that he has the power of changing his colour to suit his environment. If the frog happens to be blind, no change of colour takes place; so that it is by the help of the eye and the nervous system that the change is effected."[1] The power of reaction must be present. The true cause of the change is within; outer circumstance incites it into operation. "In fact an external condition can do nothing but bring to light some latent quality"; or, as Weismann puts it, "Nothing can arise in an organism unless the predisposition to it is pre-existent, for every acquired character is simply the reaction of the organism upon a certain stimulus."[2] Thus the denial of the inheritance of *acquired* qualities and the assertion of the inheritance of all other characteristics go hand in hand. They are both consequences of the view that the environment can only furnish the *occasion*, that is, the incentive and means of organic development.

Now, this view of the significance of heredity and of the subordinate, though necessary, rôle of the environment carries with it most important consequences for the study of the child and the conditions of his development. The first of these consequences, it is manifest, is that if we accept this theory in its full extent, we must conclude that, at least so far as his organic structure is concerned, the human being must be regarded as in some manner latently or potentially present even in the very lowest form of animal life. Biologists do not hesitate to draw this con-

[1] Headley's *Problems of Evolution*, p. 49. [2] *Ibid.*, p. 50.

clusion. "In the lowest known organism, in which not even a nucleus can be seen, is found potentially all that makes the world varied and beautiful."[1] More strictly, perhaps, biologists *seek* to find this potentiality, that is, they proceed on the hypothesis that it is there, and are engaged in discovering the conditions and manner of its presence.

But structure and function go together and, so far as the general observation of animal life shows, develop *pari passu* at all its stages. And if it be true that the promise of the human structure is latent in the lowest organism, it would seem that the promise of its functions lies there likewise. No doubt we must distinguish between the psychical and the physical. However they are related they cannot be identified. But that does not prevent us from regarding both as developed forms of the lowest life, the one on the side of its functions and the other on the side of their physical condition. Indeed we must derive both or neither, unless we are prepared to destroy all intelligible correlation between what an organism does and what it is. Hence it follows that the mental powers of man are brought within the sweep of natural evolution; and the child is determined at birth—to go no further—as a rational not less than as a physical being. No doubt, as in other cases, the environment, or, as we may say in this context, *experience* may furnish the means of modifying the inherited powers, but it cannot initiate. The child can become only what it was potentially at the first.

Now, at first sight, this hypothesis seems fatal to the possibilities of ethics and religion and all the higher interests of man; and to limit greatly the range within

[1] Headley's *Problems of Evolution*, p. 39.

which the child can be educated. It is not without reason that, as we have seen, the apologists of man's spiritual life have recoiled from this doctrine, and have either sought to endow man with some power or other which stood free from this chain of necessary causation, or have endeavoured to discredit the deliverances of natural science as hypothetical and sought refuge in faith, *based* upon ignorance. But the first of these methods is certainly doomed to fail. Its very success brings failure. For precisely in the degree to which the self-conscious ego is withdrawn from real connection with the world, in which it is placed in order to realise itself, does that realisation become unintelligible. We cannot afford to deny or mystify man's intercourse with the world, by interaction with which his powers are evolved; and intercourse is impossible if there is no real or ontological relation between these factors. And as to the second method, even while admitting that this doctrine of evolution is only a hypothesis, and that even the surest deliverances of natural science are only in process of being proved, I should consider the tenure of our moral and religious beliefs very insecure if they could be held only on the condition of discrediting natural science.

Rather than avail ourselves of either of these methods, let us seek to discover what consequences really do follow if we accept this doctrine of evolution and heredity as true.

I believe it possible that in this doctrine, rightly understood, there may be found the best defence of man's spiritual interests. The importance of the issue justifies close inquiry.

In the first place, then, it is to be noticed that the result of this view is not to naturalise man, but to rationalise his antecedents.

For this doctrine does not assimilate man to his animal progenitors, but his animal progenitors to man. It does not strip man of his powers, but endows the lower animal creation with the promise of them, asserting that they exist from the first potentially. Evolution thus comes to mean what idealistic philosophers have maintained that it is, namely, a process of levelling upwards, and not of levelling downwards. Man is not made the poorer by the enrichment of his animal ancestors. His conscious life retains its characters even although it should be proved that the crude promise of it lies in simple organisms. Hence those who believe that man's nature is essentially rational or spiritual can abide this biological issue not only without concern but with the assurance that if it be true it makes the world mean more and not less; for it brings it closer to man and even makes it share, in its way, in his rational enterprise.

Within the sphere of human psychology this conception of the higher as implicit in the lower favours man's ethical and spiritual interests still more clearly. Psychologists have been divided in opinion on this question of evolution and heredity in a way closely analogous to the biologists. And amongst them also the tendency, on the whole, has been towards assimilating the lower to the higher, or towards levelling upwards. But nothing beyond a "tendency" in this direction can be asserted thus far. For there are many philosophers who, in their metaphysical speculations, at least, proceed on the older hypothesis. By implication, if not by direct assertion, they treat sensation, perception, conception, and the higher powers of reason as if they appeared *successively*; and the child during his development is made to pass from a perceptual and individual form of experience into a conceptual or universal form, which latter is alone rational in the proper sense of the term. How he steps over this succession of gaps is not, and on this theory can not be explained.

But most important issues follow from this view. Amongst them are the limitation of the operations of the higher faculties to the formal re-arrangement of the data of sense; and the condemnation of science and philosophy to the task of restating, in a more abstract and general form, the truths already obtained in perception. The progress of scientific and philosophic knowledge, on this view, is the self-stultifying movement from the concrete to the abstract, from particulars rich in content to universals that are formal and empty. And, above all, the higher is made dependent upon the lower, and man's activities, in the last resort, are represented as sensuously determined. Many therefore and various are the devices to which recourse has to be made, in order to save man's rational interests threatened by this hypothesis. As man's life rests upon perceptions and perceptions upon impressions, impressions and perceptions of another kind than those which lead to cognition are postulated on behalf of his higher interests. Art, morality, and religion are said to have their own special and peculiar sensible data, and the conceptions proper to them are derived from these data by generalisation and attenuation. There are unique æsthetic perceptions for the consciousness of beauty, unique moral perceptions for the consciousness of goodness, and unique supersensible impressions to furnish the data for religion.[1]

[1] The reader will find an interesting statement of this view in Lotze's *Lectures on Religion*; and the Ritschlians have found it useful for delivering religion from the hands of philosophy.

It is not observed that this method re-introduces the discredited doctrine of separate faculties, and loses "man" in his parts and divisions; far less is it observed that beauty, truth, and goodness imply each other and cannot thus be held apart.

But the more consistent idealist postulates the presence of the higher faculties in the lower. He finds sense to be implicit reason, and ordinary knowledge to be implicit science. The progress of knowledge is for him a process of concretion and not of abstraction, of articulation and not of mere generalisation. The higher contains the truth of the lower in a fuller form; sense is carried up into perception, and perception into thought. And hence the higher is not determined by the lower, but is the fulfilment of its own promise within it; and the nisus of the whole process lies in that which is about to be. In a word, he uses the idea of final, not of material cause as his interpreting instrument.

So far, then, there can be no doubt that this conception of evolution, both in its biological and in its physical applications, contains no threat against the higher life of man. It lifts him above external necessitation by placing the impulse and direction of his evolution within himself. He is not product but producer, not consequence but cause. He himself is present, although only implicitly, in his antecedents; and while external conditions stimulate, he is determined to action only by himself.

But, it will be asked, does not the necessitation remain? According to this view, are not the future of the child, and his character as man, determined for him? Is not hereditary determination *fatal* determination? What can education, or aught else that the physical and social environment may bring, do for him, except simply make him what he already is? Have we not denied not only the transmission of acquired characters, but the possibility of acquiring anything that is really new?

I reply that no answer except a fatalistic one is possible to these questions if we start from the ordinary presupposition, to which I have already alluded, namely, that the more we attribute to heredity the less we can attribute to the environment; or that in taking the child from the power of the one we place him under the power of the other. If heredity and environment are thus taken as opposed, or as acting singly, the possibility of that identity *in* change which the progressive attainment of rational character implies disappears. For the first means mere fixity, and the second mere change. The first denies the improvement of the self; the second dissipates the self.

But I should like to question this assumption of the opposition of heredity and environment, or of their alternate sway over human life. The fact is that life in all its activities implies their *interaction*. The child is never under the dominion of one of them to the exclusion of the other, for they signify nothing so long as they are held apart. Except for the environment his powers would remain potential only, and mere potentiality, whatever it means, is not actuality; and similarly, on the other hand, the mere environment has no significance, and its influence is not real where there are no powers that can utilise it. The entire meaning and power of both lies *in their relation*. They are what they are through mutual implication.

And, further, seeing that they enter as factors into organic life, the increase of the one does not imply the diminution of the other. On the contrary, the larger the inherited faculty, the greater the opportunities which any given environment brings. Where the inherited endowment is meagre, the environment can do little either to develop or to repress. And, relatively to his animal progenitors, it is because the hereditary powers of the child are so great that the nature of his environment is so important. You can swing a canary's cage in the most immoral surroundings without detriment to the bird ; but to place the child there is to come near to making a calamitous result inevitable.

It is not to be considered, however, that the environment can be regarded as *causing* the character. Mere environment can obviously cause nothing ; at the very most it is only one element or factor in the cause. Nay, if we keep close to the view of evolution which we have been discussing, it will be seen that the word "cause" is not appropriate in this context, and that the influence exerted by the environment is not "causal" in its character. For it does not determine the development of the child ; it only furnishes the means for its *self*-determination. It can initiate no powers, and possibly it can *ultimately* destroy none ; for the germ-plasm theory provides for the indestructibility of life and its potencies as well as for their continuity. What it can do, and does, is to provide the conditions under which particular powers of the individual may or may not be developed. And in this respect the importance of the part it plays cannot well be exaggerated. It is, I believe, as vain to expect the normal or right development of a child's rational nature in an unfavourable environment, as it is to expect the healthy growth of the body under unhealthy conditions. The dependence of the child's welfare upon the external factor of his well-being is complete, even although its dependence on the inner factor also is complete.[1] Both are absolutely necessary conditions of his well-being, and they must be concurrent and co-operate.

But it does not follow that they are of the same rank, or that we can regard them both equally as causes, or as exercising the same parts in the determination of the child's character. Both means and end are necessary to bring about a result, and nevertheless the means is subordinate to, as well as necessary for the realisation of the end. And such, on this view of evolution, is the relation between the inner and outer conditions of character. All that the environment can do, in the last resort, is to call the child's powers into activity, and furnish the means of their realisation. The direction and the final limits of his development are prescribed from within.

We must now endeavour to ascertain some of the results which flow from this conception of the relation of inborn character and environment. The first of these is that a fresh light is thrown upon the nature of the dependence of the child upon his surroundings. According to the view both of the determinists and the indeterminists, any kind of real or ontological connection between the child and the natural system into which he is born was regarded as an obstacle to his freedom, and therefore to his realisation of a life which can be called moral or spiritual. Hence the controversy between them turned upon the possibility of liberating him *from* this system. According to the

[1] If the reader is tempted to consider this statement to be a mere paradox he may ask whether the dependence of animal life upon the action of any *one* of such organs as the heart, or the brain, or the lungs, is not complete.

doctrine we have endeavoured to explain, the outer world, so far from being an obstacle to his self-realisation, is the indispensable condition of it. The social and physical environment furnishes the whole content of his rational life. Hence the richer the world is in which he finds himself, the more constant its pressure upon him, and the more varied and more active its incitations, the more surely he attains what it is in him to be. The world is there in order to be possessed by his intelligent nature; and his intelligence grows just in the degree to which he enters upon this possession. It is there to call forth the active powers of his will, and his will grows in range and effectiveness with its reaction upon the world. He is set to realise his rational nature, not in spite of, but by means of his surroundings. And his dependence upon them, though as complete as the dependence of his body upon air and light and food and drink, is a dependence which ends in converting them into his own substance, and making them into constitutive elements of his power to think and act. It is isolation, and not connection, that implies impotence. It is the aloofness of a world whose meaning is not comprehended which brings bondage and compulsion. In the degree to which the self is free it possesses the world. It internalises it within the self; the self ideally comprises it and makes it the instrument of its will. In fact, this is the process by which the child develops towards the fulness of his stature. That is to say, his education is the opening out of his powers of converting that which originally was external to him into constituent elements of his self. When he has reached the stage at which his development ceases, one can say with much truth that all his environment is within him. To the degree in which the character has become fixed, whether in the ways of vice or of virtue, to that degree all the new forces which play upon him either leave him unaffected or simply re-inforce his existing tendencies. This is the reason why so little can be done to assist the adult wastrels; and why the very means of well-doing are turned by them into instruments of deeper corruption. Such is the power of character, once formed, over that which plays upon it, that, whether it be good or evil, it turns it into its own substance. And social reformers, as their experience grows, tend more and more to despair of doing anything real for adults, and to turn their forces of improvement more and more upon the child.

It follows in the next place that what a child inherits are not actual *tendencies* but potential *faculties*. Biologists sometimes speak as if it were possible for parents to transmit tendencies or propensities towards good or evil to their offspring; and we have already seen something of the way in which this conception has entered into the common belief and practice of our times. It arises from the direct application of natural categories to moral facts. Goodness is considered as a "variation," and as capable of transmission through inheritance, as if it were an organic structure. It is supposed to develop from age to age in a race,—"the race which has much of it having an advantage over that which has little." In short, it is made subject to ordinary evolution. Hence, in accordance with the germ-plasm theory, goodness should be present potentially in the lowest organism. "If goodness appeared in the world only in evolution's latest stage, we may nevertheless infer its existence before life began upon the earth. The Darwinian believes that no new power or faculty has been introduced from without, since the simplest form of life began the course of evolution that was to end in the most complex and highest. It is evident, then, that on this hypothesis, goodness existed potentially from the beginning, only waiting for the required circumstances to develop it."[1]

In accordance with this view one would expect that what applies to goodness also applies to evil; and that it, too, is present in the lowest organism, persists and is developed from age to age. But apparently it is not so. The process of evolution is said to be one by which evil is being perpetually eliminated or subjugated, and evil cannot, therefore, be regarded as a primary principle.[2]

I shall not inquire whether the biologist is entitled thus to mete out a different measure to good and evil; for I cannot admit the transmission by inheritance of either of them. Good and evil are in their very nature incapable of being transmitted. For they are neither structures nor functions; neither organs nor faculties; and it is only with these that biological evolution deals. They are not even modes or qualities of functions; they are ways in which rational beings operate; they are "values" discovered by the application of criteria, and have no independent existence and cannot persist. They continue to exist only so long as they are being willed, or only so long as the will is active; and they imply a nature which is not only potentially but, in some degree, actually rational. We call a man good because we believe that his formed character will lead him from time to time to do good acts. The amount—if we could really speak of "amount"—of good

[1] Headley's *Problems of Evolution*, p. 291.

[2] See *Problems of Evolution*, p. 293.

and evil in the world at any moment is measured by the actual volition of deeds which are right and wrong. Good and evil exist, whether in the individual or in the race, by constant re-creation, and they perish utterly with the acts which they characterise. Heredity, therefore, cannot touch them. Every man, *as moral*, is a new being. His history begins and ends with his will. For although the will is not detached from antecedents it sublates them, or takes them up into itself, and in doing so transmutes them.

What does persist and might conceivably be transmitted is the modification set up in the individual's powers through the doing of right or wrong actions. For every action, mental or physical, recoils upon the faculty which has produced it. And it is possible thus that there may be an accumulation, not indeed of good or evil, but of propensities to perform the one or the other. And there is no doubt that this accumulation takes place within the life of the individual. The creation of "habit," which is one of the conditions of the acquirement of increased power of any kind, would be unintelligible, if the doing of acts left no trace upon the doer.

But, if it be true that *acquired* characters are not transmitted, then even *tendencies* to good or evil cannot come by inheritance. No child is born vicious or virtuous. It is only by his own action that he can become the one or the other. He is not even pre-disposed to virtue or vice, unless, indeed, we identify the former with the innate impulse towards self-realisation, characteristic of all life. Not even the most unfortunate of human beings is born with a moral taint. What he inherits are powers, and these undeniably may vary both in a relative and in an absolute sense; so that the appeal of the environment may mean very different things to different children, and the education of the child into a virtuous manhood may be much more difficult in one case than in another. But that such education is more or less possible in the case of every rational being I must believe. The possession of a rational life implies it, or, rather, I should say that the possibility or potency of such a life implies it; for the possibility is turned into actuality, and the powers are realised only *in* their interaction with the environment.

The conclusion to which we are thus led, by our consideration of heredity in its relation to the child, is that *character* cannot be transmitted. The vital energy which passes from parent to child is variable in absolute quantity and in the relative strength of its constituents. And I do not believe that there is reasonable room for doubt that a degenerate parentage brings weakened offspring; or that, in this restricted and metaphorical sense, the sins of the fathers are visited upon the children. But in every other sense, except this of varying capacities awaiting realisation by actual contact with circumstance, each child is a new beginning; and the way to virtue, so far as internal conditions are concerned, is as open to the child of the wicked as it is to the child of the virtuous. The whole stress, therefore, falls upon the environment, and above all else upon the *social* environment, into which from birth the child enters. And the essential element in that environment is not the precept but the practice of those into whose hands the care of the child falls. For not only does the child measure the significance of the precept by reference to the practical life which it observes around it, but it is this practical life which constitutes the constant, normal environment, the very air it draws in with every breath.

The question of surrounding the child with influences calculated to evolve its powers is thus of transcendent importance. From birth to death he acquires nothing except from his surroundings. Apart from the community, from *his* community, from the atmosphere of example and general custom which he apprehends and assimilates, he is but a blank possibility and an abstraction. His very self is social in its whole make and structure. His character, if it is necessarily all of his own making and the expression of his own inner rational life, is nevertheless wrought out of the active substance of the social habitudes that surround him ; "its content implies in every fibre relations of community." The tongue he speaks is not more surely the language of his own people than are the ideas he forms, the sentiments he imbibes, and the habits he makes. Hence it follows that the best, nay, the only good education of the child, comes, as Pythagoras said, "by making him the citizen of a people with good institutions." What the limits of the inborn potentialities of a child may be no one can determine. There is a sense in which it is not possible to think too highly of his heritage. For is not reason in its very nature the counterpart of the realm of reality? And is not the world of things and men, the marvellous outer cosmos and the still more marvellous order of social life in all their inexhaustible variety of contact, there for him to assimilate and possess? But this inheritance, ideally so great, is in actual practice limited to the forces that immediately play around him. And, within the limited scope of his life on earth he cannot excel, except to a most exiguous degree, the actual life in which his lot is cast. He can rise but a little above his surroundings. The educative power of a community towards its own children is thus measured by the amount of virtue and wisdom which it shows in its own customary conduct.[1] It cannot improve them except by improving itself; and the building up of the moral cosmos is a slow process. But that a community should spend its care upon bringing what is best within it to bear upon the opening powers of its children, even taking upon itself the responsibilities and privileges of parentage when the natural parent by his own vice and folly has abdicated them; that it should venture far more for the sake of the young, risking much in order to educate them into virtue, is an indisputable condition of its welfare. Compared with this every other task that reformers and legislators can undertake sinks into insignificance: so rich is the innate inheritance of the child, and so dependent is his possession of it upon those into whose hands his life falls.

[1] New educational schemes, to the invention of which we are so much given, can of themselves do little—far less than is ordinarily expected. Example is the only real teacher of morals.

# IDEALISM AND POLITICS

## VII

### THE ACCUSATION

THE advantages and disadvantages of the practical politician in his reflexion upon national affairs compared with those of the political philosopher. The latter must be taken to mean all that he says. Mr. Hobhouse's arraignment of the English people: partly inspired by incidents connected with the South African war, but raising far wider and more permanent issues. Summary of his charge (1) against the British people as a whole; (2) against the middle class; (3) against the common people. The depth of national degeneracy. The people's attempts to fortify themselves in their degradation: their misreading of political history; their perverse use of the physical and biological sciences; and, above all, their recourse to Idealism.

This picture of the people of England has been drawn by passion, but is not altogether false. The dangers of an age of transition; but the goal of the transition should not be ignored, nor the good overlooked when evils are exposed. Mr. Hobhouse has told truths, but not spoken the truth.

The charges made by Mr. Hobhouse against Idealism in particular, and why Idealists have been slow to accept his challenge. True elements in his description of Idealism: its popularity, and the greatness of its influence upon public life. What, according to Mr. Hobhouse, are the Idealistic doctrines whose effects are so deplorable; and where did he find them?

## VII

## THE ACCUSATION

"DISCUSSION about democracy," says Mr. Morley, "is apt to be idle, unfruitful and certainly tiresome, unless it is connected with some live, temporary issue." Profitable thinking upon political, as upon other matters, usually arises from the direct compulsion of circumstance. When in the course of a nation's practical life a problem arises the political thinker will do well to assume that the circumstances which set the problem contain the terms of its solution ; indeed, the solution of a problem is nothing but the problem itself with its elements distinguished and their relation to one another made plain. If the political thinker is also a legislator, or even some fragment of a legislator, he enjoys those further advantages which his laboratory brings to the physical investigator—he can test his ideas. And nothing tests ideas so thoroughly, or so ruthlessly corrects their abstractions, as the attempt to carry them out, that is, to fit them into the complex system of forces which, at any moment, makes up a nation's life.

On these grounds, amongst many others, the practical politician is in a far better position for effective thought upon the condition of a people than the political philosopher. His point of view may not be so elevated, nor the range of his vision so extended; he cannot see all the world at once, snugly coiled within his "system." But, on the other hand, his vision is not blurred by distance from affairs, nor is it confused by the mists of many different views which are apt to come between the learned theoriser and the facts that he wishes to know. His contact with his problems is direct. He deals not only with opinions but with needs, not with mankind but with men. Hence, he does not too readily merge the wailings of his time in a universal harmony; he knows that all the hurts and pains of men are particular, and is not tempted to prescribe general nostrums. Having as his business to make the world better in particular ways, he takes upon himself some tangible portion of its burden and is liable to be taught true lessons by stern facts.

But if the practical politician has his advantages he has also his own special difficulties. The "live contemporary issue" which gives practical virility to his reflections is also apt to distort them. Circumstance tends to limit as well as to inspire his conceptions. The thing of the moment earnestly conned and closely handled is apt to obscure issues which may be greater, as an object held near the eye hides the world. Has his own political party come into power? Then are his people to him what the British nation was to the Milton of the *Areopagitica*, "noble and puissant, rousing itself like a strong man after sleep." Is the opposite party still in favour? Then are the English people those of Milton's *Eiconoclastes*, "with a besotted and degenerate baseness of spirit, except some few who yet retain in them the old English fortitude and love of freedom, imbastardised from the ancient nobleness of their ancestors."

Now, these violent alternations of opinion on the part of the professional politician are intelligible and comparatively pardonable. He resists mischief or carries out reforms in the face of opposition, and opposition as a rule rouses passion, exaggerates issues and inflames language. We make allowance for him. But we mete another measure to the political philosopher: He comes before us, presumably, with a calm mind, a wide outlook, and a quiet hold of principles which are permanent. He has no claim for allowance and makes none. All his thoughts are deliberate. He cannot be permitted, and does not ask permission, to constitute temporary circumstance into premisses for universal judgments. There is only one way of showing respect to him, it is that of attributing to his words their full weight and undiminished value.

It is in this spirit that I should like to examine the testimony which Mr. Hobhouse has borne as to the condition of the English people in his remarkable little book entitled "Democracy and Reaction." Mr. Hobhouse has made it easy for his critics to show towards his opinions that respect which is implied in the careful weighing of his words. He has displayed learning, diligence, disinterestedness and power in other fields of enquiry. Furthermore, his political opinions are ratified, though not without some significant qualifications, by one whose experience in letters and in practical statesmanship has the breadth and maturity of Mr. Morley's.[1]

I propose, then, to take Mr. Hobhouse's arraignment of the English people, and his account of the causes which,

[1] Mr. Morley commended Mr. Hobhouse's views to the attention of the public in weighty articles which appeared in the *Nineteenth Century* for March and April, 1905.

in his view, have brought about their degradation, as the deliberate expression of a calm opinion, reluctantly adopted but forced upon him by a wide and careful survey of the facts.

There is one consideration, however, which will weigh with a critic who would be sympathetic as well as just. Mr. Hobhouse's book was evidently inspired in great part by the South African War and the incidents which led to it. The character of that war, or at least of the conditions which brought it about, was such as to cause deep misgivings in many minds, and to disturb the calm of many quietly thoughtful men. Some of the events which preceded the war have left a stain upon the national honour. And nothing can quite remove it: not even the unexampled magnanimity shown by British statesmanship in restoring freedom to the conquered people. The blatant imperialism and reckless greed which helped to bring about the conflict and the sane and far-sighted imperialism which, so far as possible, has removed its evil effects, will stand upon the pages of our history in a contrast which nothing can mitigate.

If Mr. Hobhouse in his "Democracy and Reaction" had limited his condemnation to the events or to the state of the public mind at that time, I should be little disposed to object to his statements. But the question raised by him is not that of the war, nor of the Raid, nor of the arrested enquiry into the Raid, nor of the action of the Government then in power, nor of the temporary lapse of a people from the ways of political rectitude under the exciting influences of a great conflict. It is a far wider and graver question. It is the question whether these facts, amongst others, can be justly taken as symbols of political degradation—of a degradation so general as to affect the whole people, and so deep as to reach the intellectual and moral sources of their action, and to change the permanent conditions of their existence. For such is the view taken by Mr. Hobhouse, supported in some respects by Mr. Morley, and urged with eloquence and the manifest sincerity of a noble passion. We cannot pass it over, it seems to me, nor deal lightly with it. We must examine it, and enquire into the grounds of his rage and sorrow.

His charge summarily stated is as follows: "During some twenty or thirty years a wave of reaction has spread over the civilised world," and "the reaction has invaded one department of thought after another." As regards the British people "the reaction at home is interwoven with reaction abroad; and if it is to be summed up in a word, we should call it a reaction against humanitarianism." "The bare conception of right in public matters has lost its force." "Human wrongs and sufferings do not move us as they did." "There has been a far-reaching change in the temper of the time."

Following these accusations against the people as a whole, comes his faithful dealing with different sections of it. "The great middle class," he says, "has become contented with its lot; and is far more moved by its fear of Socialism than by any further instalment of privilege." "The true leaders of the middle class are the financiers, who show them how to get more than 3 per cent. on their investments." They are infected with "collective selfishness." "All they know of social and domestic reform is that it means expense; and their politics are summed up in the simple and comprehensive formula: Keep down the rates."

The common people have sunk still lower, if that be possible. They have learnt to read, but they are not educated. "Properly speaking, we have no educated classes." Principles of justice have lost their value to us for want of imagination to realise their significance. "The easy materialism of our own time wants to hear no more of principles in politics, and how they are endangered and how maintained." "Even the ordinary article of the old journalism has proved far too long and too heavy." The literature of the masses "must be diversified with headlines and salted with sensationalism"; it "must appeal to the uppermost prejudices of the moment," offer "a diurnal repast of bloodshed," "maintain itself by the athletic and sporting news, which in the main sells the papers in the streets." "No social revolution," he concludes, "will come from a people so absorbed in cricket and football." "Should the beginnings of a movement appear, society has an easy way of dealing with it. It will not hang the leaders, but ask them to dinner."

It is to be observed, in the next place, that the national corruption is as deep as it is general. It is not to superficial symptoms that Mr. Hobhouse points, any more than to a particular section of the people, such as the more crude and blatant Imperialists. Nor is it a temporary aberration that he bewails, or the transient mood of a nation given over for a time to the boisterous intoxication of material aggrandisement. It is a "far-reaching change in the temper of the time," a change that has penetrated into the inner recesses of the nation's spirit and mingled with its most intimate motives. For there has been "intellectual reaction," and "a religious relapse." "The decay in vivid and profound religious belief was in process a generation ago, but its effects at that time were offset by the rise of humanitarian feeling." Now, however, humanitarianism too "has lost its hold." The resulting temper is "a good-natured scepticism, not only about the other world, but about the deeper problems and higher interests in this world." "We have lost the stimulus and guidance to effort, and the basis for a serious and rational public life."

There is some hope for a nation as there is for an individual, as long as it retains the basis, or feels the stimulus, of a better life. Having these, though it may have been "left o' the very ledge of things," like Browning's Guido, it may still:

> "Catch convulsively
> One by one at all honest forms of life,
> At reason, order, decency and use—
> To cramp him and get foothold by at least."

But the British people can make no such effort, according to Mr. Hobhouse. They have lost interest in the principles upon which national well-being rests. Nay, they have sought to fortify themselves in their injustice, arrogance, ignorance, callousness, collective selfishness and scepticism; for they have invented or discovered theories by which to justify themselves. They have misread recent political history, perverted the main principles of physical science, adopted or distorted a philosophy in such a fashion as to make their own degenerate condition appear to accord with the nature of things, and their conduct, if not right, at least not wrong.

From recent political history they have learnt the lust of empire, the greed of commercial gain, and the means and methods of satisfying these passions.

Physical science, they have discovered, "gives its verdict in favour of violence and against social justice." The laws of biology furnish them with a scientific foundation for believing that might is right; that progress comes through conflict in which the fittest survives; that it must be unwise in the long run to interfere with the struggle; that we must not sympathise with the beaten and the weak. The idea of evolution has yielded to them a fatalistic creed, and taught them to conceive "a vast world-process in which human will and intelligence play a subordinate, and, in a sense, blind and unconscious part." Nay, humanity itself "is taken as a product of forces similar in character to those which made the ape. It does not shape its own fate. The future of society is not in the hands of statesmen or thinkers, but is determined by the play of forces which are beyond human control." Destiny is responsible for our acts. Destiny furnishes an excuse for ethically reprehensible modes of behaviour. Destiny has "paralysed the check on the moral consciousness."

And philosophy, "the most popular philosophy of our time," the Idealism to which "it would be natural to look for a counterpoise to these crude doctrines of physical force"—what of Idealism? It has had "a more subtly retrograde influence than any of the scientific creeds which it condemns." "Indeed, it is scarcely too much to say that the effect of Idealism on the world in general has been mainly to sap intellectual and moral sincerity, to excuse men in their consciences for professing beliefs which in the meaning ordinarily attached to them they do not hold, to soften the edges of all hard contrasts between right and wrong, truth and falsity, to throw a gloss over stupidity, and prejudice, and caste, and tradition, to weaken the bases of reason, and disincline men to the searching analysis of their habitual ways of thinking." To this catalogue of the deadly sins of Idealism it is scarcely worth adding that its founder, Hegel, "put the rights of the State in place of the rights of the individual"; or, that the Hegelian State was concretely exemplified in Bismarck's career, "who first showed the modern world what could be done in the political sphere by the thorough-going use of force and fraud," and to "whose achievements . . . we must add the whole series of trials in which the event has apparently favoured the methods of blood and iron, and discredited the cause of liberty and justice."

Such, in a summarised form, is the testimony borne by Mr. Hobhouse against the people of Britain. Let us look at the catalogue of its vices. "Lust of empire abroad and the vanity of racial domination"; greed of commercial gain at home; a middle class almost wholly divorced from public duties; a people not educated beyond the desire for its "daily tale of bloodshed in the news-paragraphs, and, if there were no real wars, murders or sudden deaths, would expect the enterprising journalist to invent them"; religious belief decaying; humanitarianism scoffed at as sentimentalism; scepticism about the other world and about the higher interests of this world; political history made to demonstrate the efficiency of blood and iron; physical science employed to cast its verdict in favour of violence and against justice and to yield the conception of a fatalism that makes remorse absurd and repentance impossible; idealism, converted into something still more subtly poisonous, sapping intellectual and moral sincerity, obscuring the difference between right and wrong, truth and falsity—all these together forming one current whose "united stream sweeps onward in full flood to the destruction of the distinctive landmarks of modern civilised progress."

That this picture has been drawn by passion is evident. It bears all the marks of such an authorship, for passion has never more than one colour on its palette. All its pictures are unrelieved, and all its objects have only one aspect. Nevertheless, this description is not void of all truth. If a drag-net were, at any time, drawn through the nethermost depths of our political life, specimens of the corrupt practices and evil passions to which Mr. Hobhouse refers would be found clinging to its meshes. Moreover, the times through which we have been and are still passing are particularly favourable to some of the noxious growths he has so vigorously condemned. Our moral and intellectual temper is not all that could be desired. We verily are an ill-educated, or, rather, a half-educated people. Our pursuit of truth is not serious or sustained. We are "general readers" who gain from the journalistic Press and the novel that slack knowledge and smattering acquaintance with the great principles of science and philosophy which cheapens them and makes them stale. And naturally, the first consequence of science made easy and philosophy popularised by such means is to liberate us from old spiritual responsibilities without establishing new ones in their stead. New conceptions of the invariable physical order, of the continuity of history and of the reign of law in human affairs imply results with which the old methods of a dogmatic faith are incapable of dealing, and they are incompatible with the freedom that was confused with indeterminism and with the responsibilities it was believed to imply. Matters pertaining to our moral and religious life, which once rested securely on authority, are now subjected to our own judgment. And we are not prepared for such a task. The present age exhibits tendencies not unlike those of the youth who leaves school for college, and who for the first time is required to exercise his judgment upon his studies. He exercises it badly as a matter of course; for judgment, like every other faculty, has to be educated. He draws from his reading the shallowest and most obvious conclusions: fatalism from science, doubt and negation from philosophy. Order and continuity in history, heredity within the mental disposition and inviolable law in the environment, seem to preclude liberty, and the inter-relation of good and evil to destroy the contrast between them. Every issue seems debatable; nay, every issue, he finds, has been already debated, and there is no conclusion which is not supported by some great name. The youth, under the first consciousness of his freedom and of dawning powers, delights to exercise them. He plays with principles, worrying them on first teething like a young puppy—to recall the simile of Plato. Nothing is sacred to him, and nothing is true. He becomes for a time either a sceptic who denies the possibility of knowledge, or a sophist who delights in altering the true perspective of things. Meantime, his intellectual guardian, if he is wise, looks on, not interfering over much, but bears him—

> "Go wantoning awhile
> Unplagued by cord in nose, and thorn in jaw."

He hints, perhaps, that scepticism is after all only another form of the dogmatism against which the young man is in revolt. He indicates that even sophistry is an old acquaintance. He stimulates the youth to revolt against these too;

and, above all, he gradually brings him under the lasting charm of the masters of those who know, to whom the scheme of things has ever been very great, and man's mind sane. Experience and years help, and the youth in no long time discovers that the world

"Means intensely and means good."

In these respects and under such limitations as these, I could agree with Mr. Hobhouse as to our times. There verily is in our age a tendency to irreverence towards principles, and a certain cheap freedom in the treatment of them, followed occasionally by negation and indifference. Religious belief at such a time does lose its authority, as it is being shifted from an external to an internal basis; science and philosophy do become weapons for secularising the world; and, undoubtedly, a secularised world is a poor thing. Naught within it matters much, for having lost its spiritual implications what remains of it is shallow.

But I cannot follow Mr. Hobhouse further and admit that his description of the condition of the British people is trustworthy. Least of all can I, in contemplating a time of transition, forget the goal towards which we are moving, or the spirit that is under many a diverse guise guiding the movement. He has, it seems to me, fallen into the old error of the denunciatory prophet, and read the commination service over the nation's head from lack of patience. He has been "very jealous for the Lord of Hosts." He has been most laudably ardent to prick the national conscience awake. But though "the children of Israel have broken the covenant, thrown down the altars, and slain the prophets of Israel with the sword," he must not say, like Carlyle and Elijah, "I, even I only am left, and they seek my life to take it away." There are left "seven thousand in Israel, all the knees which have not bowed unto Baal and every mouth which hath not kissed him." Beneath, beyond, all around the frothy foam of moral scepticism and intellectual sophistry there are the deep waters of the wide, swinging ocean making eternal music beneath the stars. England is not a sceptic. England is not indifferent to the issues of right and wrong. Our country is not hardened to all pity, nor is it deaf to the cries of the wronged and oppressed, whether within or without its gates.

Elijah had to leave the Court of Ahab, to eat and drink and in the strength of the meat to go forty days into the wilderness, unto Horeb, the Mount of God, ere he could hear the "still small voice" speak of the seven thousand who bowed not their knees to Baal. Can it be that our modern prophet has dwelt too long amongst the politicians, the journalists and the financiers, and mistaken the green-room of party politics for the stage on which is veritably acted the great drama of our national life?

Since he wrote Great Britain, under deep revulsion of feeling against the political sophistry of which it was weary, has sought a new instrument for its will for good. I know not how to account either for its rejection of the past Government or for its impatience with the pace of the present Government, especially in matters of social justice, if it had become hard of heart, and indifferent to right and wrong. Hence I conclude that Mr. Hobhouse has told truths, but not spoken the truth. Forgetting the *rôle* of the philosopher as a spectator of a wide expanse of time and of existence, he has not been careful lest he exaggerate evil, or in his exposure of it, lest he overlook the good. A nation depraved to the extent he describes could not rise again. For to him it is lost to *all* forms of good—so heedless of right, and so greedy for bad principles that it has perverted science into fatalism, philosophy into moral and intellectual obscurantism, humanitarianism into a ridiculous sentiment, and religion into a thing without fervour or sincerity. He has deprived the British people both of the means and of the desire of recovery ; and, if the nature of things be veritably moral the end of such a nation cannot be distant. The British Empire, vast as it is, circles within a universe which is sound at heart ; and if the Empire be corrupt, there is more against it than there is for it. It will sink inwards, as unsound things do, crashing through the crusts of its ancient faiths turned into hypocrisy. To such a nation, according to a once-revered authority, Mr. Hobhouse having put on his prophetic mantle could have but one brief message : "The Lord shall smite thee with madness and blindness and astonishment of heart ; and thou shalt grope at noon-day, as the blind gropeth in darkness, and thou shalt not prosper in thy ways, and thou shalt be oppressed and spoiled evermore, and no man shall save thee."

But I pass from the condition of the British nation in general. Mr. Hobhouse's own political party is at last in power. It is now the turn of the prophets of Conservatism to predict the ruin of the Empire from adopting principles which he would probably call the principles of virtue and peace and progress. And, in these days of the hurtling wars of opprobrious epithets there is little evidence that they will forget their message. I turn to the testimony which Mr. Hobhouse has tendered against Idealism, a matter which is more within my province, and, though in a sense limited, has still its public significance.

The votaries of Idealism have been slow to accept the challenge made by our author and seconded by Mr. Morley. Still, I cannot condemn their silence; for it ought to be obvious that a philosophical theory has this in common with a mathematical, physical or any other theory—that it cannot be either refuted or justified except at the expense of the trouble of comprehending it. In the case of Idealism, almost beyond any other, that task has not proved easy even to those who have seriously taken it in hand. Hence, in its case, almost beyond any other, recourse has been had to coarse methods of refutation, which Idealists are justified in ignoring—"joukin' and letting the jaw gae by." But, partly from loyalty to great teachers whose influence has long seemed to me as pure as their lives, and partly from the feeling that Mr. Hobhouse has gravely wronged a great cause, deepening prejudice where prejudice was all too prevalent, I am tempted to examine his statements with some care.

I begin, as before, by referring briefly to the matters in which I agree with Mr. Hobhouse. The first of these concerns the range of the influence of this theory upon the social and political life of the present time. Idealism, he truly says, is the most popular philosophy of the time. For many years adherents of this way of thought have deeply interested the British public by their writings. Almost more important than their writings is the fact that they have occupied philosophical chairs in almost every university in the Kingdom. Even the professional critics of Idealism are for the most part, like Mr. Hobhouse, themselves Idealists—after a fashion. And, when they are not, they are, as a rule, more occupied with the refutation of Idealism than with the construction of a better theory. It follows from their position of academic authority, were it from nothing else, that Idealists exercise an influence not easily measured upon the youth of the nation—upon those, that is, who, from the educational opportunities they enjoy, may naturally be expected to become the leaders of the nation's future thought and practice.

In this respect the question of the nature of the influence of the Idealists is manifestly of grave importance, and Mr. Hobhouse has done well in raising it. If that influence is even remotely like what Mr. Hobhouse thinks it is ; if the Idealists from their academic chairs are raying out not light but darkness, glossing over stupidity, sapping the moral and intellectual sincerity of their pupils, confounding the issues, nay, mitigating the contrast of right and wrong, truth and falsity, turning religious beliefs into insidious ambiguities, and substituting for practical faith in sound principles the quaking bog of universal doubt, then the need of dealing with them is imperative, for their action most sincerely concerns the public welfare. We interfere with "the liberty" of the Press and Stage in cases where the evils are far less dangerous because they are more gross. Would Mr. Hobhouse not refuse to license Idealists? Or might I recommend to him, and to those who agree with him, the use of a method of dealing with Idealism which is more lethal than licensing laws, I mean the method of refuting it by just reasoning?

There are men who would argue that the professional philosopher and his subtle speculations are so remote from the practical concerns of mankind that they can safely be ignored ; and that his influence, even upon his own disciples, fades when they leave the rarefied air of the metaphysical classroom for the open world. But Mr. Hobhouse is not of this mind. He knows that the world is ruled by its thinkers, and would probably acknowledge that professors of philosophy think—just a little. The influence of the philosophers upon morals, politics and religion can be compared only to that of scientific men upon the material conditions of life. The changes introduced by Adam Smith or Immanuel Kant have decidedly not been less revolutionary or of less practical significance to mankind than those brought about by Newton, or James Watt. Indeed, the evidence of modern history to the power of the speculative thinker in politics is so strong as not to need to be cited. Sir Henry Maine once said that he did not know a single law reform since Bentham's day which cannot be traced to his influence. Not even yet is that of his pupil, John Stuart Mill, entirely spent. And, difficult as it is to measure the forces which play within our own social and political life, it is hardly to be denied that the power exercised by Bentham and the Utilitarian school has, for better or for worse, passed into the hands of the Idealists.

Their Idealism, moreover, is "German Idealism"—which is another reason for public alarm. "The Rhine has flowed into the Thames!" is the warning note rung out by Mr. Hobhouse. Carlyle introduced a version of it, bringing it as far as Chelsea. Then Jowett, and Thomas Hill Green, and William Wallace, and Lewis Nettleship, and Arnold Toynbee, and David Ritchie—to mention only those teachers whose voices are now silent—guided the waters, as Mr. Hobhouse says, "into those upper reaches of the Thames known locally as the Isis." John and Edward Caird brought them up the Clyde, Hutcheson Stirling up the Firth of Forth. They have passed up the Mersey, where Professor Maccunn corrupts the world with his able books, and up the Severn and Dee and Don. They pollute the Bay of St. Andrews, there is a thin dilution of them in the waters of the Cam, and they have somehow crept overland into Birmingham. "The stream of German Idealism has been diffused over the academical world of Great Britain." The disaster is universal.

Nor is there any very clear evidence that the waters are subsiding, so that the innocent dove may find rest for the sole of her foot. Rumour has it that the dry land is appearing in Germany. There, they say, Idealism is dead—even as Christianity is dead in Jerusalem. But whether Mr. Hobhouse and the critics can take comfort from this fact or not, I cannot say. It may possibly occur to them that Germany and Palestine would be none the worse for the presence of Idealism and Christianity, and that the faiths instituted in their stead are not more satisfactory.

One thing alone is quite certain: it is that up to the present time and in this country we can ignore neither Christianity nor Idealism—their power is too real. And, however different this theory may be in other respects from the Christian faith, it is like it in the subtle character of its influence. Philosophy, like religion, whispers its secrets in the inner ear of mankind. These secrets creep along the blood, find their way to the nation's heart, mingle in the hidden recesses of the soul with the very springs of conduct, and therefore pollute (or purify) the whole life.

In the face of all these considerations it is evident that Mr. Hobhouse in endeavouring to turn the public mind against Idealism is trying to perform a plain public duty—provided always that his convictions about the character of Idealism are valid. But he will pardon one who does not share his convictions for reminding him of a picture seen by

Christian in Interpreter's House, and for estimating more highly the part played by "the man with a vessel of oil in his hand" than that of the man who was "always casting much water upon the fire, to quench it."

But what, according to Mr. Hobhouse, are the specific doctrines which Idealism is promulgating with effects that are so deplorable? He has, unfortunately, indicated them with far less precision than is desirable in a case which is so grave. Besides, in his diagnosis, he has mingled causes with effects, the disease with the symptoms, so that it is not easy to separate them and to direct the attack against the former. Let us specify them.

1. For Idealism "every institution and every belief is alike a manifestation of a spiritual principle; and thus, for everything, there is an inner and more spiritual interpretation."

2. Idealism gives assurance that men "need not follow where their reason takes them"; "that there is no logical foundation for the certainty which the sciences claim"; "that still less is there any rational groundwork of morality, in particular for humanitarian morality."

3. Idealism "sets the State in place of the rights of the individual," and moreover the State "is not to serve humanity but is an end in itself." "It sums up in itself both the temporal and the spiritual order. There are no limits to its authority, nor any necessary responsibility on the part of its government."

The effects of these articles of the idealistic creed are stated with much vigour and fulness. From the first of them it follows that "vulgar and stupid beliefs can be held with a refined and enlightened meaning"; that "intellectual and moral sincerity are sapped"; that "men are excused in their consciences for professing beliefs which on the meaning ordinarily attached to them they do not hold" ; that "the edges of all hard contrasts between right and wrong, truth and falsity are softened" ; that "a gloss is thrown over stupidity, and prejudice, and caste, and tradition ; that the bases of reason are weakened" ; and so forth, along the whole list of the most deadly moral and intellectual sins. From the second of them follows "a lightened intellectual conscience both for those who wish to revert to the easy rule of authority and faith, and for the society which has become afraid of further progress and is lusting after the delights of barbarism." From the last come the policy and methods of Bismarck, "blood and iron" in modern politics, "the disappointment of those who identified liberty with national self-government," "the setting of national efficiency above freedom," and so on further.

One could reasonably desire that Mr. Hobhouse had given some indication of the idealistic treatises where these maleficent doctrines may be found. We could then get them burnt by the public hangman. Still more desirable is it that his rendering of a doctrine which has filled so many volumes and led so large a section of humanity along the primrose road had been less meagre. But I think we may "ken his meanin' frae his mumpin'." He is repeating charges frequently made against Hegel by men who have never read a page of his writings. I shall endeavour to deal with them in another article.

# IDEALISM AND POLITICS

## VIII

## THE DEFENCE

A SUMMARY of the objections urged against Idealism. The objections are valid, provided vital considerations are omitted. But the omission perverts the theory. Why Idealism is peculiarly liable to perversion : it is compacted together of elements ordinarily assumed to be irreconcilable, and has the unity of differences as its starting-point. Its logic is neither Inductive nor Deductive, but both : it maintains the truth of both Morality and Religion, and in that respect is both a Pessimism which condemns and a Pessimism which approves facts. It is neither Socialism nor Individualism, but both ; and is never satisfied with the abstract "Yes" or "No" of ordinary thought.

But its rejection of pure opposites and merely exclusive categories may accord with facts. The world itself may be neither a "One" nor a "Many," but a "Many in One." The actual moral and religious life, which it seeks to explain, presents the same apparent incompatibilities. So does the social and political life. Hence, at the worst, Idealism is valuable in that it brings us back to the complexities of reality ; and in that it exposes the fallacies of abstract systems. How Idealism discredits the logic of exclusion in the province of politics. Why it can please neither the destructive reformer nor the mere Conservative. How it would maintain present institutions as against the former, and yet, as against the latter, subject them to the most radical of all changes by moralizing them.

That Idealism offers the idea of "Spirit" as the one possible explanation of objects, including political life. Its principle is valid, but its application of it is incomplete, especially in that its accent on difference and negation, except in Hegel, has been too light.

The fallacy of believing that, because Idealism maintains the spiritual nature of reality, it reduces all things to the same level. Charges against Idealism that have more truth : that its principle is trite, and too general to be of use.

But Idealism is in process of articulating this principle. It employs it as a hypothesis, which is applied and verified little by little as the experience of the world matures. The contribution made by Green to political theory, and the loss which political thought and practice have sustained by his early death.

## VIII

## THE DEFENCE

THE main objections against the doctrine of Idealism to which, as we saw in my last article, Mr. Hobhouse has given such vigorous expression, may be stated as follows:

1. That Idealism, by its spiritual interpretation of all institutions and beliefs, implies an optimism which makes the world into a place in which there is nothing to improve, —a veritable conservative, non-moral Paradise.

2. That Idealism abolishes the distinction between right and wrong by making everything right, and destroys the uses of the intelligence by making everything doubtful.

3. That, in the sphere of politics, Idealism aggrandises the State at the expense of the individual, and brute-force order at the expense of freedom and of humanitarian relations between citizen and citizen and between State and State.

I am very much disposed to say that these charges are all true. Idealism does make all things spiritual, and imply an optimism; it does deny that there is an absolute difference between right and wrong; it does assert that no particular truth is absolutely certain; it does greatly magnify the State. But I should immediately require permission to add: *first*, that its optimism implies the fight as well as the victory, and that the votaries of Idealism, like the soldiers who believe their country right and their general invincible, strike the harder for their faith; *secondly*, that for Idealism the distinction between right and wrong is real and has the majestic significance of the tragic conflict of elemental powers just *because* the difference between them is not absolute; *thirdly*, that if for Idealism no particular truth is certain, it is because the certainty of a truth never does lie in itself alone, but in the growing system of assured knowledge of which it is a part; *lastly*, that the State is greatly magnified by the Idealists because through it, and through it only, can the individual attain freedom—the *real* freedom, which is power to do right things in the right way.

By omitting these considerations, which I shall not call "qualifications" because they are of the essence of the idealistic doctrine, Idealism can be made contemptible. It can be put to strange uses similar to those to which, according to Mr. Hobhouse, physical science has been put in these times. Granted a condition of the public mind such as he has depicted, no perversion is impossible, and any doctrine may become vile. There never was, or will be, either a speculative theory, or a practical obligation which cannot be made the occasion of error. "Unto them that are defiled and unbelieving is nothing pure, but even their mind and conscience is defiled." But verily it is not easy to justify a philosophic critic for making himself the instrument of mere prejudice to a public which must depend on hearsay for its knowledge of philosophic theories.

Critics of "German" Idealism ought to exercise particular care in this respect. This theory is peculiarly liable to perversion, and to that particular form of perversion which is the bane of philosophic and political discussion: I mean that which results from accentuating one aspect of a doctrine to the neglect or at the expense of others. In this respect the political theory which flows from Idealism stands in sharp contrast with that which follows from the Utilitarianism of Mill and Bentham. The latter theory took so simple a view of the individual, his relation to the State, and his "happiness," that its good intentions were plain to the plain man. Its very abstractions helped it. But Idealism is complex. It is a double-edged weapon, not safe in all hands. This matter is important, and I shall try to make it clear.

This form of Idealism is a strenuous and uncompromising Monism. It would derive all things, as Mr. Hobhouse says, from a spiritual principle. Nevertheless, it appears to be compacted together of elements ordinarily regarded as irreconcilable. It is distinguished from all other systems of philosophy by the resistance it offers to the suppression of opposition; it would maintain contraries in all their right, and it even asserts that they are necessary to each other and to the unity in virtue of which they conflict. In all that it attempts to do it would show that differences are as original and significant as unity.

Hence, it repudiates the starting point, and rejects the whole process and method of other theories. It will begin neither from an atomic hypothesis—whether these be "atoms," or "monads," or "persons"—nor from its opposite. Neither particulars nor universals, neither the One nor the Many will serve its purpose. Its starting point, as well as its final goal, is the conception of "system," that is to say, of Unity *of* differences, or a One *in* the Many.

There is no simplest fact, and no most rudimentary judgment which is not for it a "system."

As is its metaphysical starting point, so is its method. Its Logic is neither deductive nor inductive. It proceeds neither from the known to the unknown—which, by the bye, is absurd—nor from the unknown to the known, which is impossible. It does not start from principles in the hope of deducing facts, nor from facts in the hope of discovering principles. On the contrary, all thought, the most elementary and the most advanced, is for Idealism *at once* deductive and inductive, analytic and synthetic, occupied with facts *and* principles: it is even both negative and positive. Knowledge evolves, it says, and evolution, in its hands, appears as a very nest of contraries. Evolution, it maintains, implies sameness *and* change, identity throughout the whole *and* the constant transmutation of every part and element within the whole. It even makes the identity express *itself* in the differences, and it deepens both the identity and differences as it proceeds. It both denies and asserts that the beginning and the end of the process are the same ; it makes the last the first, and the end throughout the process both real and not real.

The features of the idealistic categories of valuation have the same baffling character. Idealism is at once an optimism and a pessimism. Reality, for it, is evil in every part and perfect as a whole, sane throughout and "intoxicated in every limb." God is immanent in the universe, the very substance and truth of all finite being ; and yet finite being is all the more real and independent on that account. Idealism would maintain both religion and morality in all their rights. It trusts both the goodness and the power of God to the full, and will have nothing anywhere go wrong in the long run; and yet, knowing the evil of man's heart and how finitude infects his world, there is nothing that has not to be set right. Nay, Idealism plants its contradictions at the heart of both religion and morality. Religion, it holds, implies that the ideal, its God, is eternally real, and at the same time that the consciousness of God has to be realised in the human spirit, and that God himself is present in the process. Morality, it maintains, postulates a good that is absolute, an ideal which alone is in the full sense real; and yet it represents the good as in course of being attained, real only while in process, and the process as endless. Finally, in the sphere of politics, Idealism is content neither with public order nor with private freedom; it will neither make the State Subordinate to the individual, nor the individual to the State; it is neither Socialism nor Individualism. Yet it will curtail none of the *rights* of either. It will even make the evolution of the one depend upon the evolution of the other, and in its account of progress, deepen the significance of both the State and the individual. Its attitude towards the several items of political life is the same—towards private property for instance. It asserts the sacredness of property as private in a way that, provided it said no more, would please the most ardent owner of it; and yet it derives the sacredness, the privacy and the rights of property from the State, in a way that, provided it said no more, would meet the wishes of the most aggressive Socialist.

It is no marvel, therefore, that idealists find it difficult to make themselves understood, nor that their doctrine should be open to a cross fire from all the points of the compass. Some critics find it resolve all things into a featureless sameness; others accuse it of the opposite error of maintaining confusedly "the altogetherness of everything"; and others again select from its opposing phases those elements which offend themselves and ignore the rest.[1] No philosophy ever offered to the votaries—and victims—of the categories of exclusion, who will have every question answered with a downright "Yes" or "No," so ample an opportunity for misapprehension and caricature. Indeed, it is somewhat difficult to account for the obstinacy with which this theory refuses to be laid, so offensive is it to those who rely, like Mr. Hobhouse, "on the plain, human, rationalistic way of looking at life and its problems."

Can it be that the real world, which Idealism tries to comprehend, has the same perverse way of maintaining unity amongst differences, and that man is the same baffling mixture of many elements? Can it be that Idealism in utterly rejecting the *exclusive* assumptions of the older theories is trying to take things just as they stand? In any case it is certain that its main challenge to the abstract theorists who will see only one of many conflicting aspects is that they come to the *facts*. "Is it not true," it asks, "that the world is a 'One in the Many'? Do we not all alike assume whenever we begin to think of it and try to comprehend its facts that it is a rational order within which facts cohere and events are linked together? And what is the whole endeavour of all the sciences, or the very

[1] There is a whole school of writers on philosophy at the present time almost any minor member of which betrays his upbringing by never referring to any Idealistic statement without adding a "but" which detracts. They are as reluctant to admit that Idealism contains any truth, as Carlyle was to admit that the Celtic peoples had any virtues.

function of reason itself, except to make good this original assumption?"

Of course the task of philosophy would be greatly lightened if we could either treat the unity of the world as a fiction, or its differences as false show. Indeed, it would have no task, and might retire on an old-age pension. That method is precisely the one which idealists find their critics follow. As to religion and morals, for instance, they would either deny the reality of evil, or, making it absolute, deny the immanence or perfection of God, hoping thereby either to save morality at the expense of religion, or religion at the expense of morality. "Is it not evident," the plain man will say, "that God cannot be in every way perfect if there is evil in the world, and that morality is impossible if there be none?" But Idealism is not content with easy solution: it points to the facts of the case. It avers that if we examine religion and morality, as actual phenomena of man's experience, we shall find them to be compact of these apparent incompatibilities. What is it that presents itself in the life and convictions of the most devoutly religious man we happen to know? A trust in both the goodness and the power of God which overflows all bounds, an irrefragable optimism to which

> "The evil is null, is nought, is silence implying sound;"

and, side by side with that trust, a deep conviction of the terrible reality of sin, and of the tragic earnestness of the moral struggle. Let the religious life wane, and the conviction on both sides becomes more shallow: the goodness of God is less certain, and sin a lighter affair. Let the religious life deepen, and the trust in God becomes more tranquil: "Thou wilt keep him in perfect peace whose mind is stayed on Thee." Yet the conviction becomes more and more profound that in comparison with the antagonism of right and wrong no contrast means much, and the ardour of the good man's resistance to sin flames always higher.

Observation of the moral life of man, taken by itself, brings out similar apparent incompatibilities. Morality is both the being and the becoming of the good. It both demands the absolute and sets it in process. For Kant, for instance, there was nothing either in the world or out of it which absolutely *must be*, be in its own sole right, except the moral good. In this he rightly interpreted the moral consciousness, for always to that consciousness "righteousness is as the everlasting mountains": "Heaven and earth may pass away, but not one jot or tittle of the law." It is the moral order that gives to the natural order stability and meaning—

> "Stern Daughter of the voice of God!
> Thou dost preserve the stars from wrong;
> And the most ancient heavens through Thee are fresh and strong."

Nevertheless the moral order is sustained only by the continued process of willing the right. Arrest this process, and there is neither good nor evil any more; for they are not *natural* phenomena reporting themselves to the intelligence, but have their meaning and reality only in the medium of the self-conscious will. Thus, the good which is eternal is ever brought anew into being. It is always real, never real, realised without end.

If in a similar way we passed the actual fact of human cognition, or of man's social and political life, under review, the same results would appear. We should observe the same apparent incompatibilities. They are in the facts.

Now it may, or it may not, be true that under such circumstances no explanation of the facts is possible, and that we must either say that the world is in itself irrational or that human reason cannot deal with it. I cannot here stop to deal with this question. But the attitude of Idealism towards it is instructive. It contends that if human reason is what it is usually thought to be—that is, if its function is that which ordinary logicians say and "plain men" believe, namely, that of abolishing either unity or difference—then it can make nothing of facts. The world will not yield its truth, nor will any part of it, if it is attacked by the old method of exclusives. But it is precisely the presupposition of absolute exclusion which Idealism considers false. Whether it can prove its case or not, I do not now enquire; nor whether the principle and method which it offers itself will ultimately prove more effective. My present task is more simple. It is to point out that Idealism has, in any case, performed one great service, or is, at least, in process of performing it. It is sweeping away the false negations, the empty alternatives, the shallow simplicities of the older abstract theories, which constitute the unconscious philosophy of the "plain man" of Mr. Hobhouse. It is bringing us back to the complexities of facts. As if it were heedless whether it can or cannot explain the facts, reconciling the antagonisms and bringing back into intelligible harmony the conflicting phases of human experience, it points out their presence in every department of it. And who will deny that the first, the indispensable step towards comprehending facts is to face them?

How great this service of Idealism may prove to be is best known to those who are best acquainted with the troubled history of human enquiry, with its endless alternation of the mutally refuting theories which, to use the phrase of Plato, have "tried to go on one leg." In metaphysics—at least if we omit Plato and Aristotle's theories, of which Hegelianism is little more than a modern version —men have been choosing Being and *not* Becoming, or Becoming and *not* Being; a One that excludes the Many, or a Many that excludes the One; particulars, but not universals, or universals, but not particulars. They have sought from one exclusive presupposition to proceed to its opposite. If they have begun with a universal substance, they have tried to attain particular realities; if they have started from atoms, or real differences of any kind, they have been in quest of, and they have sometimes fabricated, relations between them. Their presuppositions, their methods, and their ends are at war with themselves. And they have all failed. The result has been first affirmation, then counter-affirmation, then the sceptical despair of reason, then indifference, then affirmation once more and the repetition of the whole round. The history of logic and epistemology tells the same tale. Knowledge, it has been assumed, must be *a priori* and not *a posteriori*, or *a posteriori* and not *a priori*; mediate and not immediate, or immediate and not mediate; deductive and not inductive, or inductive and not deductive; proceeding from and not to experience, or to and not from experience. But knowledge has refused to come under either of these exclusive alternatives, and reason will not go "on one leg." And, surely, it is not a little thing if Idealism has succeeded in casting doubt upon methods thus doomed to failure, and suggested that the origin of all the error may lie in the presupposition of exclusion which all the theories alike have made, and which none has examined.

Above all will the student of politics value the suggestion that he is not forced to choose between such elements of political life as law and liberty, the freedom of the individual and the effective power of the State. He will follow with great interest the hint of the idealist that it is theory, and a false theory, which has set these ultimate conditions of private and public well-being in antagonism; that if he comes to the facts he will find that freedom and order grow together; and that where citizen and State are at their best the functions and powers of each are at their highest. And, if that be the case, the practical politician will recognise that to enlarge the power of the State is not necessarily to encroach upon the individual. He will be prepared to consider every proposed enlargement of it upon its merits, instead of condemning it on *a priori* grounds as an evil to be resisted in the name of freedom.

On the other hand, the knowledge that the liberty of the individual is not necessarily antagonistic, or in inverse ratio, to the order and power of the State, takes away the fear of extending *his* power. We shall not, like Plato, prefer the despotism of the philosopher-king to democracy, nor, like Carlyle, endow the ordinary citizen with only the right to obey. We shall recognise that the philosopher-king in order to govern requires philosophic subjects, and that the citizen who can willingly obey the wise must himself be wise. The *a priori* fear of Individualism passes away, like the *a priori* fear of Socialism. We should not deem it necessary to abolish private property, or to put all the means of producing wealth in the hands of the State, or to limit individual enterprise, or to abolish competition, or otherwise to turn the citizens of the ideal State into blameless sheep, fed, herded and shorn by "a power not themselves," and *not* "making for righteousness." We can give the individual a firmer standing in the State, place better industrial weapons in his hands, if he can wield them, bid him contend to the uttermost, and expect thereby a stronger State with stronger, freer and therefore more loyal citizens.

Thus, once the logic of exclusion is discredited by Idealism in the sphere of politics, we should no longer be the victims of abstractions. "Socialism" and "Individualism" would be recognised as empty cries, and we should neither do anything, nor refrain from doing anything, in the name of either. We should not even endeavour to compromise between them or fix their boundaries: for they overlap. The best State is that which both does most for the individual and enables him to do most for himself. The most free individual and the best servant of himself is the man who, whether as capitalist or labourer, as lord or peasant, as theoretical thinker or merchant-prince, contributes most of the article he happens to produce, and thereby best meets the wants of his neighbours and best uses his station to serve the State.

Now, it evidently follows from all this that Idealism does not lend itself easily to the purposes of the party politician. There is no doubt that its doctrines can be used by the reformer; but there is as little doubt that they can be used by his opponent. Hence it is like the bat, the victim of both birds and beasts. It cannot utterly reject the past, for it applies the idea of evolution to human affairs: hence it appears "to throw a gloss over stupidity, and prejudice, and caste and tradition." History being continuous for it, its hope for the future lies in making the most of the present, and in drawing out its better meaning, which is the promise and potency of the future. But such a course never has appeared honest to the root-and-branch political rhetorician, nor to those prophets who come to destroy and not to fulfil. Hence Idealism has seemed to Mr. Hobhouse to "react against the plain, human, rationalistic way of looking at life and its problems," and to be "sapping intellectual and moral sincerity." Why does this theory not condemn old things right away? It would be so much more satisfactory to have done with the "old theology" and the "old politics," and to burn the barn in order to kill the rats. But Idealism cannot advocate cataclysmic changes. I believe it would conserve most of our present institutions, most of the relations in which the citizens of the State stand to one another, most even of the international relations between State and State, unsatisfactory as they are. It would by no means abolish private property, or proclaim that there shall be masters no more and men no more, or tamper with the family—as some Socialists desire; it would not destroy the far less ideal cash-relations that hold in the sphere of commerce and the competitive industries; it would not even merge the nations together, or pronounce patriotism a sin against humanity.

On the other hand, it is entirely false to say that Idealism would introduce no change in these matters, and it is utterly vain to expect that it will please the Conservative. For evolution in its view preserves the identity of animal, plant, man or State only through the constant transformation of every cell and fibre within them. Hence, there is a respect in which Idealism is the most radical of all social and political theories. For while preserving present institutions, and civic and international relations, *it would moralise them*. It would, to take one instance, leave the social reformer no rest till he had made the workshop, the mine, the counting-house, the shipyard into moral institutions. Idealism finds manual labour, the transferring and making of goods, to be occupations entered upon for the sake of obtaining a more or less meagre livelihood, and often carried on at the expense of wearing down the bodies and souls of men ; and it is profoundly dissatisfied. It would level "the trades" with "the professions," not by degrading the latter, but by making the former what his profession ought always to be to the teacher, the physician, the minister of religion, and the artist, namely, the expression of a free choice of mode of life, and the outlet of devoted energies. Such a social revolution as *that*, even although it left the external relations between men just as they stand, would reach sufficiently deep to satisfy the most ardent reformer. And I suspect that instead of pronouncing such an ideal too low, or too narrow, or the change to it not sufficiently sweeping, our radical reformer and socialist would despair of reaching it. But it is the characteristic of Idealism, with its view of the State as spiritual and of society as a moral institution that it cannot be content with less. It believes intensely in the vitality of ideals, and maintains that its hopes are "too fair to turn out false."

These last considerations have led us to what I believe to be the essential character of the idealistic doctrine in its application to politics—to what is, in fact, its central principle. Mr. Hobhouse calls that principle "spiritual."

To Idealism, he says, "every institution and every belief is alike a manifestation of a spiritual principle." I shall not quarrel with more than one word in his description of it; I object only to the apparently innocent word "alike," to which I shall come presently.

It is quite true that Idealism offers as the principle of explanation of objects, and of political life amongst them, simply the conception of "spirit." This it has done all the way from Hegel, its modern founder, to Green, whom Mr. Morley most justly regards as "the true successor of Mill in the line of political thinkers." Speaking of Green, Professor Maccunn says: "There can be no doubt that he stands or falls by the doctrine that the political life of men and nations is a spiritual revelation." "Hegel's object was his object. To find reason in human society, to show that the life of citizenship was in its essence a reasonable life, reasonable in its respect for institutions and accomplished facts, reasonable also in its sanguine hopes, aspirations and ideals—this was the central purpose and sober passion of his life." The analysis of the empirical fact of democratic citizenship convinced him that it "really does justify the contention that civic duty, rightly regarded, is nothing less than a spiritual function, or, if we prefer so to phrase it, that the life of citizenship is a mode of divine service. It may seem to savour of extravagance," Professor Maccunn adds, "thus to claim the 'secular' for the spiritual. For the secularities of politics are manifest. They are only too much with us. Who is the politician who does not know the parties and programmes, the caucuses, committee rooms, polling booths, the compromises, expediencies, trickeries? And is it of this thing that one can venture to speak in terms of religion or of a spiritual philosophy! Yet, if we follow Green, we must."

There is no doubt that in thus refusing to leave any ultimate room or rights to the merely secular, Green is rightly rendering the idealistic doctrine. And it is on this account, above all others, that it has seemed to many critics "to soften the hard contrast of right and wrong," to "sap intellectual and moral sincerity," "to react against the plain, human way of looking at life and its problems," "to weaken the bases of reason," "to prepare the way for scepticism," and so forth. In making "every institution and every belief alike a manifestation of a spiritual principle," it seems to raise them all to the same level, to leave nothing to condemn and nothing to amend. It seems to be an optimism which leaves no room for effort. The "nothingness and nullity of sin" is so clear to it, or at least the victory of good over evil is so easy and so certain that the moral struggle becomes a sham fight, and there is no call for "the dust and heat of social reform." "God's in his heaven: all's right with the world."

The antagonism of the strenuous moral and social consciousness to Idealism on these accounts seems to me to be perfectly natural. In refusing to admit differences which are absolute, in reducing all differences into relative differences, or differences within or of a unity, Idealism must seem to the ordinary critic, with his one-sided way of thought, to render them of no account. Idealism seems to the theologian to lose man in God and to be mere Pantheism; to the philosopher to evaporate things into thought and to sublimate matter into spirit; to the moralist to abolish the distinction between right and wrong; and to the logician to take away the opposition of falsehood and truth and to melt contraries down into unities of which affirmation and negation are alike false and alike true.

To offer a complete defence, if a complete defence is possible at all, is beyond my present task. I should myself admit that the idealistic votaries of this way of thought have to make it more plain to themselves as well as to the world that spirit is a principle of *difference* as well as of unity. I have tried to indicate elsewhere that it is the unique and crowning characteristic of spirit to hold difference *as difference* within its own unity, and to be able to manifest its own nature only in a self-externalising process, and by fortifying its opposites against itself.[1] But I am fully aware that the English version of Idealism has to be strengthened on this side, and that the result of doing so would be to restore the significance of the negative and to bring the theory nearer to the form in which it left the hands of Hegel.

But to admit in this way that Idealism is no perfect or complete theory, and that it has to do fuller justice to negation and difference, is not to admit that its principle is wrong, or that the conclusions of Mr. Hobhouse and the critics are just. Their criticism rests on wrong presuppositions and a discredited logic. They have not learnt that to make opposition absolute is to destroy it altogether, though it should be obvious enough that there can be no conflict between right and wrong, or between any other opposites, if they do not meet in the same field. They have not asked what is the meaning of spirit; and they unconsciously deprive it of its meaning by contemplating it from the point of view of "substance" or "mechanism,"

[1] This conception is illustrated in the second of my articles on "The Working Faith of the Social Reformer."

and applying to it metaphors derived from the physical, or, at best, from the biological world. Idealists protest and explain, and they will be heard in the long run.

Sometimes the critics, like Mr. Hobhouse, show themselves in their objections to be the victims of a very simple fallacy which would demonstrate the falsity of every Monistic theory, whether it be a form of "spiritualism" or of "materialism." It is the fallacy of concluding that things which proceed from the same principle must have the same value. It is the fallacy which charged the idea of evolution with reducing man to the level of "the ape" and "the oyster," on the ground that it maintains the continuity of life. "Every institution and every belief is *alike* a manifestation of a spiritual principle," says Mr. Hobhouse. But every idealist and every evolutionist will repudiate the word "alike," with all its levelling implications. They maintain that identity of source need not signify equality of worth, or of significance, or even of reality. May I, without insulting the critic's intelligence, make use of a very simple illustration at this point? He would say, I believe, that it is reason and reason only which can conclude that $3+5=8$. Would he also admit that it requires reason to conclude that $3+5=19$? Can a cow or a calf add numbers wrongly, or does it require a child and the working in him of a gradually dawning rational intelligence? Surely errors in arithmetic have the same source as truths; they are reached by attempts to make use of the same faculties and the same processes. And yet we are not bound to conclude that the errors and the truths have the same value. We identify their source without weakening the basis of reason, or softening the contrast between truth and falsity.

Moral distinctions are not matters of arithmetic it is true; and Idealism does not maintain that the difference between right and wrong is a matter of quantity, or of the "mere intelligence," if there be such an entity. But it does maintain that it requires reason, conscience, will, moral motives and a moral environment to seek satisfaction in false ends as in true, to do what is wrong as well as what is right. If that is not the case then wrong is not immoral, nor is it sin, either as against the self, or mankind, or God? It is only a natural mishap that has occurred to an infra-moral, irresponsible and innocent being. But ought it not to be plain that it is a condition of condemning beliefs and institutions, as well as of improving or approving them, that their source should be spiritual? Thus, the conception of "spirit" cannot be let go in matters of political and social life without mechanising that life. Men and nations cannot possess the privileges of rational spirit without its responsibilities, nor its potentialities without its risks. And of all of these the weightiest, the only ones which can have supreme importance according to the idealist, are those which turn upon the relation and the difference between right and wrong, the contrast between which he is supposed to weaken!

A more valid charge against Idealism were just the opposite. So far from interpreting political life in a new and mischievous way, its view that "the course of history and the growth of institutions is the revelation of a spiritual principle" is just the old opinion that "right is might." The critic can urge that the principle it has brought in with such a blare of metaphysical wind is not only true but trite. Carlyle, following the Hebrew prophets, thundered it in our ears. It is a doctrine taught by all men who carry the spirit of devotion into political life. Besides, it is too general to guide a people amidst the complex details of circumstance, and it is capable of abuse as well as use. It can make the conscience of the politician his accomplice, as well as his guide. It has generated the worst as well as the best governments. Civilisations have perished beneath the rule of ignorant priests who were conscientious devotees of their degraded deities.

There were no answer to these charges if Idealism had contributed nothing to political theory except the mere conception of the spiritual principle in history. The value of any such conception depends on the way in which it is articulated and applied. Like every other broad, "colligating" hypothesis, whether in science or in philosophy, or in morals, or in religion, it is capable of being an empty, otiose and even a false generalisation. Idealism is not in the least unique in that it has taken a spiritual view of human life; it is not from that that either its merits or its demerits flow. Its uniqueness lies in the fact that it has endeavoured to employ the conception of spirit in the way in which the natural sciences employ *their* dominating hypotheses. It is for it a principle of research in knowledge, and of reform in private and public conduct. Idealism would follow the self-articulation of spirit in the history of beliefs and institutions, even as biology seeks to follow the evolution of natural life from form to form in an ascending series. Its task is only begun. It is no complete theory, rounded and finished. The soundness of its results may quite legitimately be questioned in every one of the fields in which its ruling conception has been employed. After all, the category of "spirit," like that of the "space" of ordinary geometry, or of the "transmutation of energy" in physics, or of "natural selection" or "evolution" in biology, is only a *hypothesis*. Even as an hypothesis, it is only *in process* of being proved: and proof is never complete; for knowledge is never one rounded whole, one all-comprehensive equipoised system in which every element sustains and is sustained by every other element. From this point of view the claims of the Idealism which has been called "absolute" are just as modest as those of any other tentative theory by which man seeks to understand himself, and make of his world a home in which his intelligence may find some order and peace. There is a sense in which Idealism, like any other theory of human life, must await developments in morals and politics, and is altogether unable to anticipate practice. Men and States can be taught the right way, not by wide theories, but little by little, through feeling the stings of their practical errors. The idealist runs no risk of losing his head with intellectual pride. His task is too great and his performance too small. His "colligating conception" is so rich and his use of it as yet so poor and meagre.

But that principle itself he need not forego for any such criticisms as have been advanced against it. It has already shown something of that power which a regulative conception always manifests in systematic thinking, re-interpreting and transvaluating the phenomena to which it is applied. At the very worst Idealism, by means of its hypothesis of "spirit," has rendered obsolete the abstract methods which set the elements of individual and social welfare in antagonism to each other. It has shown that neither in theology, nor in ethics, nor in logic, nor in politics can investigation proceed on the old lines, or alternate between the old antitheses. What the ultimate value of its own positive contribution may be, and what manner of influence Idealism may naturally be expected to exert on our own future politics it is not as yet easy to discern. But a reader of the writings of Green, regarded by Mr. Morley and many more as the last in the line of our great political thinkers, will scarcely conclude that his Idealism can be charged with reactionary tendencies. "No political writer ever valued institutions more. He saw in his country's institutions no mere secular product of many human minds and many human wills, but rather the results of the action of that universal spirit, that 'divine tactic'—as Burke called it—which, through the instrumentality of human wills, operates throughout the whole history and growth of States." Yet he did not deny freedom, nor make institutions ends in themselves. Institutions, he held, exist for men and not men for institutions. "The value of the institutions of civil life lies in their operation as giving reality to the capacities of will and reason, and enabling them to be really exercised. He vitalises them. He humanises them. He moralises them. As we read his pages they cease to be pieces of social structure or bits of social mechanism." The "common good," the "spiritual state," "humanity," were not idle watchwords for him. They were "actual objects of value, endeavour and sacrifice, symbols through which he saw 'the moralised lives of men.'" No political writer in this country believed more thoroughly in democracy, or had a firmer faith in great ideals; but on the other hand no writer knew better what purifying fires democracy has to endure if the ideals are to be attained. Had English idealists been able to take up and carry forward the torch that fell, alas! so early from Green's hands, or had our statesmen been able to approach their practical task in the light of his conceptions and the moral ardour of his spirit, our politics would have advanced by methods not quite so tortuous, by steps not quite so timid, by paths not quite so blind, through errors not quite so costly and against resistance not quite so hard.

IX

# SOCIAL AND INDIVIDUAL EVOLUTION

The study of man, and especially of human society, is likely to rival the study of nature, and ought to be conducted in the same spirit. But the methods of natural science are not directly applicable to human nature, and man can be explained only in terms of himself.

The conditions which have made the solution of social problems urgent. The hypothesis in the light of which the solution must be sought—that the Individual and Society imply each other and that their welfare is coincident. Facts which obscure this truth, and give plausibility to the one-sided aims of the Individualist on the one hand and of the Socialist on the other. The presupposition, which these abstract doctrines hold in common, examined. How it is contradicted by the history of the growth of civilization, which is a progressive realization both of law and liberty.

When and why the ends of the individual and those of society are in conflict. The point of view from which the State and its activities are mere means of the welfare of the individual, and how in consequence the functions of the State cannot be limited except at the expense of individual well-being. But the State cannot perform its functions except by developing the individuality of its citizens. The regulation of "rights" is not their abolition but their ratification, and the social tendencies of the present day do not point to a limitation of individual enterprise; for the private and public will towards good are not in antagonism, but social and individual evolution are two aspects of the same fact.

IX

## SOCIAL AND INDIVIDUAL EVOLUTION

I do not think that there is much reason to doubt that the next great enterprise of human thought is to attempt to comprehend man, and to form some consistent theory of the social order which he has created in realizing his own powers, and which he sustains in maintaining himself. Indeed, it has already gone forth on this adventure, and gone forth armed with presuppositions that are so new as to give the inquiry great significance. Physical nature, which has for many years been an object of surpassing intellectual and practical interest, is likely in the near future to find in man himself a not unworthy rival. We are at last becoming aware of the fact that, side by side, or even continuous with, the natural cosmos, there exists another cosmos,—a stable order of human relations which, like the former, has its general uniformities awaiting to be interpreted by means of universal principles. The desire to comprehend the laws of the order of civilized society, and of directing and controlling to some extent the forces that struggle and combine within it, is destined to deepen and to spread. Wherever we turn we find men discussing what are called "social problems." All the great organs of public thought—the pulpit, the platform and the press—are eloquent with this theme. Many of these problems are old, although even these are propounded to us in a new way by our own times: but some of them are the products of conditions that never existed before. All of them alike have become more urgent, for we have become more sensitive to them; so that we cannot avoid them; we cannot even postpone them. It will be well if we can attempt their solution in that spirit of serene and patient impersonality which springs from a conviction of the sovereignty of simple truth, and which has so distinguished the pursuit of knowledge in the natural sphere. The need of that spirit is more imperative here than in any other realm of inquiry; for the facts are more complex, the personal equation is much more difficult to strike, the value of pure unimpassioned truth is higher, and error brings more immediate and more irremediable penalties.

It is well for us that, as a rule, the times which set the problem generally contribute something to the solution as well. And if the social problem has in our day become more acute in many important respects than it ever was before, the intellectual and moral conditions under which the answer may be sought have also become more favourable. The influence of natural science is itself very significant, and may be expected to affect the inquiry into the nature of the social order. Not that the methods of natural science can, as is even yet sometimes thought, be immediately applied to social problems. To every material we must bring the appropriate categories; to every lock its own key; and we cannot discover the nature of man and of human society if we begin by ignoring the qualities which distinguish them from natural things. Nevertheless, the successful pursuit of knowledge in the physical realm has created a habit of mind favourable to patient inquiry in the more complex region of social phenomena. Natural science itself, when it attempts to speculate and become a philosophy,—as it generally does,—shows a tendency to turn away from the crude materialism of its earlier days. It is beginning to recognize that its categories are abstract, and valid only within strict limits. Above all, a suspicion has arisen that a natural cosmos which has no *intrinsic* reference to one of its most marvellous phenomena, namely, the intelligent being, *i.e.* that the world with which science has been content to deal in the past is only a fragment. An important actor is left out of the play as represented by the man of science, namely, the intrinsic relation of nature to mind. But the idea of evolution, even though it may have raised more problems than it has solved so far, has led thinkers first to divine and then to feel convinced that the natural and the social orders are in some way or other continuous and constitute *one cosmos*. In other words, man and the social world which he has made are no longer regarded as contingent addenda to a natural scheme complete without them. On the contrary, we surmise that we both need nature to explain man and man to explain nature; and even that the latter need is the more imperative of the two. For man epitomizes nature; nature, amongst its many other manifestations, issues in man; and, *having such an issue*, it cannot be treated as the crude mechanism which it was supposed to be by the earlier investigators. Hence, the progress of natural inquiry will itself lead inevitably to a new attempt to understand man. On the other hand, it would not be difficult to show from the recent history of the sciences of man that they have felt a new impulse which arises from the fuller conviction of his continuity with his natural antecedents: psychology, logic, ethics and politics already show that a new spirit is abroad.

On the practical side, the pressure upward is still greater, for the conditions of practical life in civilized society have changed during the last sixty years in the most fundamental manner. Modern invention has led to the organization of industry, to the stratification of society into classes with common and yet competing professional and commercial interests, and to the establishment of an economic *world* on a most sensitive and unstable equilibrium,—phenomena to which the past offers hardly any parallel. All the familiar landmarks of social economy have been swept away. We are constrained to ask with new seriousness, "What is this social machine which I have helped to create, which reveals to me at the same moment both my weakness and my strength, and which is at once my master and my servant? And what kind of being is he who expresses his nature in this way?" The conviction is taking possession of the common mind that men, in pursuing their own ends, have to take account of one another. If at times they may be tempted to regard the peaceful gospel of the brotherhood of man as a noble but rather empty and impracticable sentiment, the ceaseless struggle in the industrial world teaches them very effectively that in order to live they must associate. The individual in his isolation and singularity has had his weakness laid bare. It has become altogether undeniable that the life of every man in civilized society is inextricably entangled with that of his fellows. In a word, the world has turned its back upon Individualism in its commercial and industrial practice, and even its selfishness has been constrained to take upon itself a more or less social form.

Now, we have only to interpret these new conditions, and press them to their ultimate issues, in order to arrive at the important conclusion that *the nature of the individual is essentially social.* That is to say, a man's relations to his fellows are not *addenda* to his personality, but the inmost content and reality of it. He cannot act as a rational being, nor be a rational being, except by incorporating them. The difference between individuals in significance and worth comes from the different degrees in which they have been able thus to incorporate in themselves these social relations, and to constitute themselves into *foci* of the general life. Man grows as an individual, expands and deepens his private personality, by rationally appropriating the social medium in which he lives—by making *its* meaning *his* knowledge, and by converting *its* higher tendencies and possibilities of better things into *his* personal purpose. If his growth is stunted, it is because his appropriation is incomplete. In the ideal individual the life of his community would receive a new incarnation. So that individual and society are not separable as different elements within a whole. Distinction, friction, antagonism, come only from their imperfection. The one is not the other, only because it is not itself. Society is an external necessity to the individual because *he* is not sufficiently intelligent to grasp its meaning, or sufficiently good to adopt its ends; and society, on its part, is a mechanical and most imperfect whole only because its members are only partly rationalized.

The same truth may be expressed conversely. If the nature of the individual is essentially social, *the nature of society is essentially individual*—or "personal," if that more highly favoured and less accurate term be preferred. I do not mean by this that society as it approaches its ideal becomes more like a physical organism in having one brain or one centre of self-conscious activity. The idea of organism thus metaphorically used has really very little value; and we contribute little to the solution of social problems by multiplying ingenious analogies between physiological and social tissues, organs and functions. Society is a hyper-organism. It shows a tendency to be *all* in *every* part, in a way to which the physical organism furnishes no adequate parallel. A society has not reached its ideal until it has as many centres of conscious activity as it has members. To the individual who does not comprehend his relations to his fellows, the community is a mechanical system and a hard taskmaster. He is implicitly at war with it, and a public danger. And a society—be it a family, a municipality, a church or a state—is really *one* only if all that are in it are also of it; only if its meaning is open to all its members and its purposes beat in every one of its organs. The truth of individuality is thus to be found in a fully organized society; and of society in a fully developed individual.

I find this truth very generally acknowledged in our day—*in a manner*. No doubt what strikes us, when we first contemplate modern social life, is its apparently irreconcilable internecine conflicts. These conflicts, moreover, are reflected into the doctrines of thinkers upon this subject, as well as into the proposals of practical reformers; so that the difference between Socialist and Individualist has become more immediately important, as well as more passionate, than perhaps any other. Nevertheless, we always find that the Socialist, while aiming in the first place at securing the solidarity of society, professes a wish to preserve the individuality of its members; and that the Individualist, while desiring above all to protect the freedom of the members, desires also to preserve the unity of society. That is to say, both parties alike seek both individual and social welfare; and it is sufficiently obvious to both parties that neither of these forms of good can be secured where either individual freedom or social order is allowed to perish. Thus, the abstract principle of the coincidence of private and general good is denied by no one. But it is one matter to acknowledge a great principle and quite another to apply it consciously, and with faithfulness and consistency, to the details of theory and practice. I take it that in this matter of the relation of the individual to society we have gained very little more than a general hypothesis. So far, we have done very little to explicate the contents of this hypothesis, or to show its practical application to the social problems that irritate and excite us.

The principle of the essential coincidence of individual and social welfare occupies in the moral sphere a place analogous to the conception of the uniformity of nature—using the term "nature" in its broadest sense—in the sphere of knowledge. This latter conception has attained the rank of a universal postulate only in comparatively recent times. There are some who would still limit the conception to the infra-human sphere, and who would fain provide, in the region of man's spiritual activities, room for absolute new beginnings and surprises. But, on the whole, reflective persons, unless they have fallen into the error of thinking that man's freedom must have in it an element of chance, agree in regarding the *order* of reality, including man, as both sure and universal. Not that this conviction of universal order is justified by our actual knowledge. Our knowledge of the connections of things breaks off short on every hand: we do not know what binds together the common qualities of common objects, or what, in a thousand instances, links antecedent to consequent. The existence of law is, in all such cases, an unverified hypothesis, and the conception of the world as a cosmic whole is an ideal after which we reach rather than our actual possession. But, on the other hand, this ideal is something more than a guess: it is a postulate of thought, without which thinking would not take place. Once convinced that the world is not a cosmos but a chaos, that there is no connection between events, that any antecedent may be followed by any consequent, thought would be both impossible and idle. All the processes that give unity to our experience and make our life rational rest upon and are inspired by the belief that the world is one and rational, an intelligible whole in which every phenomenon has its own place. And the evolution of our rational life, together with every fresh insight into the nature of reality, is simply a progressive ratification of this faith of reason in the outer order of the world; it is a partial realization of the ideal of knowledge in the crudest intellectual endeavour, and the ideal is only very imperfectly achieved and actualized in the most mature.

Now, it can be shown that the conception of the moral cosmos, the conception that every particular good has its own place and meaning in a scheme of universal good, constitutes in a similar way the beginning and the end of our practical moral life. This is the parallel hypothesis which the gradual growth of individual character and of social life progressively makes good. Morality moves *within* this hypothesis; it finds its basis in it as a postulate, and its goal in it as an ideal. The recognition of an act as obligatory, the consciousness that a thing done is "right," is the recognition of it as an instance of a good that is universal, unconditioned, existing on its own account, and binding just for that reason. Every right action is a fresh reification of a universal law of goodness, and therefore a contribution to the welfare of all; and every wrong deed is a public calamity. Hence the distinction of private from public good is, in the moral sphere, entirely false. There is no duty to self that is not also a duty to others, and no duty to others which is not the most supreme and most intimate good of the self. Morality is no alternation of egoism and altruism, or compromise between private and public welfare, but *a process of giving individual form to universal principles.* It is hardly necessary to say that this process is in every sense incomplete and imperfect. The principle of the whole is most inadequately realized and exemplified in the details of human action. The universal and the particular elements of the good are most incompletely reconciled, and are often in direct conflict. But this comes from the fact that society is not a consistent whole, and that its members are incomplete individuals. There is neither perfect law nor perfect liberty. The evolution of the individual's powers is hindered by the hard necessities of an imperfectly moralized social system, and the evolution of the public good is baffled by the narrow views and the unsocialized wills of individuals.

In the presence of these facts, which broadly characterize modern life, with its unceasing conflict of the interests of individuals with individuals and of class with class, it is not easy to maintain one's faith in the reality of the moral cosmos. It is more easy to sympathize *both* with the Socialists and with the Individualists who, for different and even opposite reasons, despair of reconciling the two primary conditions of man's welfare, and of identifying public and private good. Instead of the reconciliation of these two vital elements, they would postpone, even if they do not desire to suppress, one element in favour of the other. They differ only in regard to what shall be put in the fore and what in the back ground. The Socialist, weary of the strain and the strife of the competitive world of private interests, would take away the occasion of these apparent evils,—or as much of it as is supposed to lie in the unrestricted possession and use of wealth,—in order to secure a closer social unity. The Individualist, on the other hand, would resist what seems to him to be the mechanization of society and of the individuals which constitute it, in order to maintain that personal independence and enterprise to which he is prone to attribute social advance so far as it has been secured. As a matter of theory they might both be equally ready to admit that, in an ideal state of matters, the intimate unity of the whole and the independence of the parts would coexist. But in practice they despair of this ideal. They cannot see that, as we have shown, this ideal is in process of being actualized, and that the evolution of both individual character and of such social communities as the State, are simply evidences of its operation. They see only the imperfectly unified elements of the ideal; and they assume an attitude of negation and antagonism to either the one or the other of them. They fall into the service of an abstraction, and therefore also into conflict with one another. Social and individual ends to these modern prophets and reformers assume the appearance of being mutually exclusive. The very highest practical solution that is hoped for is a form of compromise between them; and the utmost they expect in the way of theory is some definition of the limits within which social and individual activity should respectively be confined.

Such a view is apt to appear much more reasonable than a more outspoken and unrestrained optimism which identifies social and individual ends, and represents both as evolving together. But I am inclined to think that it is in reality less scientific and less useful for practice. It is, indeed, only another example of the tendency of ordinary thought to play fast and loose with great principles, more especially in the domain of ethics and social science. It would be admitted that, within the sphere of physical knowledge, the principle of uniformity, or of the rational coherence of the parts within the whole, must be held in its integrity. A world which allows any place for pure contingency would be all irrational. Its laws or universals would hold only now and then, and therefore *never absolutely*; and a law which, within its own domain, holds only now and then or which is not absolute is, of course, not a law. But it is not so generally recognized that it is not a less unconditioned demand of the moral consciousness that the world of morality should be in like manner a true cosmos. In a word, there cannot be "one lost good."

But even apart from these ultimate conditions of intellectual and moral activity, we should be very slow to prescribe limits to the possibilities of the moral progress of man. *Nature*, whether in the human or in the infra-human sphere, is apt to be wider than man's thoughts, and to be moved with purposes which he very imperfectly divines, and never knows except in part. We are only slowly learning what a majestic thing the world is, and the mind of man which can explore its wonders. But this consciousness of the majesty of the world and of the mind of man—a consciousness which ever grows within us as we witness natural science gradually withdrawing the veil from the face of reality—is an inheritance of his age to which the modern moralist may also lay claim. He may regard the moral powers dwelling in man as on their way to the institution of an order of social life whose laws are as universal and necessary as those of the natural cosmos. Their necessity would have a different history, it is true, and be the very expression of freedom; but they would not, on that account, be the less necessary, the less sovereign, the less constant and harmonious. And it is evident that such an ideal order would fulfil the desire of the Socialist. But it would also satisfy the Individualist. For it would stint no member of that society of any human quality, deprive him of no power or propensity or opportunity to do right; but leave to him a responsibility which he can divide with no one, and therefore moral possibilities to whose scope there is no final limit. I should lay it down as a necessary consequence of the postulate on which morality rests that social evolution means individual evolution, and *vice versa*; and, therefore, that to endeavour to secure the one by limiting the other is to be false to both. And I should charge both Socialists and Individualists with a certain disloyalty to their own principles if, while acknowledging the postulate of the coincidence of public order and individual liberty, they refuse to follow that postulate into the details of theory and practical life.

But it is time that we should look at this matter a little more closely, in order to see how it comes that the concrete ideal is so uniformly set aside in our day in favour of these conflicting abstractions. When we translate this view of "the concomitance of social and individual evolution" into common words, it seems to mean that, as civilization advances, the functions of society as a unity and the functions of individuals within that society are simultaneously enlarged. For evolution means just this increase of function, this capacity of responding in new ways to the demand of the environment—of doing more things and doing them better. And it may well be asked, How is it possible that society can do more and more for its members and at the same time allow, and even enable, them to do more and more for themselves? Is it not true, rather, that each of them has its own proper and peculiar province, that neither of these provinces can be enlarged without mischievous encroachment upon the other, and that the discovery of the true limiting line is the most imperative need of our times? We want the intellectual insight of the social and political theorist to indicate the direction in which the line of division between them runs, and the prudence and strength of the man of affairs to maintain the observance of that line at all costs. All parties practically agree in thinking that the recent development of social functions has carried with it restriction upon the members of society and a certain limitation of their powers. They differ only in that the Socialist welcomes this encroachment upon the individual's province because it confines his power for social mischief, while the Individualist bewails it, because it lowers his capacity and opportunity for securing his own and his society's well-being. It is mainly upon these grounds that proposals to nationalize the land or the instruments of production are advocated and resisted. It is tacitly assumed that individual enterprise and liberty on the one hand, and communal action or "state interference," on the other, are antagonistic. Human welfare is held to be best secured by maintaining an equilibrium between them, and equilibrium means the equality of *opposing* forces. Indeed, it is considered to be too obvious to be even questioned that the more the state, or the organized community, undertakes and performs, the less there remains to be done by the individual *qua* individual.

Nevertheless, obvious as these conclusions may seem to be, I believe they can be shown to imply a view as to the nature of the relation of society to its members which is not less false in theory than mischievous in practice. This view rests, in fact, upon a mechanical metaphor which is not applicable within the sphere of intelligent life; and it is definitely inconsistent with the conception of the growth of personal intelligence and will through the ideal inclusion of social tendencies, and of the growth of society by fuller self-manifestation in the individual character of its members. In the mechanical sphere the equilibrium that rests upon resistance is the closest relation attainable, and there *must* be exclusion and extrusion; but, wherever we enter into the region of organic existence, mutual exclusion gives way to mutual inclusion. This is preëminently the case in the sphere of intelligence and morality, which constitute the medium in which human society maintains itself and develops. *There*, what the part gains it gains both by means of, and for, the whole; and what the whole achieves makes achievement on the part of the members all the more easy. This doctrine is as old as Plato, who knew that the best education was membership of a good state, and that the good state is best realized by making it an institution for educating its citizens in all virtue. From this is would evidently follow that we can never benefit the individual by limiting the state's power of efficient activity, nor the state by hampering the effective will and limiting the opportunity for independent activity on the part of its members. On this view the Individualist would desire *more* "state interference," and the Socialist, on his part, would as soon deprive the individual of his intelligence as of his private property. The former would know that a highly organized state is the means to the production of strong men, and the latter that strong men alone can make a powerful state. In one word, the theory that the mutual limitation and artificial equilibration of individual and social powers is the practical ideal is radically inconsistent with the conception of the coincidence of perfect law and perfect liberty which is admitted to be the beginning and the end, the essence and constitutive principle of moral life, social and individual.

It is inconsistent also with the actual course of civilization. Impossible as it may at first seem to be, that both society and its members may at the same time enlarge their sphere of activity, history shows us that this has actually been taking place. Indeed, I am not sure that anything else of the highest moment has been taking place. For this more intense integration and fuller articulation of the moral cosmos, this synthesis and analysis at one stroke, this growth of society as an active unit and of its members as free and effective personalities within it, is the very essence of civilization. A higher organism differs from a lower just in these two ways: it is more effective as a whole, more intensely at one with itself, less indifferent to its parts, more capable of concentrating itself at any point and making it, as it were, the centre of interest and activity and the temporary "seat of the soul," and, at the same time, its elements are much more unique in structure and effective in function. This is precisely the phenomenon which we observe when we contrast the ancient and rudimentary, with the modern and developed State. The State which assumed every function to itself and denied all to the individual, the oligarchic or monarchic despotism, always had the most limited functions; and though it claimed to do everything, it could really perform very little. To do more, it had to make room for the individual and call forth his powers. On the other hand, an individual rich in resources of intelligence and will, who, by some misfortune, found himself a member of a crude and unorganized state, would find his powers restricted by it. In order to express his resources he must first lift his social environment to his own level. A highly organized State is really a treasury of resources on which the individual can draw in doing his work and developing his character. "Our mother, the State," is no sentimental expression. It expresses, rather, as Plato shows, the authority which superintends the individual at his birth, fosters him in his childhood, guides and protects him his life through, gives him his station and its duties, and puts into him the power to fulfil them. It is the stable background of all his welfare, and just as truly the indispensable condition of his rational well-being as are the earth and air of his physical life. The civic States of Athens and Sparta, first experiments as they were in public liberty, represented a most stupendous advance in freedom on the earlier forms of society. These States did more for the individual; that is to say, they protected his life and enlarged it, providing him with the conditions of well-being in a way that was impossible to the Eastern despotisms. But these States did more for their members, and fulfilled larger functions, just because they accorded to their members a larger liberty.

If, on the other hand, we contrast these ancient states with a modern municipality, we find that their service to their members was as much less effective as the recognition of their private rights was more limited. After all, life was not so safe on the streets of Athens as in London or Paris. Nor did the city-state of Athens keep the streets clean and light them, secure the conditions of public health, build hospitals, provide for the poor and distribute justice, as a modern city does. On the other hand, the liberty of the individual, in the sense of a capacity for conceiving worthy purposes and great ends and of bringing them about,—which is the only liberty worth having,—is as much greater in modern times as social life is more highly organized. No doubt, the laws of the State are generally prohibitive in form and always restrictive in character; they define and bind and limit. But to regard them as mere hindrances to individual development is like representing gravitation as a hindrance to movement, or like thinking that joints and sinews and muscles and nerves place a mammal at a disadvantage as compared with a mollusc. To dissolve the State in order to make its members "free," might seem a desirable though an unattainable ideal to Rousseau; but any student of history knows now that to slacken the bonds of the State is to pull down the sky and let loose the foundations of the great deep upon its citizens.

But, it may be asked, do we not find in spite of theory that circumstances continually arise in which individual and social ends come into collision? Is not the problem of their relative priority being continually set, in different ages and to different peoples? Is it not necessary that we should give precedence either to social ends as being more comprehensive and permanent, or to personal ends as being more immediately imperative and more valuable in so far as, from the moral point of view, "character" must have the first place? Must we not, in the last resort, either regard society as means to personal ends, or individuals as instruments of the social purpose? And is it not one of the best features of the moral life of the present day that it is turning its back upon the Individualism of the past age, and giving definite priority, at least in theory, to the more universal conditions of social well-being?

I should answer these questions by saying that what has really been gained is a better explanation of the individual and a deeper insight into that which constitutes his well-being. We are passing beyond the stage at which public and private ends can be opposed in this abstract way, and beginning to ask whether there are any legitimate social ends that do not find their goal in the individual, or any legitimate personal ends that are not genuinely social in content. If the ends of society and those of the individual come into collision, it is because both society and the individual are in contradiction with themselves. The conflict arises because either the individual or the society has blundered and sought an illegitimate end, even from its own point of view. A social will that does not justify itself in particular benefits to the individuals who constitute the community must delete itself; and an individual end which is anti-social tends to destroy the individual himself. Indeed, I am inclined to think that each of these constitutes the best criterion for the other; that is to say, that the particular purpose of the individual can be best judged in the light of its significance for society, and that a public end can be best judged by its value for the particular citizens. In any case, it is not true, as is too frequently supposed, that there are public ends to be achieved by public machinery, and private ends that must be left to the individual acting by himself, or in voluntary combination with his fellows. On the contrary it might be held that there are no social ends as such, and no personal ends as such.

Let us take the first of these statements. It can be shown by analysis of social ends and activities that the individual is both their *terminus a quo* and their *terminus ad quem*, and that social or public agencies are in reality nothing but public means of satisfying private desires. If the state maintains an army or navy or a judicial system, or runs the penny post; if a municipality manufactures gas, cleans the streets or runs the tramways, it is surely only because this is the most effective way of securing safety, justice, comfort and convenience for the individual citizens. Nor does the public nature of the means defeat in any way the privacy of the ends secured. My correspondence with my neighbours is as much my own as if I carried my letters myself; and I go whither I wish on my own business even although I may employ the municipal tramway cars. In most cases I am free to employ or not to employ the public machinery as I think fit; in some cases I am obliged to contribute to the maintenance of the public machinery whether I employ it or not. But in all cases alike, even when I contribute to public education, or to the maintenance of judges or of prisons or hospitals, without myself making use of them, it would be difficult for me to show that I do not derive any advantage from these institutions; and it would be impossible for me to show that their end is not personal, individual, even though I should not happen to be one of those individuals for whom the State directly provides. In one word, all social activities are means and not ends; and organized society, in this respect, occupies the middle place between the individual's will and the individual's perfected purpose, as all instruments do.

I postpone for the present the other aspect of this truth, in order to indicate the consequences that follow from what I have just said. If State or municipal action occupies the place I have indicated, then the problem of its extension is a much more simple matter than it is generally supposed to be. Once it is clearly seen that the individual is not supplanted but served by the State, and that the State, in all its activities, has no other aim than this service, the bitterness of the controversy between Socialists and Individualists might be expected to disappear. Any new proposal would be estimated from the point of view of its utility as means, and of its effectiveness as an instrument; and the great questions of individual and social rights[1] would not be raised, as they are at present, whenever

[1] Society has no right which is so unconditioned as the right to make the most of its members: and the individual has no right which can compare with his right to do his duty, which is to fulfil his part as a member of society, and therefore to serve society.

a municipality contemplates a new enterprise. It would be adopted without hesitation in all cases where there is reasonable security that the civic machinery is likely to be a better instrument than private enterprise.

No doubt every such new social activity implies a certain dislocation ; and it must also be confessed that the dislocation is not in every respect analogous to that which takes place when a new private competitor in business enters the field. In a word, the principle we have laid down cannot be acted upon abstractly. The amount of dislocation involved in a new civic enterprise might make it imprudent in one community when it is not in another. In one city voluntary combination, or private enterprise, might clean the streets or run the tramways better than the municipality. In another, owing either to the defects of private endeavour or to the great practical intelligence of the civic authorities, the municipality might be intrusted with these functions. And the same truth holds, *mutatis mutandis*, as regards the State. But the essential point is this—that there are hardly any limits that can be set off-hand to the functions of the city or the State. They may be very narrow, and they may be very wide ; but they can always be extended *pari passu* with the capacity of the community to evolve good servants. A city in which the general intelligence is high, and which can recognize and rightly appraise practical wisdom and moral integrity in its officials and agents, may with advantage undertake functions which, in a community where the intelligence and the morality are lower, would only lead to disaster. Once more we see, in fact, that the efficacy of the social will depends in an absolute way on the intelligence and probity of the private will. There is no way of enlarging the functions of the public organ except that of deepening the meaning of "personality" in the individual citizen.

But "to deepen personality" is to socialize the man; and here arises the other aspect of the truth, according to which the individual has been regarded as subordinate to society, and morality represented as the pursuit of an altruistic ideal. In one sense the altruistic ideal is a false ideal; it is false if it is meant that under any circumstances the individual should seek the good of others *as distinguished from his own moral good.* No man can ever be required to sacrifice his character. I should hold as a matter of principle that every individual in Britain to-day has in his own personal concerns enough to occupy him, and that the man who considers that he has any call to be altruistic, in the sentimental sense of the term, has a most imperfect conception of duty. Duty is never supererogatory to the genuinely moralized consciousness, but an obligation laid upon him which he can set aside only at his own most private and personal peril. It is the novice in morality and not the veteran who carries with him into the service of his neighbour or of his state a supercilious sense of benevolence and of condescension, and thinks that he is working merely for others. The veteran has a better notion of the quality of duty and goodness. He is no meddler in many matters, but stands aside from affairs until they come to him as absolute imperatives which he dare not disobey because they involve his very manhood. When this *is* involved he may spend his life and pour out his soul like water in the public service; but the public service in that case is his own most intimate and most real private good.

But while there must remain in the moral life an intensely

individual element, so that the rights of personality can be sacrificed to nothing in the heavens above or in the earth beneath, and the individual's good can be postponed to neither city nor state nor humanity, it must not be forgotten, on the other hand, that all this sacredness and supremacy of the individual's personality comes from its identification with that which is more than personal. It is the moral law, the *universal* good, the *objective* right, the eternal purpose written in the heavens, of which no jot or tittle can in any wise pass away, that gives validity to his claim to his own way. Hence, he can resist the will of the community or of the State only if he has identified himself with a will which, in the concrete sense, is more universal than either. In fact, the content of the morally authoritative will must always be *the common good*; just as the common good must always assume a personal form.

When this is borne in mind it is seen that we are entitled to resist every invasion of personality, in whatever high name it may come upon us. The common good attains reality not by invading but by constituting personality, by becoming, that is, the desire of the heart of the people. It cannot therefore come into collision with private good, although it may well conflict against private wills more or less ignorant of the good. Society develops not by limiting but by expanding private rights: only, on the other hand, the private rights must be more than private claims, that is, the rights must be *right*, and therefore universal.

Among the rights of the individual which, on this view, are constituted by society and ratified and further evolved by its progress is that of private property; and a reference to it may serve to illustrate the principle I have tried to expound. It is not infrequently held that one of the most characteristic and significant of modern tendencies is to restrict the right of the individual to external goods and subordinate his use of them to considerations of public utility. What is the ultimate meaning of the factory and other acts which limit the right of so-called "free bargaining," except that they imply the denial of the boasted "right" of the individual "to do as he likes with his own"? And looking to the future, it will be asked whether there is any legislative tendency more probable than that of the further limitation of individual liberty on behalf of the interests of society as a whole. Are we not on the way to a condition of matters in which the state shall be the only capitalist and employer and the individual be deprived of all rights of property other than those which would belong to him in the capacity of a civil servant?

I would answer these questions in a way radically different from that of the militant socialists. I would distinguish between the definition and regulation of rights on the one hand and their restriction or abolition on the other. It is at least possible that to define and to regulate a right is to render it more secure. The so-called invasion of private rights to property I regard as a symbol that the social consciousness of the sacredness of property is deepening. The state, as a matter of fact, instead of depriving all alike of the power of saying, "This is mine and not yours," is endeavouring to indicate more accurately what *is* a man's own, and to protect it more completely. An illustration may help to bring out this important point more clearly. There was a time when the "rights of property" extended over persons; when a man might sell or buy his neighbour and dispose of his children as he pleased. Would it be held that, under these circumstances, property was more sacred and the independence of the individual more fully recognized? On the contrary, they were little prized and little protected. But in the degree to which the State became conscious of their worth, to that degree it set itself to render them secure by means of restraining enactments. But the restraint fell upon the *abuse*, not upon the use, and it made the latter more secure by prohibiting the former. Indeed, it seems to me that the prohibitive legislation of any progressive society is just the immediate consequence and expression of this more adequate consciousness of the conditions of individual welfare, and is, in reality, negative only in form. It also seems to me that the public mind of our day is evidently growing more sensitive to the significance of material wealth, just as it has in the past become more sensitive to the meaning and worth of individual life and liberty. With the organization of industry the magnitude of the issues that depend upon the use and abuse of material wealth has become much more evident. The public will is slowly but deliberately setting itself to regulate its material forces. But regulation is not abolition in the social sphere, any more than it is in the natural. It is no disadvantage to the good citizen or to society at large that the legislature should more and more effectively block the paths that lead to wrong action. The good citizen does not wish to send women down to work in pits, to employ little children in factories, or to sweat his employees. He is not wronged by any legislation that prohibits these methods of making wealth; he is rather sustained in his attempt to do what is right; and, amongst other things, he is enabled to hold his own against industrial competitors who are not restrained by social and humanitarian considerations. I think it possible to go further, and to say that even the immoral or unsocialized person is not really wronged by any such regulations, nor deprived of any of his rights. Liberty to do wrong is scarcely a *right*, but the use of it is the perversion or negation of a right. The wrong employment of a right always endangers it. There is hardly any right more fundamental than the right to be free. It is the origin and condition of all others, for freedom is the element within which alone a distinctively human life is possible. Nevertheless the state can step in, under certain circumstances, and take it away, immuring the individual within four walls. And this is done not merely in order to protect society against the criminal. It is better for the criminal himself to be walled in than to follow his evil ways unhindered, even although he may not acknowledge it. Punishment may very well be, and always is, when it fulfils its purpose, the only way left to us to protect the criminal against himself and restore to him his violated humanity.

I do not think, therefore, that the social tendencies of the present day point to a limitation of individual independence and enterprise, even although legislation is prohibitive as against certain alleged rights and the positive functions of society are being constantly enlarged. I think we may look forward to the future not without confidence. But that confidence were sadly misplaced if it were true that law and liberty were like two sections of a confined surface ; if social ends and individual ends were mutually exclusive ; if the prohibition of the misuse of wealth and of the power it gives threatened the right to private property, without which the rudiments of positive freedom were impossible. But there is no such antagonism between the public and the private will, nor between the ideals of a progressive society and of the citizens who live within it. Social evolution and the evolution of individual character are but two aspects of the same fact.

# SOCIAL RESPONSIBILITIES

## X

## PRESENT CONDITIONS

THE mass of unobtrusive civic services constantly rendered in Glasgow by its good citizens. The tendency of social reformers to overlook the good elements in civic life, and to rely on denunciation, and on revolutionary methods of reform.

To improve civic life we must understand it, and to understand it we must recognize its positive value; for nothing is constituted by its own shortcomings. To reform society we must make more of the forces of social welfare already at work; and to make more of these forces the obligations of citizenship must be felt more deeply and widely.

Evidences of a slack spirit of citizenship: the subscribers to good causes, and the workers on the committees in charge of social enterprises are comparatively few in number; the pulse of social life beats low in the breasts of many men who, in private and business life, are upright and generous, and they have a low estimate of their civic obligations.

Reasons why business men in particular should earnestly care and take trouble for the affairs of the city. A contrast between the methods employed by practical men in conducting their own affairs, and those too often followed in the local and imperial parliaments. The relative indifference to the affairs of the city and the State due to the want of realizing the value of our social inheritance, and the conditions under which alone it can be maintained unimpaired.

# NOTE

THESE four lectures on Social Responsibilities were delivered at the invitation of the Scottish Christian Social Union, and addressed primarily to the business men of Glasgow. Their object is to deepen the sense of social responsibility amongst such men, as the most secure and practical means of raising the level of social life, and of dealing wisely and effectively with its very difficult problems.

In the first lecture, which is Introductory, some indications are given of the fact that the affairs of the City and of the State are treated in a more frivolous way than those of a private business; and it is assumed that the reason for this lies in that many men are not aware how directly and vitally their well-being depends upon Society, and that of Society upon them. The second and the third lectures are intended to give a popular exposition of the intimacy of the relations of Man and Society, and of the many and deep obligations of social service which spring therefrom. In the last lecture some indications are given of the means that must be employed in order to make this service ultimately effective in a broad and permanent way.

## X

## PRESENT CONDITIONS

I UNDERTAKE this course of Lectures with much diffidence ; it is quite unlike anything that I have ever attempted before. If anyone were to question my right to speak on such a theme, and to address myself specially to the business men of Glasgow, I should find it somewhat difficult to give an answer.

But one thing I can say : it is not because I think that the business men of Glasgow are indifferent to the public welfare, or callous towards the social good. I have been in Glasgow for nearly twenty years as student and teacher, and have learned something of the number and variety of the social undertakings, and of the depth and volume of the stream of benevolence that flows unbroken through the years in this city. I have been still more impressed by the care, the time, the conscientious labour that are constantly being devoted in unobtrusive ways by faithful and unselfish men to the just and economical management of our charitable and other public institutions. There is a great mass of good social work carried on daily in Glasgow, for which the main reward is just the doing it ; and much of this work is done by its business men.

Now, social reformers do not often dwell upon this

aspect of the truth. They are, as a rule, more impressed with the evils of Society than with the good which keeps these evils in check. The poverty, the thoughtlessness, the unhappiness, the listless helplessness of the many thousands of their fellow-citizens arrest their attention and move their feelings more readily than do the quiet, unobtrusive, every-day virtues which, after all, characterize the great multitude of well-doing men and women, and sustain the concrete and more or less harmonious life of the society. Hence the social prophets are generally too denunciatory in their methods, and, not infrequently, have very little hope for the future except in some radical change of our laws and institutions. They desire some new beginning for our social life under new conditions, or even upon some entirely new basis. Nor can it be said that they are in every sense wrong. There is no doubt that many of our laws and institutions require to be changed. We desire with great unanimity many reforms which we know not how to bring about. So that in many respects the legislative enactments lag behind the moral convictions and purposes of the times. And these latter are never quite secure until they are embodied in stable institutions and fixed laws.

Nevertheless, I think our social purposes would, on the whole, be more sane if there existed a clearer consciousness of the value of our laws and institutions just as they stand ; and that social reform would move more steadily if we were more fully resolved to make the best of them. Without in the least denying the need for many changes, being certain, rather, that a more fully moralized social life would of itself bring many changes, I still believe that what is most to be desired is a larger volume of good work on present lines, and the injection of a higher meaning into our present ways. This, at any rate, is the aspect of reform to which I shall venture to call your attention.

Now, a clearer consciousness of the good that is already in the world, is, I believe, the same thing as a clearer understanding of the *meaning* of the social world and of the great principles which bind its structure together. For to understand an object is to see through its defects to the positive qualities that constitute it; and nothing is ever made up of its own shortcomings. Hence, we must place our faith in evolution rather than in revolution. Any good that can be done in the future must first of all be firmly fixed in the good at present working in the world. To reform society we must recognize the need and form a clear estimate of the possibility of making much more of the forces of social welfare already at work amongst us.

How, then, is this to be accomplished? I am tempted to offer a very simple answer, in which we shall all agree: It is by bringing more men, more good men, to share in the great enterprize of improving our social life. The workers in this field, numerous as they are, are all too few. The obligations of citizenship are not felt so widely nor so deeply as they ought to be.

In order that we may realize this fact, I must discuss shortly the present condition of matters, and endeavour to put quite plainly the results of my own observation. If in any respect they are partial or incorrect, your wider experience of the practical affairs of the city will enable you to modify them. Is it not true that, many as are the workers in the various departments of the social field, their number is not great in comparison with the whole number of good men in the city? If you look through the lists of subscribers and donors to the many good causes that exist in Glasgow, do you not find very much the same names? If you are engaged on committees or occupied in benevolent social enterprizes do you not very generally meet with the same men and women? Are there sound reasons for denying that there are many thousands of men in this city whose interest in civic matters is at least not palpable? Or are we not forced to the conclusion that the circle of those who are generous of their time and of their means for public causes is comparatively narrow?

Again, if we turn from these private institutions to those civic matters which concern the welfare of the city as a whole, and which are gathered in the hands of our public representatives on the Town Council, is it not all too clear that purposeful, serious, persistent interest in them is far less general than it ought to be? The pulse of social life beats low in the breast of many a man who, in his private dealings with his fellow-men, is upright, honourable, just, and generous. I cannot account for the fact that social evils which are so patent and so universally deplored continue to exist among us, and that the movement towards a better life is so slow, except by saying that we have not learnt to mass together the will for good which undoubtedly exists amongst us, or to set free the latent moral forces and direct them towards social ends.

The ordinary citizen does not always seek to pay his social debts. And the main reason, I believe, is that he is not aware of the extent of his borrowing. He considers that if he provides for his own and his family's needs, if he pays his taxes, and if he contributes some modicum of his means to his church or to some of the educational or charitable institutions of his city, he can cry quits with his social world, and go about conscience free. Of earnest care, of loving thought for that social world he shows much too little. He will scarcely trouble to cast his vote in the elections; if he does cast his vote, he is apt to do so on some petty, passing issue, as on a matter not worth much reflection. If the affairs of the city or the education of its children fall into wrong hands—if men of narrow minds, and even of doubtful integrity, gather up the reins of government, he only stands aloof the more, as from some low concern which does not much affect him. He does not desire the doubtful honours of civic authority; he believes he is a better man than many of those who seek them; and their mistakes justify him the more, in his own eyes, for standing apart from the unseemly scramble.

Is this an exaggerated account of the state of mind towards the city and its civic institutions of many men who are honourable in business, kindly, generous, and neighbourly in all the relations of their private life? I think not. I believe you will acknowledge the facts. I am not even sure but that some of you may feel inclined to defend them.

The matter is one we may contemplate with some care; for the destiny of the city—nay, we can take a wider survey and say that the welfare of the State as a whole—depends in very great measure on the possibility of directing the more serious and active interest of just these good men upon its affairs. This is particularly desirable in the case of the good business men, whose life is directly practical. For I do not think that the business spirit rules sufficiently widely in the conduct of our civic and imperial affairs—not that we can lay all the blame upon the individuals who are actually engaged on these affairs. Under present circumstances, they cannot easily do better. It is not possible entirely to prevent the inferior members of any public assembly from pitching the key of its discussions. And, above all, these men are *our* representatives—the victims, as well as the exponents of social forces which they cannot control. There is no way of raising the level of our representatives except by raising the level of public life as a whole. And it cannot be denied that, with all the defects they may have, they sacrifice much more time and devote more care and thought to public affairs than most of the men who criticize them.

But after making every allowance of this kind, I believe the business men of this city would agree that the affairs of the city (and of the empire, too, for that matter) are conducted in a spirit, and in a manner which, were they applied to the affairs of a private company, would be called frivolous and dangerous. For instance, either through your influence, or more probably through not exercising your influence, there are men sitting on the City Council whom you would not make your partners in business, or whom the shareholders in a great company would endeavour with much earnestness to remove from the directorate on the first opportunity. Nor do I think that the practical men in this city would approve altogether of the way in which the business is conducted. Most of the best work of the City Council is of course done in Committees, whose labours the public does not see. And besides, the public cares more, or at least is more fully informed about, the "scenes" on the Town Council than about its solid business. But allowing again for these facts, I may say that, in our local and imperial Parliament, there is much more mere oratory, more dialectical defeats and triumphs not in the least relevant to the practical business of governing well, than you would be able to approve on any private board of directors with less than a tithe of the city's affairs to manage.

In fact, a private business whose reports read week by week like the discussions in our Town Council would not be considered safe by its shareholders. And nothing, my Lord Provost, proves so clearly the toughness of the social fibre as the fact that it can stand the strain of our treatment of it. We grumble at the treatment, but we do not earnestly strive to change it. An impartial spectator, looking at our ways, would conclude that, in comparison with our more private affairs, those of the city and the empire concern our welfare in a remote and superficial way. We are relatively very indifferent to them ; and we are indifferent just because we are ignorant, and our social thinking is full of fallacies.

We are not aware of the magnitude and worth of our social inheritance. We have never realized either the difficulty of the process by which our inheritance has been gained, or of the conditions under which alone it can be maintained in its integrity. It is not seen that it is the product of the efforts of countless generations of men, slowly constructing out of the chaos of ill-regulated desires and colliding purposes both the stable institutions of civilization and the temperament which respects them. Not knowing either the nature or the worth of our inheritance, not realizing either the frailty or the strength of the forces which bind the social structure together into the most complicated and delicate of all the products of human nature, we do not care for it as for our most precious possession, nor strive to increase its worth, establishing it ever more firmly on the broad basis of a more enlightened social consciousness. We take Society as a matter of course, and its laws as laws of nature. We enjoy its benefits as we enjoy the sunshine and the air. The very stability of our institutions and steadfastness of our social ways give them the appearance of standing of themselves, and of needing neither our care nor our help.

# SOCIAL RESPONSIBILITIES

## XI

## MAN DEPENDS ON SOCIETY

The conclusions of the previous lectures resumed. No reform could mean so much as that which would issue in a more active social spirit and a more enlightened social conscience. The weakness of appeals to sentiment, as compared to a clearer version of what is right.

Fallacies which obscure our view of our civic obligations: first those of the Individualist, secondly those of the Socialist. A sketch of the characteristic errors of both; and of the way in which a true social theory exposes and corrects them. The errors in each case spring from ignorance of the depth of the interdependence of the individual and the social whole of which he is a part.

Plato's exposure of the errors of the Individualist. The extent of the individual's social borrowing. How in this case we cannot repay our obligations without enriching ourselves.

## XI

## MAN DEPENDS ON SOCIETY

I VENTURED to say in this place last week that the obligations of civic life sit all too lightly on the minds of many men, otherwise blameless and estimable. I even held these men to be, in a considerable degree, responsible for defects in the conduct of public business both in the imperial and in the local assemblies. These defects are perhaps most visible on the larger scale of the former: so many are the really important reforms which everyone would like to see carried out; so extraordinarily narrow are the limits of the legislative outcome year by year; and so slack is the hand which controls the national expenditure, in spite of all the eloquence with which the nation is regaled. If we ourselves were more earnest in our citizenship, more resolutely bent upon extending downwards the quiet joys of national sobriety, industry, thrift, and social justice, we should be able to find more efficient instruments. But, as things are at present, we tolerate incapacity in public business, and the irrelevance of mere rhetoric, with far more patience and placidity than we show towards inefficiency in the methods of a company in which we happen to hold shares.

If these conclusions are correct, then it follows as a matter of course that no problem, imperial or local, has more genuinely practical importance than that of breaking down this civic indifference, which lies at the root of the incompetence of our public representatives. It is far more important than any particular reform in our laws or institutions. For if the social conscience were more generally active, and civic duties were more unconditionally imperative, reforms, wise in their conception and far-reaching in their beneficent effects, would follow almost of themselves. The community whose morals are genuinely socialized is like a strong man in mind and body, fit to meet any ordinary emergency. It has little to fear in facing the future, for the nature of things is at its back.

How, then, is this more active social spirit to be made more general? How are more good men to be brought to regard the affairs of the city and the State as if they were their own? Not by an appeal to sentiment, or by stirring the emotions—at least in the first place. The value of sentiments depends upon the convictions from which they spring. They are worthy only if their object is worthy. And if at any time our best feelings do not cluster round worthy objects, it means that we have not recognized the true nature of these objects. All genuine reformation comes from clearer vision of what is right. And this is what I implied when I said that our indifference to the social good rests on ignorance, and on the fallacies of which ignorance is both the cause and the victim. I shall mention only two of those fallacies at present, for our time together is very limited.

The first I shall call, at the risk of some misunderstanding, the fallacy of the Individualist; the second the fallacy of the Socialist. Both of these terms have many meanings, all these meanings continually change, and only the foolhardy will try to fix them in a definition. But I should try to account for the Individualist by saying that he has only an obscure vision of the dependence of the individual upon society; and the Socialist, by saying that he has only an obscure vision of the dependence of society upon *him*. The former, at the heart of him, believes he can get on pretty well without society; he wants to be let alone by it and to carry on his private affairs without its interference; and he would fain resist the extension of public enterprise, because it seems to invade the personal province. He has a very strong view of his private rights, and a less strong sense of his public duties. Indeed, his duty to society is apt to take the form of charity, which he may dispense, or not, according to the promptings of a benevolent heart.

The Socialist is not so easily described. He is apt to desire the profits of Individualism without its pains; and his mind is less clear even to himself than that of the Individualist. It ranges more widely and adventurously. But he is much impressed with the evils that individualism brings. Individual enterprise is to him the outcome of private greed, and brings competition and collision, and hard hearts and merciless methods. He would have the work of the world done, of course, and its rewards distributed. But the work must be done, and its fruits enjoyed, not so much by any one in particular, for that might bring back private enterprise, as by every one in general. The extension of municipal and State enterprise seems good to him for the very reason that it seems evil to his opponent: it narrows the sphere of the private will, which he holds to be at bottom bad.

Neither description is kind; but neither is intended to

be complete, for what we have to do with at present is their characteristic errors.

Now, it has seemed to me that the social theory of modern times promises in no way to tell more beneficially on our practice than in exposing and removing these errors. It shows the Individualist that he cannot do without society, and even that he must not seek to narrow its enterprise as if it were a bad thing in itself. It shows the Socialist that the private will, so far from needing limitation, needs expansion in the only way in which the will can be expanded—namely, by being enabled to conceive larger fields of enterprise, and made more free to carry them out. Nay, modern theory goes further—though we cannot stop to show how at present—it reveals the interesting and apparently paradoxical fact that social and individual enterprise grow together: that the communities where the individuals have the largest and freest manhood are precisely those which do most for their citizens. What a rich growth of fruitless discussion, which bursts forth with such amazing vitality whenever a city or a State projects anything new, would disappear were this truth seen and believed!

The real source of the errors on both sides is the same; or, in other words, both errors are branches which spring from the same trunk. Both the Individualist and the Socialist regard the State or civic community, and the individuals who constitute it, as more or less exclusive and independent of each other. The correction of their errors comes from recognizing more fully that the State or the city and its citizens have only one life; so that each in repressing its opposite is destroying itself. In other words, the Individualist must be brought to see that his dependence on society is much more close than he deems, and the Socialist that the welfare of society depends on providing for the individual the means for the most vigorous growth of an independent personality—means which include, amongst other things, full rights of private property and full scope for private enterprise.

In this lecture I shall take up the first of these tasks. I shall try to show, not that the Individualist's sense of his own rights is too strong, nor that he values his independence too highly, but that he owes his rights, his independence, and the sphere for their exercise, to society; and that, in consequence, his obligations to society are as sacred as his obligations to himself.

There is in Plato's *Crito* a passage which brings this forth with so much clearness that I am tempted to quote it.

Socrates is in prison, awaiting the hour of his death. He is advised by his friends, who have provided the opportunity, to escape from prison rather than suffer the unjust sentence of his fellow-citizens. But the voice of the laws of the state of Athens keeps "murmuring in his ears like the sound of the flute in the ears of the mystic," and "prevents him from hearing any other."

"Tell us," say the laws, "what complaint you have to make against us which justifies you in attempting to destroy us and the state? In the first place did we not bring you into existence? Your father married your mother by our aid and begat you. Say whether you have any objection to urge against those of us who regulate marriage?" "None," I should reply. "Or against those of us who, after birth, regulate the nurture and education of children, in which you also were trained? Were not the laws which have the charge of education right in commanding your father to train you in music and gymnastics?" "Right," I should reply. "Well, then, since you were brought into the world and nurtured and educated by us, can you deny in the first place that you are our child and slave as your fathers were before you? And if this is true you are not on equal terms with us, nor can you think that you have a right to do to us what we are doing to you. Would you have any right to strike or revile or do any other evil to your father or your master, if you had one, because you have been struck or reviled by him or received some other evil at his hands?—you would not say this? And because we think right to destroy you, do you think that you have any right to destroy us in return and your country as far as in you lies? Will you, O professor of true virtue, pretend that you are justified in this? Has a philosopher like you failed to discover that our country is more to be valued and higher and holier far than mother or father or any ancestor, and more to be regarded in the eyes of the gods and of men of understanding? also to be soothed and gently and reverently entreated when angry, even more than a father, and if not persuaded obeyed? And when we are punished by her, whether with imprisonment or stripes, the punishment is to be endured in silence; and if she lead us to wounds or death in battle, thither we follow as is right: neither may anyone yield or retreat or leave his rank, but whether in battle or in a court of law, or in any other place, he must do what his city and his country order him, or he must change their view of what is just; and if he may do no violence to his father or his mother, much less may he do violence to his country."

"What answer shall we make to this, Crito? Do the laws speak truly or do they not?"

*Crito.* "I think that they do?"

*Soc.* "Then the laws will say, 'Consider Socrates, that if we speak truly you are going to do us an injury. For, after having brought you into the world, and nurtured and educated you, and given you and every other citizen a share in every good we had to give, we further proclaim to every Athenian, that if he does not like us when he has come of age and has seen the ways of the city, he may go where he pleases, and take his goods with him; and none of us laws will interfere with him. . . . But he who has experience of the manner in which we order justice and administer the State, and still remains, has entered into an implied contract that he will do as we command him. And he who disobeys us is thrice wrong—1st, because in disobeying us he is disobeying his parents; 2nd, because we are the authors of his education; 3rd, because he has made an agreement with us that he will duly obey our commands. . . . We do not rudely impose them, but give him the alternative of obeying, or convincing us that they are unjust. That is what we offer and he does neither.' . . .

"'Listen, then, Socrates, to us, who have brought you up. Think not of life and children first and of justice afterwards, but of justice first, that you may be justified before the princes of the world below. For neither will you nor any that belong to you be happier or holier or juster in this life, or happier in another, if you do as Crito bids. Now you depart in innocence, a sufferer and not a doer of evil, a victim not of the laws but of men. But if you go forth returning evil for evil and injury for injury, breaking the covenants and agreements you have made with us, and wronging those whom you ought least to wrong, that is to say, yourself, your friends, your country, and us, we shall be angry with you while you live, and our brethren the laws in the world below will receive you as an enemy; for they will know that you have done your best to destroy us. Listen to us then and not to Crito.'

"This is the voice which I seemed to hear murmuring in my ears like the sound of the flute in the ears of the mystic; that voice, I say, is humming in my ears and prevents me from hearing any other. And I know that anything more which you may say will be vain. Yet speak if you have anything to say."

*Crito.* "I have nothing to say, Socrates."

*Soc.* "Leave me then to follow whithersoever God leads."

"The very existence of the State," says Plato elsewhere, "implies that virtue is not any man's private possession. . . . All of us have a mutual interest in the justice and virtue of one another. . . . He who appears to you to be the worst of those who have been brought up in laws and humanities would appear to be a just man and a master of justice if he were to be compared with men who had no education, or courts of justice or laws, or any restraints upon them which compelled them to practise virtue."

I do not deny that there is more of State compulsion in this passage from the *Crito* than is pleasing to modern ears, or is consistent with the welfare of the State itself, not to speak of that of the individual. Plato did not recognize, as fully as later thinkers have done, that the State in pouring its treasures into its citizens makes them free. Nevertheless, the dependence of the individual upon society is not exaggerated by him, nor is the reverential service that he owes to his city and his State. Indeed, I doubt if these can be exaggerated; we possess so little that we have not borrowed from them.

"But I have my individuality," you reply, "and its indefeasible rights which the city and State must in all circumstances respect." And the reply is right. The State that does not respect these, nay, the State that does not deepen the meaning of personality and enlarge the range of its rights is not safe or progressive. But what is that individuality? And whence has it come? How much is there of it that is not due to the State and its manifold institutions? Apart from the power of reaction on its environment which is implicit in all rational life, I should answer "Nothing." And even that power itself would remain undeveloped, unrealized, a meaningless and impotent possibility, were it not for the social system into which it is born, and from which at every moment of its existence it derives its maintenance. If we examine the personality on which the individualist justly sets so high a value, and the rights of which he is so conscious, we shall find that every shred and element of their content are derived from the State, in which he has been nurtured. "He grows with his world, . . . and when he can separate himself from that world, and know himself apart from it, then by that time his self, . . . is penetrated, infected, characterized by the existence of others. Its content implies in every fibre relations of community. . . . He grows up in an atmosphere of example and general custom, his life widens out from one little world to other and higher worlds, and he apprehends through successive stations the whole in which he lives, and in which he has lived. Is he now to try and develop his 'individuality,' his self which is not the same as other selves? Where is it? What is it?" If any one doubts that anything more than an empty form will remain of his personality after its social content has been removed, let him try the experiment. Let him ask what language he would speak, what habits he would have, what ideas of right and wrong he would entertain, what religious creed he would hold? As there is no cell or fibre of his physical organism which has not been borrowed and elaborated from his natural environment, so there is no element of his individuality which he does not owe to this social world within and upon which alone his rational nature can be sustained. May I suggest a small exercise in Book-keeping? Will you set down on one side all the services you have done to society, and put a good price on every one of them; and, on the other side, will you set down all that society has done for you? It is an exercise, I believe, which would prove every "mere" individual to be, indeed, a bankrupt.

Now, what follows from all this? Manifestly, it seems to me, that the indifference of the individual to his social obligations is in no sense justifiable. His duties towards society are only comparable to the duties of the child to the mother who has carried him under her heart; for he is born, nourished, developed into individuality within the social matrix. He owes to his city and the State a service that never grows weary, a loyalty that never fails, a love that forgets all faults, or rather, remembers them only to endeavour to remove them. Nay, he owes everything to them except the bare potentiality of becoming a rational being, which potentiality would never be realized without his city and the State.

Is there, then, any means of paying back obligations which are so vast, and so obvious? There are many, I would answer; and they have this unique characteristic that in paying them back man enriches himself. The first, the greatest service he can render his city and State, is that of fulfilling the duties of the station in life in which he is placed. For social life is articulated through and through into limited spheres of activity, more or less suitable to the powers of its particular organs. No public activity will make up for the neglect of these more private duties. But in performing these honestly and well the individual is also serving the State. In an ideal condition of society, I am sometimes tempted to believe, no other service can be required of a man except that which his peculiar station, his profession, trade, or craft may bring. But we are far, very far, from that ideal state when everyone, being virtuous and wise, bears his own share of the burden of the general good—which, by the bye, is not only a burden but a privilege. In the meantime, the man who either by his wisdom or his riches, by his happy temperament, his virtuous will, his ready sympathy, his wide intellectual outlook, his social status, or by any other form of wealth within him or without, is endowed beyond his neighbours, is called upon to undertake many a task outside his narrower sphere. I do not deny that even if he confines himself within his immediate personal or family concerns, and wraps himself up in his more private virtues his value to the community is great. But by doing so he will deprive himself of the opportunities of a larger growth: for the wider atmosphere of the city and of the state is to that of the family as the open air is to a closed room—colder and less kindly and sometimes rude, but also bracing.

Virtue was never meant to be cloistered, my friends, and the world of human society needs all we possess of it. We have a right to call upon each other to be good citizens, and to endeavour as best we may to pay the debts of honour to the great municipality and the greater empire within which it is our privilege to lead and to spend our little lives.

# SOCIAL RESPONSIBILITIES

## XII

## SOCIETY DEPENDS ON MAN

The notion that the provinces of individual and social interests are relatively independent and exclusive, and that neither can be extended except by invading the other, rests on a metaphor, and has been adopted without examination. It has blinded the Individualist to the truth that in limiting the functions of Society he may be injuring himself.

The Socialist, to whom we now turn, would not desire to weaken the Individual, any more than the Individualist would desire to loosen the Social order. Nevertheless, by abolishing private property, he would reduce the individual into a condition of tutelage and deprive him of the opportunity of realizing his rational nature. His aim should be to strengthen the institutions of Society by moralizing them.

How the magnitude of the modern City and modern State has obscured their dependence upon the spiritual worth of the individual citizen ; and how minor organizations, within the State, tend to withdraw his interest from, and to destroy his loyalty to, the latter.

But the City and the State own no quality which they have not drawn from their citizens, and they can be maintained only by being continually reproduced by the rational activities of their members.

This truth illustrated by reference to a private business concern, which can prosper only as long as it is conducted well. The stability of the City and the State depends in like manner on the active loyalty of the citizens ; and they will not be safe or progressive unless social obligations are regarded as debts of honour to be punctually paid.

## XII

## SOCIETY DEPENDS ON MAN

In the last lecture we were considering one aspect of a common fallacy : the fallacy which represents the individual man and the society in which he lives as two things relatively independent of each other, having exclusive rights and separate provinces, neither of which can be extended except by invading the other.

This view rests on a metaphor. It has been adopted without examination. It has been assumed as a matter of course that human relations are like relations between physical things. It is entertained by men who are not conscious of possessing any theory of society ; and it rules their practice all the more absolutely because they are not aware of it. It produces both resistance to, and the advocacy of, social changes on false issues. It prescribes no higher duty to the wisest statesman than that of compromising between extremes, both of which are bad—as if there were no principle in civic and imperial matters which is intrinsically good. He attempts to find some *via media*, to mark the boundaries which should separate Municipal or State enterprise from private enterprise. And the attempt necessarily fails, for no such line exists. Man and society, like a plant and its environment, enter too intimately into one another to permit us to represent their functions as altogether distinct. Each needs the other in order to act at all. Their dependence is mutual and absolute, and they prosper together; for, in truth, they have but one life. Private and communal enterprise, and private and communal efficiency grow together.

From the ordinary point of view—the point of view occupied by the Individualist who opposes himself to society, and of the Socialist who opposes society to himself—this parallel growth of functions appears to be impossible or a mere theoretical paradox. But on examining the individual in the last lecture, we found that in opposing society he is really opposing himself. For he *is* his society individualized, its impersonal forces focussed. There is in him no content whatsoever, whether intellectual or moral, which he has not borrowed from it. His personality, were it analyzed, would show nothing rational that is not social. His speech, opinions, habits, beliefs, moral purposes, religious faith—deprived of which he would not remain a rational being—have been appropriated by him from the common social stock.

Not only does society enter into his personality, as does the physical environment into the physical organism, but society provides him with his station in life, with those relations to his fellows which, in the case of good men, become *duties*, that is, opportunities for realizing his intellectual and moral self. Cut off from society he has neither a rational life nor a sphere in which to exercise its powers: he is like a branch severed from the tree, all the functions of his manhood are arrested. This much we said to the Individualist who too frequently carries in his heart, if we may believe what is always on his lips, a deeper sense of his rights against society than of the rights of society against him.

Let us now turn to the Socialist. He is the victim of the same fallacy as to the relative independence of the State and the individual, but he accentuates the other aspect of it. Not willingly, I admit. He would no more abolish the individual than the Individualist would abolish the State. He would even develop his powers, giving to many more men, to *all* men, the opportunities of realizing themselves to the uttermost. His intentions are good, his heart is in the right place; but his head may be wrong all the same. And if his Socialism carries him towards the appropriation of the means of industry by the State, towards the abolition of private property, then he is very far wrong. For, in spite of his good intentions he would reduce the individual into a state of dependence and tutelage, where the responsibilities, and therefore the opportunities of realizing his rational and moral nature would disappear. It is not by abolishing private property, my friends, nor even by weakening the sense of its sacredness that good citizens can be created. It is by extending and deepening that sense, till men recognize that what is another's, as well as that which is their own, demands their care and protection. The distinction between *meum* and *tuum* must remain, under all social changes. If the State appropriated all things to-day it would have in reality to distribute them again to-morrow. Nay, its very appropriation would in itself be distribution; for its assumption of the means and materials of production and distribution would not be the abrogation of them, nor would it lift away the toil of dealing with them. The same industrial and commercial operations would have to be carried on, and carried on by individuals; and I am not sure that there would be more "cakes and ale" to distribute. But as society progresses the accent that is placed on the two aspects of private property will be changed. It will fall not so much on "*Thine is mine*," as on "*Mine is also thine*." Progress comes not by destroying the relations between men in society, merging either them or their possessions in a common mass, but by moralizing them. The individuality of man must be kept sacred and intact as the centre of rights, and even the possessions of others must share its sacredness. For, as the individual apart from society is nothing but an empty name, so is society apart from the individual. And in what remains of this lecture I shall dwell upon this truth. It is too much forgotten by us all, Individualists and Socialists alike.

The very magnitude of the modern city, and especially of the modern state, obscures this truth from our view. In small, isolated, rudimentary societies, like the civic States of Athens or Sparta, the dependence of the State upon the individual's personal worth and active patriotism was obvious. The Athenian State was a little community surrounded by rivals, and at any moment the courage of its citizens might be required to defend it against its enemies. Their temperance, justice, wisdom, and all the virtues of peace were in constant demand to resist the forces within that made for its disintegration. The State was frail as well as small, and it was easily overturned; for it was the first experiment of mankind in associating wills that are free—which is the essence of a state.

But now all is changed. It is rarely, indeed, that the cry of a modern State, in peril for its existence, startles its citizens. In this country, not even in times of war, have we really heard that cry. Echoes of it have reached us from other lands and other times; but we have not ourselves witnessed the dreadful drama of a dissolving State, nor seen, as our neighbours once saw across the channel, the boiling up of the great deeps of society, the confused mingling of all its forces, which reduced the wisdom of man into folly and melted his strength into water. We have found the British State ever stable and strong, although we have had our times of suffering and distress. It seems to move, all too slowly perhaps, but with the peaceful security of a star, in obedience to tried laws of public welfare, towards fuller individual liberty and broader social justice. We may acknowledge that its welfare is our own, and that it is the ultimate source of all our benefits; but its very greatness and security conceals its dependence upon ourselves. "What am I to it?" we say: "Less than is the single leaf to the forest oak."

Nor is it from its magnitude and stability alone that any service we can render to it seems of so little importance. The modern State is exceedingly complex. There are within it numberless minor organizations—industrial, commercial, educational, religious—which are more or less remote from the direct interests of the State, and which claim and occupy all our powers. In the ancient civic State the services of the individual to it were as direct as they were manifold. He was *its* soldier in time of war, he was *its* priest, *its* judge, *its* legislator in times of peace. But the defence of the modern State is in other hands than those of the ordinary citizen, and so are the administration and the institution of its laws. Instead of making these laws, and laying his hand directly on the helm of the State he has but one voice amongst many thousands in electing a representative who may himself have hardly more to do with the making, or the refusal to make, laws than a Chinese doll whose head can be put in motion, now horizontally and now vertically. Even in a great city the part of the individual in guiding the education of the children or regulating the affairs of the public is exceedingly small. What matters it whether he performs his part or not? The city and the State do not depend on him, is the all too facile conclusion to which he is prone to come.

And, finally, the organization of interests in modern society further manifests the weakness and reduces the significance of the individual. The old individual relations between men in different grades of society and in different occupations are giving way to class relations. Knowing that he is too feeble to hold his own amongst forces whose influence travels far and wide through the modern economic world, worker joins with worker, master with master, merchant with merchant. The interests of individuals similarly placed in society are now massed together, and the shocks of their collision travel through the whole community like a blind earthquake. What is the individual amongst such forces? Is it not vain for him to profess a larger loyalty than that which he owes to his class, or to pretend to care for the State as a whole which somehow combines, if it does not harmonize, these warring elements?

Look where we will we find the individual in the presence of powers he cannot control, any more than the little boat can sway the waves of the swinging ocean. And the natural tendency of man's sense of his insignificance is to paralyse his will and arrest his service. This is *one* reason, at any rate, why men who have the good sense to take a tolerably true measure of themselves are tempted to retreat from the turmoil of public affairs and, like Voltaire's *Candide*, to "cultivate their gardens."

But this attitude also rests on a fallacy. Stable and vast as is the modern State, powerful and complex as are the forces which collide and combine within it, they do not constitute a *natural* system. There are laws of society—laws of its economic failure or prosperity, laws of its political or moral growth and decay, laws as sure as those which guide the stars. But they are not physical laws, which man cannot change or modify, but controls by obeying. The State owns no quality, its laws no meaning or power, except that which is derived from and maintained by the will, the emotions, the intelligence of individuals. It cannot exist for a moment except within this rational medium.

We have spoken of the State as a most rich inheritance, the accumulated gain of the practical wisdom of many ages of men who have shed their lives like forest leaves to make the soil on which the good customs and institutions of modern society grow. No one can measure the worth of the civilized State, many as are the defects and deep as are the wrongs that still find harbour within it. No effort of reason can set forth, one by one, the elements of social good that intervene between the individual born in such a State and the unimaginable limitations of a life of savagery.

Nevertheless, there is not one item of all these elements which can become a man's own, except in so far as by the exercise of his own intelligence and will he gains it for himself. Man is not a passive recipient of any spiritual gift. We cannot inherit nor bequeath virtues, much as we might often desire to do so, either as children of parents better than ourselves, or as parents of children whose steps we fail to guide. A man's moral and intellectual possessions are the conquests of his own sword. All the spiritual wealth of the world—its learning, its enterprise, its growing purposes—will pass him by, leaving him utterly poor in soul, unless he arrests it, and personifies it anew in his own attainments. Hence society persists only by constant reproduction. It has no more stable basis than the appearing and disappearing wills of men. Not for one day will it "go of itself." There can be no suspension of the moral and intellectual functions of the citizens of a State without bringing death, any more than there can be a suspension of the functions of the organs of a living body.

If we examine this truth in the sphere of any private enterprise it becomes plain. How long do you say can a great business concern last if, upon its Board of Directors or amongst its workmen, you substitute folly for good sense, laziness for industry, extravagance for thrift, carelessness and disorder for caution and method, dishonesty and faithlessness in contracts for honour and rectitude? A great business ordinarily takes many years to grow, and every element in its growth is the product of the constant exercise of business virtues. In slowness of growth it is like a tree, or a good character; and like these, too, it may be cut down, almost in one day.

Now, what is true of a private business is also true of the city and the State. The truth is less obvious in their case precisely because the interests involved are greater, and enter more constantly and more deeply into our daily lives. We do not recognize our privileges nor the responsibilities they bring any more than we feel the weight of the atmosphere : their pressure is constant, and we *live* amongst them. Nevertheless, the responsibilities are present, and must be constantly fulfilled, if the State and the city are to remain secure. One ill-considered act of doubtful probity on the part of a Town Council may shake public faith in it to its foundations and indefinitely lower its powers for good for a long time to come. All the great assets, which entitle our governors to rule and make us their willing subjects, are easily squandered. It looks at times as if the dignity and honour of the Town Council were at the mercy of the crudest of its members ; so directly do they depend on the combined good taste and good sense of all concerned. It is so much more easy to destroy public confidence than to produce or restore it. We cannot afford to have *one* Town Councillor whose tastes are low or whose ways are devious—except at a public loss difficult to measure. We cannot permit him even to substitute for personal selfishness the selfishness of a class, and become the tool of an "Interest" or the mouthpiece of a "Trade" without danger to the community. Indeed, one of the things I like least in our city life, and which gives me most misgivings, is that the interests of a single trade should, to so great an extent, decide our choice of rulers.

But what we have said of the governors we may repeat of those who elect them. Here, too, the stability of the city and the State depends on the active loyalty of their best citizens. I could imagine, I am not sure that at one time I did not actually witness, an eruption upwards into the light of the worst elements of our city life : an unseemly combination of the bitter prejudices and of the sordid motives of reckless men who cared little for the good name of the city, with the ignorance, intemperance, selfishness of the worst inhabitants of the slums. What thoughtful man could help feeling at such a time how thin was the social crust on which our civic life rested, in the false security of irreflexion? And when I look abroad at our vast empire and consider what consequences would follow if the ignorant masses—ignorant, I mean, of the practice of the private virtues and of the duties of citizenship—were once to realize their power and combine, I cannot but feel how directly the welfare of the State depends upon its good men.

This is not the place to address our working men; and even if it were, I should not by a single word imply that they are less careful of their own character or of that of the State than others. But I should say to them, that the Empire is now in the hollow of their hands. They can bring it down in ruin, or they can guide it to still greater issues. But whether they will do the former or the latter, depends upon the enlightened and unselfish patriotism of every man amongst them. And their responsibility recoils upon those who have been favoured with better opportunities of learning the worth of citizenship and of doing what is right to the State. The State is not safe unless public opinion is enlightened opinion; and the task of converting public opinion into educated opinion is so vast as to require the best powers of us all.

There is no doubt that the individual depends upon the State, there is just as little doubt that the State depends upon the individual. Our debts to the city and the State are measured by our obligations, and they are immeasurable; and it will not be well with either city or State if these debts are not, always in our eyes, *debts of honour to be punctually and fully paid.*

## SOCIAL RESPONSIBILITIES

### XIII

### SERVICES THAT SOCIETY NEEDS

THE City and the State are the greatest of all our benefactors, and they need our help. Their power for good, and the extent of their functions depend on the intelligence and integrity of their members.

Ingratitude to Society is due mainly to ignorance; men know not what they do in being indifferent to great causes. Illustrations of this indifference; and the immoral motto of "The Trade". The error of believing that the equipoise of the State can issue from the strife of class interests.

Our own duties to Society are best learnt from our criticisms of other men. The fear of "the growing power of the masses". Why it is well-founded; and what is to be done to avert it; (1) to deprive the masses of their most dangerous agitator, namely their wrongs; (2) and if their wrongs are fanciful, to enlighten their minds. The exceeding weakness of the means at present employed to secure an "enlightened public opinion", even while it is recognized that it must rule.

On the other hand, the advocate of methods of revolution can best help Society by endeavouring to moralize its institutions as they stand. The workshop must become a school of virtue; and labour once more ennoble man. Masters must care for their men as for their machines; and the men themselves must become more jealous of the good name of their class. Social relations are meant to be moral relations, and Social rest can come only when this is achieved.

## XIII

## SERVICES THAT SOCIETY NEEDS

If there is any man more pitiable in himself or more contemptible in the eyes of his fellows than another, he is the man who from amidst prosperous circumstances can look at his benefactor in dire need, without endeavouring to relieve him. Ingratitude is one of the most monstrous of the vices that disfigure humanity.

Well, gentlemen, I have been speaking in these lectures of a benefactor to whom we owe a great deal—much more than we can measure. Plato, as we saw, thought that man owes more to the State than to father and mother: and I am not sure that he was wrong. What in your life do you value most? Is it not that you have been born of good parents, brought up on a virtuous hearth, educated in a good school and college, so as to meet the duties and opportunities of life with a clear mind and a strong will? That you have been provided with a sphere in life where you can exercise the powers of your manhood in performing your duties? That you have acquired wealth, or influence, or learning, or brought up children on your own hearth to inherit your means and to continue the good life? Then, without exaggeration of feeling or ornament of rhetoric, I may say that the city and the State in which you have found yourselves have been your partners in the attainment of them all. All these things, the best of life's endowments, are a joint product. You owe them to yourself; you owe them also to the social life that throbs within you. Society supplies nothing but opportunities; but it supplies them all. You may use them or you may abuse them, but you can neither do, nor have, nor be anything without its constant fostering—constant as that of the air you breathe, and just as essential to your life. Here, then, is a benefactor indeed.

And, as I tried to show in my last lecture, it is a benefactor which needs your help. The State is simply the product of man's rational effort, sustained only by the continued well-doing of its members. No man anywhere does a private wrong, or omits to do a private right thing but that society suffers. No man does well but the State gains. The powers of the State, or city, its capacity for conceiving and carrying out good purposes, rise or fall with the virtues of its members, as the water in the inland lake rises with the rains which fill the hillside rills and falls in time of drought. We sometimes inquire as to the limits of the activity of a State or city: it is an idle question. These depend on the intelligence and integrity of its members. A corrupt or ignorant city can do little; and it is far better for everyone that its powers should be kept low: an enlightened and just community can do much, increasing the happiness and the useful functions of its citizens at every stage of its own advance. Always in city or State the measure of its power is that of the wisdom and uprightness of its citizens.

It is not possible to reflect upon these matters, or to penetrate even a little behind superficial appearances without concluding that the city and the State both deserve our services and need them.

"What services, then, can we render?" you may be inclined to ask.

The real answer lies in your own circumstances, your vocation, and your character. In no two cases is the answer precisely the same, and no man can find the answer for another. Besides, the man who dictates his duty to his neighbour offers him an indignity and is himself presumptuous. Duty binds only those who discover it and impose it on themselves. The doing it is a privilege confined to the free. If a man's social conscience is awake he will discover far more of these privileges than he can employ, and find that more good causes call for his succour than he can support.

But we have been assuming (have we not?) that there are men, and even good men, who have not reflected much on these matters, and whose sense of their social responsibilities has been asleep. Good causes call for their help and they do not hear. The hospitals would be closed, the hands of charity would be empty, the education of the children would stop, the city would starve, all the generous enterprises of civilization would be arrested if the rates and taxes were converted into free will offerings, and no one offered anything but these men. They verily know not what they do in being indifferent to such great causes.

But even these men really want guidance only in one matter. Let them value society more highly, and all manner of good results would follow.

They would never use society as mere means, but always as an end. They would respect its rights, they would protect its honour, they would guide its enterprise, they would ennoble and strengthen its purposes. But, instead of all this, what is it we too often see? You have been present at meetings where candidates for civic or imperial responsibilities have sought the public confidence; you have heard them "heckled," you have perhaps observed the questions asked of them. Have you ever heard Capital press upon the candidate the rights of Labour? Have you seen Labour anxious for the rights of Capital? Not as a rule, I venture to say. "The so-called 'rights' of capital are all too well sustained," says Labour. "Labour is sufficiently clamorous already," says Capital. And both speak true, at least in this respect, that each side has only an obscure and faint vision of the interests of the State as a whole, and sees clearly only its own. I have been ashamed in this city to hear the wealthy cry against taxation irrespective of what taxation brings, and the poor cry for civic gifts irrespective of what they cost.

But if you would observe this spirit at its worst, where it exposes its degradation most shamelessly, you would find it where the amalgamated interests of a class of men are so powerful as to threaten the capture of the State. You will find it active wherever the State or city has privileges to grant or to refuse. This is one of the evils which, as even its advocates would admit, "Protection" has to encounter, and which must be set in the balance against any benefits it may be supposed to bring. But you will find it also in countries where trade is free. Does the working man, through his labour representative in City Council or Parliament, place his own interests first? Then, he repeats the errors of the privileged classes of the past, and makes social wrongs reverberate further down the ages. Let him rather send to City and Parliament men who care first for the city and the State, and justice will come the sooner. Does the trade in drink combine its vast powers and direct them on the choice of public representatives in the City Council or Imperial Parliament so as to possess instruments of its own purposes, tools for its own ends? Is it true that there can be, or even actually was inscribed on their banner, "Our Trade our Politics"? Then I call it an immoral motto, and say that those who profess and act upon it are enemies of the public good.

It is no answer to say that the extravagant assertion of their class "rights" is but a reply to the extravagant denial of them by others, even although the answer is not void of all truth. Nor is it an answer to say that where every class presses for its own claims, justice will arrive to all as the result of their collision. It is not true. The just equipoise of rights never comes in this way. Mere class legislation is never right. The State can provide for a class, or protect its interests, only when by doing so it is providing for and protecting its own more universal good. What will arrive by such methods is care for the strong and neglect of the weak, the conversion of the State into a warring arena, and the ultimate triumph of the clamorous. It is not the strife of interests that maintains the equipoise of the State or city, but its just men.

If the ordinary citizen wants work to do for society he will find employment in combating this spirit, and exhibiting in his speech and conduct a nobler view of the State and of the ends it is meant to serve.

But he will obtain a closer and clearer view of his duties if he listens to his own criticisms of the city or of the State. For it is a characteristic of the imperfectly socialized nature, that is, of our stunted moral life, that it sees the defects and duties of others more clearly than its own.

Let us, then, listen for a moment to the criticisms of the grumbler and the social pessimist.

Is he well to do? Has he been born in the soft and dangerously enervating lap of wealth, or social privilege? Then he will tell us that the greatest danger to the State comes from the growing power of "the masses."

Is he poor? Does he find the struggle for a livelihood severe? Has society been a mother to others and only a step-mother to him, slow and niggard to reward his toil, swift to bring penalties upon him for faults that are not always his own? Does not she refuse him the opportunity to win his bread, just as it suits herself; and when in age or sickness he can win it no longer, provide for his grey head and his bent form no better shelter than the work-house? "Then,"—he concludes, not without emphasis—"then must her ways be overturned, and a new social structure set up on other foundations—where there shall be capitalists no more, nor competition and poverty any more, and where no one can say, 'That is not thine, but mine.'"

Now, what answer shall be given to these men? To the first I would reply that I believe his diagnosis of the tendencies of the times to be accurate on the whole. The working-man's assertion of his rights is verily growing stronger; his power over city and State is on the increase. He is gradually learning to combine with his fellows, and a dim sense of his latent might is slowly broadening within him. And already his power is divined by others; for demagogues pander to him, agitators excite him, and politicians bow their knees to him. What, then, is the duty of those who witness and fear this new phenomenon, and whose fears, I admit, are by no means idle?

The answer is not difficult. See to it that you do not leave "the masses," as you call them, in the hands of the most dangerous agitator of all—namely, their own wrongs.

I know that "the masses" are ignorant, and that they often blame society for evils which arise from their own wasteful ways. But when they have just complaints against no one except themselves, you have little to fear from them. Men in the wrong have usually little force. Never at any stage of society or in any country,—not in Russia to-day nor in France when Revolution came—has the agitator much power to move the masses, unless he has been nursed on the milk of their wrongs.

But perhaps our individualistic critic cannot admit this, and maintains that the discontent of the masses and their growing aggression has no other cause than their own ignorance and their own bad will. Then it is another duty which sits at his door, and calls for him to a wiser *rôle* and a better even for himself than that of merely grumbling at his times. If he would save the State from the dangers he foresees, let him show the masses that their wrongs are fanciful and their social nostrums false. I do not doubt for a moment who our ruler is about to be in State and city. It is "public opinion." The organization of modern society makes it easy to spread opinion and to mass the motives of men. There is no place now where authority can sit in sheltered quiet. The politician flies his kites to ascertain how the winds are blowing, for he dare not launch his projects "if the winds are adverse." If, as a candidate for City Council or Imperial Parliament, he seeks votes, he also seeks to ascertain the desires of his audience, promises to fulfil them with alacrity if he can, and, if he cannot, his language becomes nebulous or sophistical. The occasions are far too rare when the candidate for power in the city or the State will set himself, through foul weather and through fair, to *form* the public opinion that he fears? Are our statesmen not followers of it rather than its leaders?

Well if this be the case, let our critic see to it that, so far as in him lies, the public opinion which we are doomed to follow shall be an enlightened opinion. But of all the matters that concern our general welfare there are none so neglected in school or college as those of our civic life. The youths in our Universities are taught Latin and Greek, some of them learn something of beast and bird and flower, of chemical agents and physical forces, and even of the laws of wealth, and of literature and history. It is right, nay, it is imperative, that they should know these things, and know them better. The battle between the nations is to be fought more and more in the fields of the intelligence; and men must be fitted for their special professions if the State is to prosper. But who explains to students the structure of the State? How are they to learn the laws on which our own social welfare rests? Who reveals to them the intricacy of the elements which compose the modern State and the delicacy of its machinery? How shall they judge between projects of reform which are wise and plans which are foolish? Where, above all, can they learn reverence for the State, or get some glimpse of the nature of the rights and duties of citizenship? Only through the heated debates and passionate utterances of struggling politicians, and in the hurried pages of a daily press, the one and the other of which are committed to foregone party conclusions.

I am not forgetting that the good sense of the Town Council of Glasgow and the generosity of some of its citizens have led them, in our own University, to endow in part one lectureship, whose emoluments are not much less than those of a man-cook or a head-butler. Something can be accomplished even with these small means. A beginning can be made to deal with social phenomena in the serene, passionless spirit, and with the impersonal devotion and severity and purity of method which we apply to the investigation of natural objects.

But I look forward to the time when Glasgow, nay, when the country as a whole, shall do much more to raise the level of knowledge of the nature of the State and of the laws of its true advance. You will yet purify the wells of citizenship by enlightening the minds of the citizens. You will first teach your teachers. And I venture to say that the time will come when there shall be no college or secondary school in the land where something is not done, amongst the rudiments of many subjects, to give to the future citizen a glimpse of the vast powers that move in our social life and of the nobleness of its service.

Or has the critic who fears the growing power of the masses any wiser strategy to recommend? For my part I do not believe there is any short cut to this great end of forming the "public opinion," which will rule us whether we shall educate it or not. It is a long way round; but the longest way round in some matters is the shortest way home.

Here, then, perhaps, is a service to society which some of you may, directly or indirectly, desire to perform.

But I must turn for a moment before I close to our other critic, who is, as a rule, at the other end of the social scale and advocates methods of revolution.

To him I would say, as I have already hinted in a single sentence, that his one hope lies not in overturning the relations that bind man to man in society, but in moralizing them. His own method is more easy, I admit: it is almost always more easy to overturn than to improve. But after every social overturn comes the restoration, and restoration, as a rule, very much on old lines. The main relations that now divide man from man, giving to each his own station and rights and duties, are essential to society. If they are destroyed they must be restored, for society cannot exist without them. But they may be moralized. I sometimes believe that it is the one paramount enterprise of society to moralize its institutions, and that it will find no rest till it achieves this task. And by this I mean that the ordinary, daily connexions in which man is bound to man in his business, in public works, in offices, in his avocation as master or servant, as capitalist or labourer, the pursuit of which constitutes the very substance of his life, must be such as to develop, and not to crush or corrupt, the manhood that is in them.

Benevolence descending upon the needy from above has its value. It is good, at least for the West End, that it should wrap its skirts more closely around it and occasionally visit the slums of the East. Tax the land, if that is just, provide houses for the homeless, and pensions for needy age, if you are sure that by these means you do not defeat your ends. But neither voluntary gifts nor compulsory legislation can reach the social evils if the stable relations amongst which we make our bread are not made into opportunities of a good life. Capital must discover that it has duties. Labour, my friends, must be ennobled. Its conditions must be changed so that it may *make* men and not destroy them.

The workshop must become a school of virtue, as most of the old workshops were and as the professions are now. More masters must care for their men as they care for their machines. They must seek inventions that shall induce industry, honesty, thrift, manliness amongst their workers, even as they seek for cheaper and better material for their industry or better methods of dealing with it.

But, on the other hand, what the masters can do for the men is restricted or enlarged, it is limited, defined by what the men are willing to do for themselves. The enterprise of raising the moral level of these substantial relations amongst which we spend our lives, is a task that demands the co-operation of both sides. The men themselves must become jealous of the good name of their class, and recognize in every thriftless, intemperate, irregular, dishonest workman the enemy of their good.

I am quite certain that the care of the master for the man and of the man for the master is a sound principle in economics: I cannot doubt that it is also sound social doctrine. Social relations are meant to be moral relations. I believe it is inscribed in the very structure both of man and society that they shall find no rest except in the right, and find no true joy or happiness except in the pursuit of it.

GLASGOW: PRINTED AT THE UNIVERSITY PRESS BY ROBERT MACLEHOSE AND CO. LTD.